Your Second Child

by
Joan Solomon Weiss

SUMMIT BOOKS
NEW YORK

Published by SUMMIT BOOKS
A Division of Simon & Schuster, Inc.
Simon & Schuster Building
1230 Avenue of the Americas
New York, New York 10020
SUMMIT BOOKS and COLOPHON are trademarks of Simòn & Schuster, Inc.
Designed by Irving Perkins Associates
Manufactured in the United States of America

3 5 7 9 10 8 6 4 2
9 10 8   (pbk.)

First Edition
Library of Congress Cataloging in Publication Data

Weiss, Joan Solomon.
Your second child.

Bibliography: p.
Includes index.
1. Parenting—United States.   I. Title.
II. Title: Second child.
HQ755.8.W43   649'.1   81-8974
AACR2

ISBN 0-671-25618-1
0-671-25619-X (pbk.)

Acknowledgments

THIS BOOK COULD NOT HAVE BEEN FINISHED, or even started, without the help of so many others. I neeeded, first, the patience and understanding of my husband, Allan, and the inspiration of my children, Brian and Michael. More practically, Sheilah and Donald Ziccardi provided me with a place to work, complete with fully stocked refrigerator, and Rose Actor gave me the peace of mind of knowing that my children were well cared for while I worked. My agent, Barbara Lowenstein, and editor, Jonathan Segal, gave me the confidence to try my luck in this bewildering business of book publishing.

There is, unfortunately, not room enough here to name all the parents and the second children who shared with me their experiences, their disappointments, and their delights. Nor is there room to list individually all the professional experts who shared with me their knowledge. But I would like to thank them all for their contributions to this book. And I would like to list and thank those individuals and groups who provided me with special assistance, ranging from manuscript review to emergency babysitting to research help to generous and continuous support. They are Ellen Gottfried, Fran Levinson, Judy Ashworth, Ann Harvey, Hugh Harvey, Pat Levinson, Steve Meltzer, Annette Kranson, Jerry Kranson, Susan Philliber, Sandy Weiss, Bob Gottfried, Roseanne Welch, Bob Levinson, Ilene Heyman, Madeline Firetag Lizt, Gloria Mazin, Janet Wein, Louise Schwartz, Fran Whittelsey, Louise May, Martin Lizt, Lorraine Wechsler, Fran Fabian, Lee Mackler, the Maternity Center Association, and the Mothers' Center of Queens.

I am grateful, also, to my sister, Diane, to my parents, Leo and Pauline Solomon, and to my in-laws, Gerta, Emil, and Jules Weiss, for encouraging me when I was discouraged and for being there when I needed them.

Lastly, I would like to acknowledge the valuable contribution of Lorraine Carsons, who helped give me the courage to start the book, but sadly, is not here to celebrate its completion.

—Joan Solomon Weiss
February 1981

*To Allan, Diane, and Brian, first children all,
and to Michael, my second.*

Contents

Foreword by Virginia Pomeranz, M.D. 11

Introduction 17

CHAPTER

1   Planning for Your Second Child 25

2   Pregnancy and Childbirth the Second Time Around 51

3   Preparing Your First Child for Your Second Child 83

4   The Highlights and Hazards of Second-Time Parenthood 112

5   The Second-Child Syndrome: Slow but Steady? 133

6   The Combat Zone: Children at War 169

7   Playing and Learning Together 197

8   Making One Room Big Enough for Two 217

9   Meshing Schedules and Making Time 235

Bibliography 259

Index 279

Foreword

FOREWORDS ARE SOMETIMES ECSTATIC RAVES penned by a close friend, relative, or debtor of the author to discharge some tangible or other obligation. This foreword is not. I met Joan Weiss, the author, only when she interviewed me while she was working on the text. We are not related. I am not her children's physician. But I am delighted to write the foreword for her book, because I think it is an excellent book—a book which should be read by every parent of a second child, and every parent of a first child who is contemplating a second.

Your Second Child is easy, lively reading. Ms. Weiss's thorough exploration of her subject is laced with interesting personal anecdotes and spiced with wit, and her accounts of the results of scholarly studies are both lucid and accompanied by appropriate caveats. (*Your* family may find your *older* offspring the more "creative" and sociable, the *younger* the cerebral scientist-to-be. The statistics are nonetheless fascinating.)

I'm particularly pleased that the author has shown parents how to steer clear of three major pitfalls. One is guilt—the feeling that one owes the first child an apology for introducing an interloper, or that one has done the second a disservice by depriving him or her of sole parental attention from the start. I have not met an adult of either sex who was an only child and wanted to *have* only one child. I have the distinct impression that only children conclude, when they have grown up, that an only child misses something—even though many only children from six to sixteen claim they consider their only-child status fortunate, and many a sibling of that age will declare himself or herself cruelly cursed. Actually, both children will thank you later; probably, *much* later.

A second parental pitfall is anxious overprotection of the

younger child from assault by the elder, and/or vice versa. In fact, if you leave siblings alone and interfere only when the noise level exceeds your personal tolerance—or the dissension threatens to escalate to lethal warfare—and then separate them, you'll find that your children truly enjoy each other's company. And deprivation of that companionship will soon be viewed as the worst possible punishment. It can be pretty difficult for the elder to continue to resent a toddler who clearly believes the sun rises and sets on big brother or sister.

Third, Ms. Weiss correctly cautions against comparisons between siblings, usually to the detriment of one or the other. As she reminds us, each child is individual and unique, and a parent need only let each know, in quiet moments, how much those qualities are appreciated and cherished. (I recall a story I once read of six adults standing at the bier of their recently deceased mother, each silently treasuring the same thought: "I was her favorite child." What a wise woman!)

Ms. Weiss also lays to long-deserved rest a pervasive superstition that has haunted second-time parents-to-be: If the first child was "easy," the second is bound to be a source of intense suffering. Of course, that's not so. I have known families with as many as five perfectly charming children—not peas in a pod, but each a joy in his or her own way. (Carbon copies of even the nicest child are not half so much fun as two or more distinct personalities.) And interestingly, I cannot remember knowing two "difficult" children in the same family; either parents learn from prior experience, or Mother Nature is just not that nasty.

One question which could not have arisen in earlier times, and has even now been treated too little in the popular press, is timing. In these days of mostly reliable family planning, parents can choose to space their offspring to suit their lifestyles—to "cluster" the kids closely, to pack one off to kindergarten before conceiving the second, or something in between. The author includes an extremely well-balanced discussion of that topic, citing authoritative views and conflicting considerations which puzzled parents can apply to their own circumstances. In this and other subjective areas, this book is blessedly nonjudgmental; these are highly personal decisions, best made by first arming oneself with all the relevant facts. The facts are here, presented in an even-handed, objective manner. Readers, thus equipped, can arrive at the conclusion that is best for *them*—their economic situation; their, and their first child's, personalities; and, most of all, their own attitudes and feelings.

Ms. Weiss presents not only the theoretical and philosophical aspects of second-time parenting, but the practical side as well. There is a wealth of sound, down-to-earth advice on matters ranging from feeding, diapering, and sleeping space to the purchase of two-child strollers—much of it stemming from the author's own experience and that of the scores of other parents we meet in the pages of her book.

Second-time parents will find this fine book both helpful and reassuring. Those wondering whether or not to make their single child a sibling will conclude—rightly, I think—that the many advantages to both parents and children far outweigh the few problems that may arise. (The sole exceptions, as Ms. Weiss properly points out, are those parents who have discovered that parenting is not really for them at all. There *are* some people just "not cut out for bringing up babies.") And those pondering the potential trials of time management need look no further than the fact that the author, herself the mother of two small children, has found the hours and energy to research and write a full-length book and to do it very, very well.

—*Virginia E. Pomeranz, M.D.*
Associate Clinical Professor of Pediatrics,
Cornell University Medical College

Your
Second
Child

Introduction

YOU'VE FINALLY GOT IT MADE. All those middle-of-the-night wake-ups to bare your breasts or pop a bottle top are just a memory now. No more burping baby to the theme song of the Late Late Show. No more dribble on your best designer clothes. Your cute little baby has grown, right before your tired eyes, into a talkative, toilet-trained toddler.

But despite the "good life" that seems just ahead, you may decide to throw caution to the wind and do it all over again. If so, you won't be alone. Many parents have taken the stretchies and Swyngomatic out of storage, making ready for their second baby, even before their first baby has been shuttled off to nursery school.

THE CHALLENGE OF TWO CHILDREN

Some second-time parents have undoubtedly been taken in by the tale that it is "easier" with two children. In reality, your second child will bring both pleasure and pandemonium into your life and a green-eyed monster into your home.

On the bright side, the second birth itself is likely to be quicker and easier since the mother's body has been "readied" by the first labor and delivery. And Mom and Dad are no longer novices at the parenting business. By the time they are faced with child number two, they are calm enough to realize that a drippy nose does not signal pneumonia. They are experienced enough to stay on track, not changing their child-rearing methods with every new fad they read about or every old friend they talk to. Although they are not as affectionate in the beginning, they eventually become even warmer toward their second child than their first—

17

less likely to spank, more likely to praise. And they are not as likely to interfere or intrude with their second, giving advice when it most obviously is not wanted.

There is also something to be said for having an older sibling. It gives a kid a chance to play Robin to big brother's Batman, or Han Solo to big sister's Darth Vader. First children can be charming companions and eager teachers, as well as gallant leaders in playground warfare. They can serve as models of behavior to strive for, examples of behavior to avoid. As an added attraction, they often break down parental resistance to all sorts of forbidden toys and daring adventures, smoothing the way for the family's youngest.

But to be realistic, the onset of sibling rivalry will challenge all your parenting skills. You may find wet sheets in your first child's bed after months of dry nights; nails, once well-shaped and shiny, bitten down to the quick; innocent eyes brightened by a murderous gleam. There are many ways your first child will tell you that the last nine months should never have happened. Some signs of jealousy will be so obvious you can't miss them, some so subtle you will hardly notice them. Your eldest may even act extragood after the birth, and delight you by hugging the baby with apparent affection. But watch out! Those hugs may literally take the baby's breath away.

Before you know it, the Cain-and-Abel syndrome will strike your secondborn as well. Try reading a book to big sister, and little sister will try ripping up the pages. Try hugging your firstborn, and you will soon have one clinging child on each wellworn knee. Jealousy is a painful emotion. It is hard to see your children suffer from it, and it is hard to know what to do about it.

You will be going through your own emotional turmoil as you adjust to your larger family. You may find yourself "split in two," not knowing whose needs to tend to first. Rock your younger, or read to your older? Satisfy your bawling baby's hungry stomach, or your precocious preschooler's hungry mind? The constant demands of your two children may make you feel angry, and your anger may make you feel guilty. Some parents also feel fear—fear they will lose their special relationship with their first child. That *can* happen temporarily, especially between the mother and the firstborn. Because she is the one who gave birth, and is usually the new baby's chief caretaker, she may be held responsible for the appalling turn of events. Some first children take refuge with their fathers until they overcome their feelings of rejection. The bond between father and child often remains strong even after the mother is forgiven.

Fear sometimes takes a different direction—the fear of not being able to love the secondborn as much as the first, or even of resenting the second child for making the first so miserable. Will you ever be able to open your heart to this cute, but trouble-making, stranger? Will you be able to deal with another go-round of dirty diapers and spit-up suppers? Will you be as excited, this time, at the first fleeting smile, the first tiny tooth, the first faltering step, or will it all seem like a boring rerun that should never have aired again?

SECONDBORN, SECOND BEST?

If you think your world has gone slightly out-of-focus as your family has expanded, just think how it must be for the new addition. Many a second baby is greeted by torn and tired parents, a hostile, unhappy sibling, and a crib that has been slept in before. It is certainly a far cry from the joyous hysteria and straight-from-the-showroom furniture that awaits most firstborn babies. There are fewer flashbulbs popping the second time around, fewer flowers waiting in welcome, fewer friends phoning in congratulations. Things are really subdued if the secondborn is a second boy or a second girl, robbing the event of its one big chance for novelty.

At home, the newborn may be kissed only on the sly for fear of antagonizing big brother or sister. Feeding may be done by bottle, not breast, for the same reason. The baby's cries may go unheeded by parents too hardened to notice them or too busy to answer them. As the months go by, the secondborn baby is usually talked to less, looked at less, and touched less than was the firstborn. But as soon as the little one learns to get around, knocking down sister's blocks or making off with a piece of brother's jigsaw puzzle, there is lots of touching to be had—often of the violent variety. And retaliation may seem too big a risk.

Outsized and outranked, being second means always having to say you're sorry.

As the years go by, being second means being a "tag-along," trying to race on a used one-speed tricycle after big sister on a new ten-speed bicycle. It means sleeping on the bottom of the bunk bed and praying, every night, that the top doesn't fall in. It means wearing hand-me-down clothes labeled with nametapes that are only half right.

All in all, growing up is quite a different experience for children born second. If you wonder whether these differences leave a lasting mark on the developing personality, you've got a lot of company. During the past century, hundreds of researchers have been intrigued by the notion that firstborn children are different than secondborn, who are different than those who follow. Scientists have investigated the effects of birth order on intelligence, achievement, emotional health, creativity, conformity, and countless other attributes. Many of the results have been contradictory, but some are well-documented, and indicate that birth order does, indeed, make a difference. A second child is less likely than a first to shoot for the stars or to land on the moon. But despite earthbound aspirations and accomplishments, a second child is more likely to be well-liked, confident, and creative.

SEEKING HELP

As a current or future parent of two children, how can you help your youngest make the most of being secondborn? And how can you help yourself live through the fights, the tears, the jealous tantrums, and the double duties of having two children? If you have looked to your local bookstore for helpful advice, you probably haven't found much. Apparently, most publishers assume that bringing up one baby is pretty much like bringing up another. But I began to doubt that assumption even before my second child was born. The pregnancy itself was a very different experience. I was more nauseous than I had been the first time and a whole lot crankier. With an active two-year-old to care for, I couldn't spare the time for leisurely bubble baths or rejuvenating naps. And I was totally preoccupied with preparing firstborn

Brian for his soon-to-be sibling. I spent half my time reading him books about birth and babies, and the other half trying to get him out of his crib and into a bed, off the bottle and onto a cup, out of diapers and into Underoos.

After the birth of Michael, our second child, my husband and I encountered a number of situations we were at a loss to handle. What to do about Brian's mischief-making while I was nursing Michael? What to say to Brian while everyone cooed over the baby? How to keep the apartment quiet enough for Michael's naps without cramping Brian's sonorous style? How to cope with two simultaneously screaming children? I was especially upset when I went to cut Brian's nails and noticed there was nothing left to cut. Why was he so distressed? What were we doing wrong? Brian's feelings of rivalry toward the baby did have one unexpected, positive effect: After watching me change Michael, he decided that diapers are definitely not for big boys going on three. So Michael's birth succeeded where months of our coaxing, pleading, and blatant bribing had failed.

In order to make some sense out of our family's new experiences, I started making written notes of my feelings as a second child, of my feelings about having two children, and of some typical interactions between Brian and Michael. I soon realized that a fascinating story was unfolding in front of me. I also realized that the story extended beyond my own family. As a professional science and medical writer, I decided to put my reporting skills to use. I haunted the libraries, hunting down hundreds of articles on birth-order research and sibling relations. I also hunted down some long-lost friends, and their friends, and their friends. When I wasn't talking to experienced parents, I was talking to experienced doctors and therapists. I conducted numerous in-depth interviews of obstetricians, pediatricians, psychologists, psychoanalysts and social workers. From what I read and heard, I learned more than I thought I would ever know about second children. My research has helped me to cope with *both* of my children better and to enjoy the double dividends of a two-child family.

Through this book, I hope to share my new insights with three different groups of parents—those who are deciding whether to have a second child, those who are expecting a second child, and those who already have two children but don't quite know what to do with them. For those of you still in the decision-making stage, I have started off with a discussion of the practical and psychological factors to consider in expanding your family. The decision is an important one, as important as your decision to start a family, because it involves the creation of a new life. What will that new life do to your finances? Your career? Your marriage? What will your two children do to, and for, each other? If you decide to go for broke (perhaps literally), and have a second, your next decision is a matter of timing—how soon to put your plan into action? You may have heard that children spaced too closely won't be smart; you may have heard that children spaced too far apart won't be friends. This discussion will bring out the realities of various age spacings, and suggest ways to arrive at a spacing right for your family.

For parents with a second child already on the way, I have written a chapter exploring the pregnancy and childbirth: How can you expect them to differ from your first experience? They will, from day one through month nine, in ways you can't even imagine. Your figure may change at a different rate, in a different way. Your aches and pains may have moved around, and some may be worse. Your mood may be brighter, but if it's darker, don't be surprised. Your labor probably won't be as long, but your childbirth will be as lovely. Those are just hints of what is ahead for you during this, your second pregnancy.

One of the most obvious differences between a first and second pregnancy is the addition of a first child. And one of the most pressing concerns of parents is the preparation of that child for the new family member. It is not an easy task. It requires understanding, sensitivity, and finesse. If it's done poorly, it can mean a future of rivalry and resentment between your two children. If it's done well, the rivalry will be there anyway, but there may be a little less resentment and a little more love. In the chapter on preparation, I present ideas for parents spanning from before the pregnancy, through the birth, the hospital stay, and the homecoming day. If you are pondering such innovations as sibling-preparation classes, siblings at birth, or sibling visitation, that chapter may help you clarify your thoughts, make up your mind, or change it.

If you are currently faced with the reality of two children, you will find practical suggestions in this book for dealing with the double demands of your daily life—ways to cut down on household chores, ways to coordinate your children's schedules, ways to make time for your own interests. There are also suggestions for making the best use of the space you have, even if you don't think you have enough. Yes, two children can live together in one room, although it is not the ideal arrangement. They may even learn to like it if you do it up right.

To focus in on the second child, this book explores various facets of birth-order research. How does the secondborn position affect emotions, abilities, interests, and achievements? The research also answers these burning questions: Who tends to be taller, first children or second? Who are more careful about contraception, women born first or later? Who marries first, firstborn men or their younger brothers? The birth-order chapter concludes with a discussion of how you, the parent, can help your secondborn overcome the drawbacks linked to his birth position, and make the most of the advantages.

What about the relationship between your two children? The sibling experience, long neglected, is now being explored in depth by mental health researchers. What they are finding is that sibling rivalry is common and normal, but only one side of the sibling story. More important is the bond of love and loyalty that develops between most brothers and sisters and that deepens with the passing years. This book addresses both sides of the story—the fighting and the friendship—suggesting ways to cope with the negative feelings and ways to encourage the positive ones.

Throughout this book, parents speak for themselves. They relate their feelings, their problems, their particular methods of coping. Professionals who work with children also express their views, providing yet another perspective on the two-child family. And secondborn children have a chance to tell it their way. Have they been treated differently because they are second and youngest? Have they been overshadowed by their older siblings, or given enough room to establish their own identities? Has their birth order stamped their lives for better or for worse?

Shortly before I completed this book, I attended a meeting at

Brian's school which dealt with sibling relations. The guest lecturer delivered a speech on ways to prepare a child for the birth of a sibling. Then the floor was opened for questions, and the usual questions came: How do I keep my older child from being so jealous of my younger? How do I explain to my son why his baby sister keeps grabbing his toys? But then, the unexpected happened. One of the parents made this observation: "All these questions come from the same perspective—that of the older child. What about the *second* child? No one sees things from that perspective. There's no information on the second child, just nothing written at all."

I had intended to remain silent at the meeting, just to take it all in. But I couldn't contain myself. I fairly jumped out of my seat and announced my current project to the group. "So, at least second children will be getting some of their due."

I left that meeting with renewed confidence in the importance of this book. Yes, there are parents out there who are determined to do as well by their second child as they do by their first. Perhaps this book will help them to bring up second children who are not second best.

1. Planning for Your Second Child

YOU FINALLY GAVE YOUR PARENTS the grandchild they were clamoring for. You made your sister an aunt, your brother-in-law an uncle, and your second cousin a proud third cousin. But apparently that wasn't enough. You may have been still lying, knees-up, on the delivery table, gazing with wonder at your first baby, when the pressure started for number two.

"This time I gave you a girl. Next time I'll make it a boy," your obstetrician may have announced, ignoring your modest contribution to the event. "Your next labor will be a breeze compared with this one," your aunt may have said during visiting hours, as you smiled weakly, wondering if you would ever again be able to sit on a chair without cushions. If you were a first-time father, you were probably also given a gaze into someone else's crystal ball. Perhaps your mother passed on the word: "We expect your next child to be named after *our* side of the family."

Once you arrived home from the hospital and the general hysteria subsided, you may have been allowed to turn your full attention to the child on hand. But if that child has since passed the age of two and you are still not expecting or not telling, you are probably feeling the heat again. For many couples, their child's second birthday party is the breaking point. Half the guests may be accompanied by a snoozing sibling or a pregnant mother. You hoped the talk would revolve around all the new things your two-year-olds are learning. Instead, you overhear conversations about stretch marks and breast pumps and swollen ankles, subjects you dimly remember and long to forget. Then, the inevitable question, "How about you?" as your friends try to drum up potential playmates for their own second children. Apparently, the two-year mark *is* a time of decision and action for many

25

parents; the most common timespan between a first and second birth is between two and a half and three years.

Even if you don't respond to the pressures of your friends and of passing time, events may occur in your own life to remind you that a decision must be made. Your closets are becoming over-crowded with used maternity outfits and outgrown baby clothes: Should you give them to the Salvation Army, or keep them, just in case? If you have decided to move, should you economize and buy the two-bedroom model, or will you really need the third bedroom? Should you take on that new, long-term project at work, or should you let it pass, hoping that you will soon be asking for parental leave from your job?

If you were forming a family twenty or thirty years ago, the decision probably would not have been yours to make. Birth control was not nearly as effective then as it is now, and social pressure was a lot more effective. Something was considered wrong—either mentally, morally, or sexually—with couples who didn't have children. And one child just wouldn't do; at least two and preferably three or four were the necessary credentials for acceptance as a complete family.

While pressure obviously still exists regarding family size, at least there is a variety of pressure groups to choose from. Your relatives most likely extol the joys of oft-repeated parenthood. A national organization and several books trumpet the joys of non-parenthood. Still another organization and other books promote the satisfactions of a one-child family. Certainly, much of the written material is impassioned propaganda, but it serves the useful function of countering the strong large-family tradition in this country. It makes it clear that you do have a choice. That choice does not end with the initial decision to become a parent. It extends to the decision to have a second, or subsequent, child. And with it comes the responsibility of careful, deliberate, plan-ning. Every child deserves to be a planned child.

WAS ONCE ENOUGH?

But how can you best approach the decision the second time around? It is a good idea, initially, to think about how much you enjoy being a parent. If you are like most first-timers, you melted at your child's first toothless grin; you photographed her first swaggering steps in living color, or captured them on film for the big screen; you steadied him during his first dizzying ride on the carousel, and you enjoyed the music and movement almost as much as you did when you were a child. It is easy, and fun, to be a parent at times like those. But on a day-to-day basis, how much time and effort do you give to your child? Do you give it because you feel you have to—or because you really want to? And how about the bad times—the cold that keeps your child, and you, awake all night; the food hurled acrosss the room to land on your just-washed walls; the temper tantrums at the supermarket just as your turn comes to check out; the hitting and the biting and the talking back. Of course you don't like the demands and the difficulties, but are you able to put them into perspective and still feel positively about yourself and your child?

Some parents learn, from their reactions to their first child, that they were not cut out for bringing up babies. Brenda, the mother of four-year-old Matthew, was surprised by that discovery. She fully expected to like motherhood and to be good at it. She enjoyed Matthew's infancy and felt she handled it well. "But by the time he was about eighteen months old, I found it rough going. He was very strong-willed and stubborn. I had a hard time controlling him and letting him know who was boss. I just couldn't deal with it. I found myself being verbally abusive, so I went for counseling." Brenda and her husband decided not to have another child. "I don't think I could go through those terrible two's again. I'm too impatient. It took a while to admit it to myself, but in the role of mother, I just don't have it."

Of course, problems with the first child don't guarantee problems with the second. Your second child may well be very different from your first, requiring a different parenting approach, maybe one you are more comfortable with. In addition, you may have learned from any mistakes you've made as a first-time parent. But if you feel, like Brenda does, that you just don't have it, that your patience is short and your temper shorter, you would be wise to consider stopping at one.

Even if you did have it the first time, will you be able to muster it all over again? As you surely know by now, you have to give a child a lot more than a child will give you. And if you don't want the child enough, you might not be willing to give enough. "I was very patient with Adam because I was so excited to have him," said Lenore, a woman who has almost decided not to have a second child. "I wanted him so much, I even managed to appear cheerful in the middle of the night. I was able to put up with the vomit and the cradle cap and the other joys of motherhood. But that was six years ago. I'm not dying to have another, so I don't know if I could put up with all of that again." Lenore, however, still isn't sure. She is storing Adam's old carriage at her mother's house. And she instructed her friends not to give away the baby clothes she lent them. "I always had a fantasy of two children that went along with the house and the picket fence. The carriage and the clothes are keeping the fantasy alive."

Fantasies of family life are common. Before marriage, many couples fantasize about the number of children they want and even about the sexes they would like them to be. They may discuss the relative merits of having two girls and then a boy, versus having the boy first and then the girls—or how about the boy in the middle? The fantasies are fed by television images of firm but benevolent parents helping their confused but lovable children through the skirmishes of sibling rivalry and the agonies of adolescence. For the postwar generation, family life was served up, with an extra helping of sugar, by *Ozzie and Harriet* and *Father Knows Best*. More recently, *Eight Is Enough* and *The Waltons* did the same thing, only the portions were larger.

CONSIDER THE COSTS

But the alluring images of television familes are given stiff competition by the real-life arrival of a couple's first baby. The subsequent arrival of the hospital and medical bills can really bring the new parents down to earth. (How *did* Robert Young ever support that brood?) The financial cost of bringing up a child is a real and valid concern, and as the cost of living increases, it becomes a more important factor in family planning decisions. A recent study of 1,600 American women examined the reasons why they wanted the number of children they did. Of those who wanted just one child, 38 percent cited "financial costs" as the main reason they wanted no more. (The next most important reason, health problems and old age, was cited first by just 12 percent of the sample.)

The economic costs of rearing children are substantial. The Population Reference Bureau in Washington, D.C., has broken down those costs into two parts. One is the "direct maintenance cost" consisting of such out-of-pocket expenses as food, clothing, and education, including four years at a public university. The other is the "opportunity cost," or the income that one of the parents foregoes by staying home for a certain period to care for the children. Using information from a number of government and private sources, the Population Reference Bureau (PRB) estimated the direct costs in 1980 dollars to be more than $85,000, assuming a moderate standard of living. The opportunity cost varies, depending on the caretaker's educational level. A woman who has completed college can expect to forego more than *$53,000* in income, according to Thomas J. Espenshade, author of the PRB report. (That figure is based on several general assumptions: that before a woman has a child she works only halftime; that she drastically reduces her hours of paid work after the birth; that she takes on a somewhat heavier work load when the child enters school; and that she returns to her previous level of halftime work when the child turns fifteen. These calculations were done only for women, not for men.) Grand total of both costs: nearly $140,000.

If you are startled by that statistic, try this one: Approximately 30 percent of annual income is typically spent on a firstborn child in a middle-class family. Most middle-class parents think they spend just about 8 percent of yearly income on each of their children.

For parents considering a second child, the financial news isn't all bad. A second child will probably not be as big a financial drain as your first. Studies show that a second child costs only about half as much as a first to raise to age eighteen. Less than 15 percent of the family income is typically spent on a second child, compared with the 30 percent figure for a first. Certain economies of scale hold down the costs of a second child, points out Dr. Espenshade. Food can be purchased more economically, for example, and housing can stretch further as two children often share a room. The recycling of baby equipment, clothing, and toys also spells savings. However, considering the figures of 30 and 15 together may give you reason to pause, and a very good reason to consider the financial consequences of increasing your family size.

CONSIDER THE WORK

Another of the realities that is brought home with the baby is the amount of work child-rearing entails. The type of work may change as the child moves from one stage to another, but it won't go away until the child does. The sheer physical drudgery is the worst at the beginning—the feedings and the burpings that seem to go on forever, with one session almost merging into another; the diapers that always need changing because if you are not quick enough the stretchies will need changing too; the bottles that need scrubbing and the sheets that need washing. And, of course, there is the baby, who always seems to start crying just when you think you have found a quiet moment to yourself.

If you feel as if you're putting a lot of time and energy into child care, you're right. A recent study estimated that a first child generates 9,274 hours of extra housework from the time he is born until he graduates from high school. That translates to more than four years of full-time employment for whoever is doing that housework.

If you feel overworked by one child, how will a second affect you? That same study indicates that having a second child creates still more housework—an average of 3,672 hours more. But that figure is less than half the amount generated by the first. So the story for work is about the same as the story for money—having a second child increases but does not double the duties.

Once again, however, the perceptions of parents do not always match the realities, and the realities vary from family to family. For Bob and Sharon, parents of Jesse, four, and Gail, one, the addition of their second child seemed to more than double the demands. "I feel like I'm constantly being pulled in different directions," said Bob. "I seem to be on demand nine-tenths of my waking hours. If it's two parents and one child, you can share the duties and one can rest. But when it's two on two, you don't get too many chances to sit down. It just seems to get bigger and bigger."

Jenny is the mother of Marty, three, and Gary, two. She emphasizes that children are hard work, and that the work is not appreciated by those who don't do it. But, in her experience, two children are no harder than one child. "In some ways, it's even easier. They play together and teach each other. Some of the pressure is taken off the parents."

A study of 245 mothers, each with two children, was conducted by sociologists from East Carolina University. Seventy percent of the women reported that two children require "a little more work, but not much," than one child. Sixty percent reported having "less time to myself" after the second child was born. And close to 80 percent said there was "more noise" in the house with two children than with one. But the overall sentiment of the mothers was that "there is more adjustment from none to one than from one to two." Apparently, once you have given up on privacy in the bathroom, once you have figured out how to cut up your roast beef with one hand while rocking a baby carriage with the other, once you have mastered the art of diapering a toddler who is performing somersaults on the changing table, you feel you can handle anything—even another child.

FOR BETTER OR FOR WORSE?

But having one child, or two, or more, can have an effect you don't expect. Some couples find their marital relationship severely strained by parenthood. They may discover, early on, that they are unable to agree on child-rearing tactics: Is it better to rock the baby to sleep or let her cry it out? Is it okay to let little Joshua play with the doll he got for his first birthday? And how about the gun he got for his second? Those aren't usually the issues that divorces are made of. But when two people are exhausted from lack of sleep (a common characteristic of early parenthood), the smallest disagreement can escalate into a very cold war.

Another problem area may be the division of labor: Who should do what, and how often? "Carl has only given Jesse one bath in the entire four years of his life," Carolyn complained. She found him equally uncooperative in other areas of child care. "He felt he had his job to do and I had mine, and that's the way it was. I was very upset by his lack of involvement. Sometimes I felt I only needed him for his paycheck. Other than that, it was me and Jesse." Carolyn and Carl have decided that Jesse will not be getting a brother or sister.

But many couples weather parenthood very well. In fact, some judge their marriages as better than ever after the birth of their first child. The addition of a second child, however, can change the picture again, for better or for worse. Which way will your marriage go? Read a different study, you will get a different answer. One study showed that marriages are more likely to "get worse" than "improve" after a second child is born. Another found that two is not enough: Couples with three children are the most satisfied.

Surprisingly, there is one study that clarifies the picture a bit. It relates marital satisfaction not only to the number of children in the household, but also to whether those children were planned. The researchers found that in families with unplanned children, marital adjustment declined after the birth of the second child. But when family size was planned, couples with two children were better adjusted than were couples with one child. Planning seems to be the key, for the happiness of the children and the parents.

SECONDS, ANYONE?

Apparently, a second child means more expense, more work, more noise, and for some couples, more fights. Yet the two-child family is the most popular family size, and becoming more so all the time. In 1952, just 25 percent of women considered a two-child family ideal, according to opinion polls. That figure rose to 45 percent in 1974 and to 51 percent in 1980. The Bureau of the Census recently reported that women aged eighteen to thirty-four expected to have, on average, 2.072 children during their lifetime. Of the women who already had one child, 58 percent expected to have at least one more.

Many factors motivate people to have a second child. Some people do it to avoid smothering their current child with too much parental concern. They think that the second child will take some of the pressure off the first, and "spread the grief around" a bit. Other people do it because their parents did it, and they liked growing up in a two-child family.

"I was very content with the size of my family," said Kenneth, recalling his own happy boyhood. "I did a lot of things with my older brother. We played a lot of ball, we played together in the house. I think I would have been lonely if I was by myself. I wouldn't have liked it. And I wouldn't like it for my child either." Kenneth and his wife recently had their second child. (Some adults with unhappy memories of life with a brother or sister use similar reasoning to decide against having a second child. One such man told his wife, "The worst thing we can do for our son is to present him with a sibling.")

The list of common reasons for having a second goes on and on. Psychiatrists call the following reasons "wrong" reasons: the fear that an only child will die and leave a couple childless; the attempt to satisfy family pressures; the hope of having another wage-earner in the family when the second child matures; the wish for companionship in old age; the desire to have the family name carried on. At the time of this writing, Dr. Elizabeth Whelan, executive director of the American Council on Science and Health, was herself trying to decide whether to have a second child. She suggests two additional motivations: "If you really enjoy your first child and think that child is great, it might be tantalizing to see what another would be like. Or, perhaps, you might think your first child is more like your husband (or wife). So you might want to try again to see if you could have one more like yourself."

Yet another reason some couples have a second is an attempt at sexual balance—or "a girl for you and a boy for me." But wishing it so does not make it so; even if you take your temperature regularly and have sex on schedule, sex control is not yet a popular scientific reality. If you take the gamble, you may well be disappointed, and your second child may turn out the loser.

"A girl may feel pressured into playing the boy, or a boy into fulfilling his parents' needs for a girl," says Dr. Tess Forrest, an analyst specializing in family relations. "Children in that position often become torn in terms of their own identity, and develop sexual identification problems."

THE ONLY CHILD: SPOILED BRAT OR SOLID CITIZEN?

For some couples, the decision is not between one child and two children, but between no children and two children. They most definitely do not want an only child. Some pretty nasty things have been said about children without siblings. "Being an only child is a disease in itself," wrote an eminent psychologist around the turn of the century. Other authorities have applied such adjectives as selfish, spoiled, aggressive, egotistical, domineering, and overindulged to an only child's personality. Although such a negative appraisal has not withstood scientific scrutiny, it has had a long-lasting impact on family planning decisions. In 1967, only 6 percent of women planned to have one child. But there has been an upward shift since then; in 1979, 13 percent of women expected to have just one child. Perhaps the word has gotten around—being only isn't half bad.

Research indicates that only children tend to be high achievers. They are likely to perform well in school academically, and to achieve occupational success as adults. They are also inclined to be independent and to have high levels of self-esteem. (Of course, those personality attributes are based on statistical averages; they do not apply to every only child.)

A common belief is that only children are lonely children. Actually, most only children are socially outgoing and fare quite well at making friends. But some do feel the lack of a sibling. In a survey of 105 "onlies," ranging in age from eight to sixty-six, more than half the children said they would like other children in the family, and three-quarters of the adults said they had wished for brothers or sisters during at least one period in their lives. The major reason given by the adults: the desire for companionship.

A study of 300 married women in the Buffalo area of New York supported those findings. The women from one-child families were the most unhappy with their family size. Almost half reported that they liked growing up in a one-child family "not at all." Fewer than 10 percent of the women from two-child families said they liked that size "not at all." Those findings were cited by Dr. Kenneth Terhune in a report to The Center for Population Research, a division of the National Institute of Child Health and Human Development. He interpreted them as representing "an important clue that something is missing" in the family life of an only child. "No study has examined the emotional gratification of having siblings with whom to share experiences and to confide. No study has examined the ability to become close to others, to relate to them on an intimate basis. It may just be that having non-family playmates cannot fully substitute for siblings in such regards."

Scientists might not be sure of it, but most parents are. They want their first child to have a brother or sister. In providing a sibling, they feel they are providing a companion. Good reason or bad reason for having a second? Alone, it's not good enough. Each child deserves to be wanted for his or her own sake, not for the sake of anything or anybody else. But if you do decide to have a second child for the best reason of all—simply because you want one—you are not doing bad by your first.

BEYOND CAIN AND ABEL

Sisters and brothers won't necessarily like each other, but they will have a powerful and lasting impact on each other. They provide each other with experiences in sharing, in cooperating, in compromising. They force each other to confront and deal with the painful emotions of jealousy and greed. They enable each other to develop resources to deal with other difficult situations later in life.

The two-child family is, admittedly, a competitve family size. That fact is emphasized in literature advocating one-child families, and is described as a drawback. But is it really so bad? Considering the society we live in, it can be considered an advantage. Whether they are ready for it or not, children are faced with competition in school. Adults are faced with competiton for jobs. And all through life there is competition for friendship and love. The sibling experience provides an early opportunity to learn to deal with being competitive. It prepares children for what is really out there.

Sisters and brothers don't only provide lessons for the future. They can also provide a lot of fun for the here and now. They are often close companions who play for endless hours, somehow dreaming up activities that don't bore the older or frustrate the younger. Their feelings of friendship become obvious in their response to outside attack. Whether the aggressor is a scolding parent or the park bully, siblings are often quick to come to each other's aid.

Family life in general can be a richer experience for children with siblings, and for their parents. The home is a livelier place, family gatherings more festive. Dr. Brian Sutton-Smith, Professor of Education at the University of Pennsylvania and authority on sibling relations, has quite a bit of research material in his own family—five children, aged eleven to twenty-seven. "The emotional range is greater in a family with siblings," he says. "The lows are lower, but the highs are higher. There is more of a quality of uproarious happiness. Sure, kids can fight like the devil, but they can also have great times together."

The bond between siblings usually remains intact even after they have grown and moved out of their parents' home. True, most siblings aren't best friends in adulthood. But then they are not as apt to be "dropped" as friends are. More important, siblings are often turned to in times of crisis. Many parents are comforted by the knowledge that their grown children "have each other."

So a second child will not be a hardship for your first, especially if you deal intelligently with the problems of rivalry that will inevitably come up. But does a second child fit into your own life plans? Having another child may mean a delay in developing your career and in pursuing other interests. It may mean extra years of dragging your kids along on vacation instead of getting away from it all with your mate. It may mean that you will still have a child around the house at an age when you would rather have put all that far behind you.

One way to think about the decision is to consider "alternative gratification"—things you like to do with your time other than rearing children. For example, ask yourself whether you enjoy child-rearing as much as you enjoy the hours you spend reading, or working, or jogging. Try to figure out how that alternative stacks up against another child. It is important not to make moral judgments during this process—not to condemn yourself as "selfish" or "irresponsible" if you decide against second parenthood. Time is a limited and precious resource. You should be honest with yourself in deciding how you want to spend it.

If you do choose, after careful deliberation, to spend some of that time having and rearing a second child, you will probably be glad you did. Remember that study of 245 mothers which uncovered complaints of more work, more noise, and less time alone in a two-child household? Those same mothers had some good things to say about having second children: "They are company to each other"; "My husband and I have one apiece"; "They are twice as much pleasure." And most of the mothers—about 94 percent—said they had "never" wished that they could return to a one-child family (quiet as it may be).

Having a second child is a risk. Your second child will be different from your first, and you will be, in many ways, a different parent the second time. It is also a challenge. All your resources of time, energy, understanding, and love will be put to a severe test by your two children. But it is also a great opportunity. Your second child will give you the chance to experience all the joys and satisfactions of parenthood yet another time.

A MATTER OF TIMING

Once you have decided to go ahead and do it again, you are faced with another decision: When? You may be tempted to do it right away, to get all the diapering and dirty work over with and get on with a more normal way of life. But could you handle two kids in diapers at the same time, two kids who can't talk, or walk, or eat anything but Cheerios by themselves? And you may have heard it's not so great for the children themselves to be too close—the older child may be robbed of his babyhood, and each child robbed of your time.

On the other hand, you may feel you need a long breathing space between children. You just can't face the demands of infancy so soon again, especially not while your first child is still so demanding herself. But if you do it that way—waiting until your first child is a schoolchild—will your children ever be friends? Or will their interests be so different they will never play together, never share friends or share secrets, never be interested in the same thing at the same time?

Today, more parents are opting for a longer wait—but not *too* long. The average interval between a first and second birth is two years and eight months, according to Census Bureau figures. (Not since World War II has that interval been so large.) Recent figures from the National Center for Health Statistics provide still another perspective on child spacing. In about 45 percent of families, there is a two-to-four-year age difference between the first and second child. In about 25 percent of families, the age difference is less than two years, and in the remaining 30 percent, it is more than four years.

The Bureau of the Census suggests two possible reasons for the trend to larger spacings. One is the trend to smaller families. In two-child families—now the most popular size—there is a longer interval between children than in families with three or more children. Children just don't come as fast or often as they used to. The second reason—one that explains both longer spacings and smaller families—is birth control. Today, most couples can have the number of children they want pretty much when they want them. And they apparently don't want a lot of children of almost the same age.

Still another reason becomes apparent in talking to parents about their spacing decisions. Some of them feel their children will be intellectually deprived if they are spaced too closely. That factor played a part in the decision in my own family to try to space our children at least three years apart. I remembered a psychology professor in college stressing the importance of a three-year separation. I didn't recall if he provided any proof of intellectual advantages, but the number stuck in my mind. My husband and I did try for it, but didn't quite make it. My due date would have placed our children two years, seven and a half months apart in age. Everyone wondered why I wasn't devastated at being two weeks late. However, I was still four months short of the magic number, and certain that we had doomed our children to mediocrity.

I don't know if my college professor read them all, but there have been a lot of published reports on age spacing and intelligence. To my relief, they don't all say what he said. In fact, many of them contradict each other. Here is a sampling:

One study looked at the scores of college students on the American College Entrance Examination. Boys did better the farther apart they were spaced from their siblings, but girls did better the closer the age spacing. Another study examined the school grades of boys and girls from four suburban Boston communities. Again, boys did better if they were spaced farther apart —but spacing had no effect on the academic achievement of the girls. Yet another study indicated that general intelligence is highest when births are separated by two to four years, an intermediate spacing.

Some research suggests that a wide spacing is advantageous for the younger child, but may not be ideal for the intellectual development of the older. Still other research shows that spacing makes no difference to the intelligence of either younger or older.

As a whole, the research gives a slight edge to wider spacing. But any differences caused by spacing are so small, and so many other factors play a role in intellectual development, that psychologists do not recommend using this body of data as a basis for family planning decisions.

If you can't make your children much smarter by spacing them farther apart, can you make them healthier? Some people believe that closely spaced births can harm the mother and the second child—that her body needs a year to get back to "normal" before undergoing another pregnancy, and that the new baby is more vulnerable to disease or death if there wasn't enough time between births.

But no known dangers result from a short interval between one birth and another pregnancy. Even if you get pregnant the first time you ovulate after the birth, you are inviting no increased medical risk, according to prevailing obstetrical opinion. However, there are some doctors who advise waiting at least one full year from the birth before becoming pregnant again. One I spoke to admitted basing that recommendation on "feeling, not on anything scientific." If your first delivery was a Caesarean birth, such a suggestion has more scientific validity. Your doctor will probably advise a six-months' or even a year's wait to become pregnant to give the scar time to heal and you time to recover fully from the surgery.

Even breast-feeding mothers need not worry about spacing for health reasons. Pregnancy will not harm the milk, though the supply may decline after the first few months.

So close spacing is not harmful to a child's intellect or to maternal or infant health (except in the case of a Caesarean delivery). But that does not mean that spacing is not important. It can have dramatic effects on family life, on the relationship between your children, and even on your marriage. Some people focus on just one part of the picture. For example, they will try to space the births in a way they feel will benefit the children, even if it is not right for the parents. Stuart and Terri realized that was what they were doing—neglecting their own feelings for the "good" of the children—but they went ahead, anyway. "We didn't want the separation between our children to be longer than three years," Stuart recalled. "We felt they wouldn't relate well if there was a bigger age gap. So we tried for a second, even though we weren't dying to have a second child at that particular moment. It was strictly for the children." Stuart then engaged in some wishful thinking. "It would have been nice if we could have delayed having a second child for a few years, until we were ready. Then, when we did have the baby, Sammy would mystically go back to being three. That would have been great."

Some parents go the opposite way. They choose a spacing that is most convenient for them, and figure the children will manage somehow. Sounds heartless, but it is actually a better idea. Parents who are happy with the family structure will likely provide a happier home environment for their children. But the best idea is to consider everyone's needs beforehand. Of course, you can't see into the future and predict whether a particular age spacing will enhance or undermine family harmony. But the following breakdowns should give you some idea of what to expect.

Under Two Years Apart

These are known as "cluster" births. Some parents want their children to be close in age so they will be playmates and move along at the same pace of development. The whole family will be better off, the parents reason, because they can devise activities and outings to interest everyone. No dragging along eleven-year-old Michelle to a Saturday afternoon cartoon festival because that's where five-year-old Julian wants to be. And no wheeling along a sleeping baby to her brother's Little League game. Children of almost the same age will, presumably, want to do the same things, and want to do them together.

Another reason for closely spaced births is to go through the baby-care stage just once. Some parents don't enjoy the physical aspects of it, can't tolerate the sleepless nights, and want to put all of that behind them. "I was totally exhausted the first few months with Todd," Susan recalled. "He napped only fifteen or twenty minutes at a time, and was up every two hours at night. The prospect of dragging out the early childhood rearing years was unbearable. I would rather have them over with at the same time." Susan had her second child, Paula, eighteen months after Todd was born.

Still another motivation for having children close in age is to free yourself for out-of-home activities. It can mean less time out of the job market, and a quicker return to other interests that don't blend well with babies. Age can also be a factor. Women who are over thirty when they have their first child—and more and more women fit into that category—commonly want to have another child quickly. They may fear that a delay will affect their fertility, or perhaps create complications during pregnancy or delivery. And they may be afraid they won't have the energy to take care of a baby if they wait too long.

Parents who opt for "cluster" births are generally glad they did it—once the first few years are over. While they watch their friends still struggling through the infancy stage, they can savor their relative freedom. They are able to socialize more, travel more, go out to dinner without lugging along booster seats, bibs, and bottles. As an extra bonus, their children may well be good buddies. Many reports indicate that closely spaced children have more interests in common, play with each other more, play with each other's friends more, and are lonelier without each other.

Dr. Brian Sutton-Smith, the sibling researcher and father of five, strongly advocates spacing children less than two years apart. His main reason is their greater capacity for friendship. "This is a time of incredible loneliness and alienation. Children can't just go outside and find friends to play with. They need siblings as playmates. The closer they are in age, the more they'll play together." Dr. Sutton-Smith has followed his own advice, up to a point. His first four children are each two years apart. His fifth came along ten years later.

So family life may be fairly pleasant after the first few years— but first you have got to get through those first few years. And that's not so easy. The friendship that will probably develop later between your children is nowhere in evidence when you bring your second baby home from the hospital. If your first child is old enough to poke and bite and squeeze very tightly, that may just be what he tries to do. If he is a little too young for that now, he may get around to it a little later, when he is stronger and the baby more of a nuisance. He may try yanking toys away, knocking the baby down when she first tries to stand up or to walk, throwing things at her and pouring things over her. The physical aggression of older to younger is bad enough, but before too long, the second child learns to retaliate, and you may find both your children tormenting each other.

Jealousy, of course, knows no age limits, but younger children do not have the emotional tools to deal with it. And as babies themselves, with few friends or interests outside the home, they are more affected by the intrusion of a baby into their private sanctum. Suddenly, the parents who were his alone must be shared, a difficult accommodation to make for one so young.

Another potential drawback of close spacing is the tendency to treat the children too much alike. Because their ages are similar, parents may not pay much attention to the differences between them. They may overemphasize family togetherness and group activities—to the detriment of a child's developing individuality.

How about life for the parents? What is it like with two tiny tots? "Drudgery" is the way most parents who have been through it describe it. With children so young, child-care duties are more than doubled. In addition to the physical chores of feeding, diapering, washing, and all the rest, there is the added dimension of differing schedules. Finally got one child to nap? The other one might get ravenously hungry just about then. Finally got them both to sleep, and you are beginning to nod off yourself? One awakens with colicky cramps, waking up the other, and you have two screaming babes on your hands.

The first year or two can be a real trial for parents, individually and as a couple. So much of you is demanded by the children, there may not be enough left for each other. "Since our second child was born, my husband and I have had marital problems," confided Cathy, the mother of children born a year and a half apart. "I think it's because there's that much more responsibility for me, more things to cope with during the day. By the time Peter comes home from work my tolerance is gone. I don't want any demands made of me. I don't want anyone to touch me. After having two kids hanging all over me all day, I want my body to myself. It's hard on Peter. I'm not as active sexually anymore because I'm just too tired."

Parents who have their children close in age also have to put up with pressure from outsiders. Some people express sympathy, assuming it was an "accident." Others express disapproval that you would dare be different. "How *could* you have two, one after another?" they may ask. Lois, the mother of two boys a year apart, has had her fill of such comments. "Most people were negative and sarcastic about my having two children so close. Even my best friends made sly remarks. I really resented it. It made me feel uncomfortable and uneasy."

If you do choose to have your children within two years of each other because of the positive aspects of that spacing, there are ways to deal with the drawbacks. Every effort should be made to treat each child as an individual, with separate needs, talents, and abilities. And every effort should be made to assure the older child he is still loved, to provide him with some private time with you every day, and to stimulate his interests outside the home—all without neglecting the newcomer. The baby also needs a fair share of your attention and love. (If you feel you are putting in too much effort, and are on the verge of personal and marital collapse, turn quickly to chapter nine, which suggests ways to save energy without depriving yourself, your spouse, or your children.)

Two-to-Four Years Apart

This age spacing is most typical. That in itself is a reason why some parents choose it. Following the crowd makes them feel part of it. Also, if everyone else is doing it, how bad can it be?

Some parents choose this intermediate spacing because that's what the "experts" say is best, or that's what the "books" say is ideal. The reason behind the recommendation may be unheard, unread, or long forgotten, but the voice of authority clinches it —three years, take a little or give a little, it will be.

Parents who do offer their own reasons for their choice often stress the negative—what they want to avoid—rather than the benefits of this particular spacing. If the children are closer, they say, there would be "too much work." If the children are farther apart in age, "they wouldn't be friends," or "the older would get so used to being an only child he couldn't accept the younger."

But there are positive aspects to a two-to-four year spacing, and some parents do recognize them. Practically speaking, things are easier if the older child is older than two. By the time the second is born, the first is learning to do things for himself. He may be feeding himself, dressing himself, going to the bathroom himself. His sleep habits are probably pretty reliable, so you will only have one child to contend with in the middle of the night. Best of all, your first child may be old enough for some kind of toddler program or even a full-fledged nursery school. So while he is otherwise occupied, you just may be able to fit in a nap when your baby does. If your baby is inconsiderate enough to stay awake during those precious hours, you may find yourself enjoying your time alone together. You can finally kiss your second child without worrying about arousing jealousy in your first.

Your first child will feel jealousy of the newcomer—you can count on it—but you can encourage him to tell you about it with words, not actions. "A child over the age of two is more likely to understand what is going on and to verbally express his feelings," says Dr. Virginia Pomeranz, New York pediatrician and Associate Clinical Professor of Pediatrics at Cornell University Medical College. "He may be able to tell you exactly what he thinks about that new little creature who is occupying so much of your time. He doesn't need to show you with violence."

And he might not feel quite as badly about the latest turn of events as would a younger child. He is no longer getting constant attention anyway, so he is not as apt to notice if he gets a little less. And there are things he cares about outside his home—playing games with his friends, making castles out of sand, sleeping over at Grandma's house. So the baby doesn't ruin *everything*.

The adjustment seems easier, for all concerned, when the older child has passed his second birthday. But does that adjustment come at the price of friendship? Will your children be too far apart in age to want to play the same games? Probably not. Even children who are three or four years apart in age find ways of playing together. And they may start even before the baby is a year old, Dr. Elizabeth Whelan of the American Council on Science and Health points out. In fact, the younger child usually learns how to play at an earlier age than his older sibling did. And as they grow older, their age difference becomes less and less important to their skills and interests, so they may become even more compatible playmates.

But while they may play together a lot as they grow up, they may fight a lot, too. Some research reports indicate that sibling rivalry is most intense between children spaced two-to-four years apart—especially if the older child is a boy. There is also evidence that siblings with this age difference find life generally more stressful.

To confuse things further, not everything that is true for a two-year separation is necessarily true for a three-year separation, and a four-year separation may be quite another story again. Many psychologists stress the importance of at least a three-year interval between births. During the first three years of life, they say, the child is engaged in a process known as "individuation-separation;" he is learning how to function separately from his mother, and to face difficulties on his own. If the child's sense of security is threatened by the birth of a new baby before that process is completed, he may develop permanent personality changes. Recently, Italian psychologists compared thirty-two firstborn children who had siblings less than three years younger, with thirty-two firstborns who had siblings more than three years younger (all sixty-four were high school students at the time of the study). Those with more closely spaced siblings scored higher in "affiliation," the need to associate with other people, and in "succorance," the need for help from others. In sum, they were more dependent. The investigators attribute that trait to their siblings' coming too soon.

A four-year separation is even better than a three-year gap, according to some experts. Dr. Joan Lasko, a pioneer researcher in the field, found that a four-year-old is easier to handle than a three-year-old when a new baby is born. And mothers tend to be harsher with an older sibling who is three than with one who is four.

So a two-to-four-year separation may not be as ideal as you thought, even if "everyone" is doing it. Each spacing has its advantages and drawbacks. The idea is not to consult a table of national averages and try to place yourself right smack in the middle, but to consult your own feelings and the needs of all your family members.

More Than Four Years Apart

This age spacing has a lot to recommend it, but it is often arrived at by circumstances, not choice. If the first child has serious health problems early in life, the parents may be too busy coping with them to think of coping with another child. Or the first child may have the type of personality that leaves the parents so tired at night, they can't imagine even conceiving another child, much less bringing one up. In some cases, a miscarriage or stillbirth helps to explain a large age gap between first and second child. Or financial concerns may explain the delay. Some parents simply can't afford to have a second child so soon, or would like to save up more money to prevent a future financial crunch. (The financial advantages of a wide spacing become even more apparent fifteen or twenty years on, when only one college education has to be paid for at a time.)

However it is arrived at, this spacing makes a lot of parents very happy. They actually have the time to enjoy the infancy of their second child, to nurse him in comparative peace and quiet, to play with him with energy and without interruption. If the older child is considerably older than four, parenthood can be easier and more pleasant still. Dr. Burton White of Harvard University has for many years supervised observations into the homes of preschool children. He found that spacing makes a big difference to the entire family—the closer the spacing, the greater the problems for everyone involved; the wider the gap, the more delightful the experience for parents and children alike.

A recent study done of mother-infant interaction has confirmed the wisdom of widely separated births. Babies born at least three and a half years after their next older siblings were looked at more, smiled at more, and played with more than babies who came along sooner. Ironically, the intermediate spacing of one and a half to three and a half years spelled the least maternal attention for the new baby, according to researchers Michael Lewis and Valerie S. Kreitzberg of the Educational Testing Service.

"The spacing in my family is ideal," says Arlene, mother of eleven-year-old Jennifer and six-year-old Brett. "Each child got all they possibly could from me. I was able to devote myself entirely to Jennifer for her first five years. Then when Brett was born, Jennifer was in school, so Brett had plenty of attention as a baby. Even now it works out well. If I want to do something with Brett, Jennifer can busy herself. And I can do things with Jennifer when Brett sleeps. Their demands are of different kinds, so I'm able to meet them."

Arlene also points out that there is hardly any competition between her daughters, and little evidence of sibling rivalry. "They understand there is a large difference between them, so they don't expect to be doing the same things. I can put them to sleep at different times without getting complaints."

Many five- and six-year-olds genuinely enjoy the arrival of a new baby. Because they are somewhat independent of their parents, they tend to be less resentful than are two- or three-year-olds. They can play a bigger role during the period of pregnancy and their mother's hospital stay, helping prepare the home for its latest addition. And they can really help their parents in caring for the baby—fetching diapers and bottles, folding baby clothes, even trying a feeding if they are old enough and willing.

But there may be just a little jealousy beneath their helpful, mature exterior. After being the "only star" for so long, they suddenly have to share the sky with another. They may find their parents more tied to the house now, less available for weekend ski trips and cycling through the park. Instead of being taken out for dinner, they may be left behind with baby and babysitter. So life has changed for them, and not all for the better.

As the children grow older, it may be the younger who feels more competitive. He just can't do what his older sister or brother does, no matter how hard he tries—but that doesn't mean he stops trying. "Bruce is extremely jealous of his older brother," says Rona, mother of Wayne, eleven, and Bruce, five. "He won't let Wayne show him how to do anything. It's like a blow to his ego. But he'll try desperately to accomplish the same things. Wayne rides a two-wheeler, so Bruce has one, too, and even though he needs training wheels now, he's practicing so hard we might take them off soon. His competitive feelings are really causing him to extend himself."

Many parents avoid a wide separation between births for fear their children won't be friends. It is true, children of very different ages don't play together as much as children closer in age—they are simply not interested in many of the same activities. (Parents can encourage some mutual interests, as discussed in chapter seven.) But their age separation does not mean the children will not feel the loyalty of any brother or sister. The younger child may well idolize the older, sometimes even into adulthood. And the older child generally feels protective of the younger, as Dr. Pomeranz witnesses in her pediatric practice. Many of her seven- or eight-year-old patients won't let their baby sisters or brothers come to the office without coming themselves. They look the doctor in the eye and say, "Don't you hurt my sister!" or "You're giving her a shot? Please don't make it hurt too much." And so the baby has a third "parent" to see to her welfare.

Despite positive feelings toward each other, siblings widely separated in age are usually pretty independent of each other. They don't tend to take on the personality characteristics of the other. This situation seems to be especially advantageous for boys. Research shows that when boys are spaced widely apart, they tend to be more outgoing.

Girls also benefit from wide spacing. Widely spaced older sisters have more friends in school than those closer in age to younger siblings, research indicates. Widely spaced school children and young adolescents of *both* sexes are more happy-go-lucky, controlled, and fervent, already beginning to make college plans.

An interesting aspect of this age is that some parents who aim for it never quite make it. As their first child gets older and starts school, they begin to like their newfound freedom. The thought of giving it up and going back to the routines of infant care may become less palatable with each passing year. And so, though they never intended it, they may finally end up as a one-child family.

MAKING UP YOUR MIND

Now that you have looked at some of the general characteristics of various spacings, you still have some work to do. It is time to look inward, at some of your own characteristics and those of your family. Having children close in age demands a lot of energy. Do you have it? Closely spaced children can undermine a rocky marriage. Is yours strong enough to withstand the stress? Having children farther apart may mean a long break in your career, and more total years of child care. Are you ready for that? Do you want that? Your decision on spacing requires a careful appraisal of your financial resources, your life situation, your goals. And it requires the mutual consent of both parents.

Once you have decided that you want a second child, and when you want one, you still have one decision to make—when should you start trying to have one? If pregnancy was practically instantaneous with your first child, it will probably be fast again, but maybe not as fast. And if you think you will need a year, because that's what it took before, that could very well be the case. But don't count on it. If you start trying too far in advance, you may be caught unawares and unprepared. In general, a three-to-six-months' leeway is a good bet if you want to get reasonably close to your "ideal" spacing. (Statistically, two out of three couples who are trying to achieve pregnancy succeed within the first three months. About four out of five are successful by the end of the sixth month.) But if you want to make your second child a Gemini, because that sign is compatible with your older child's Aquarius, the odds are against you. As carefully as you plan, nature may have other plans.

2. Pregnancy and Childbirth the Second Time Around

As YOU BEGIN YOUR SECOND PREGNANCY, memories of your first are probably vivid. You may have spent the entire nine months walking on air, even if you could barely stand up toward the end. Or you may have experienced periods of despondency, though you still can't figure out why. Whether you felt like a beautiful Madonna or an ugly blimp, you are probably wondering what you will feel like this time. Will the pregnancy and birth be as good—or as bad—as you remember them to be? Will you feel radiantly healthy again—or as sick as a dog again? Will your figure expand to the same incredible proportions as it did last time? Will labor be easier and shorter, or harder and longer?

One thing is for sure: Your second childrearing experience will not be quite the same as your first, physically or emotionally. Every pregnancy is different, every birth unique. Some of the reasons have nothing to do with the fact that this is number two. They may simply reflect changes in your life circumstances. You are poorer this time or richer, and so more or less anxious about your family's financial future. Your marriage is either stronger or more vulnerable to stress, making this pregnancy either easier to get through or a time of tension and discord. Perhaps you have more pregnant friends to share with and compare with this time, or maybe your best friend has just moved away. Anything that affects the amount of stress you feel, and the amount of support you have, will influence the psychological and physical course of your pregnancy.

The amount of planning that goes into a pregnancy also helps determine how well it will go. If a baby is not wholeheartedly wanted at a particular time in a couple's life, the aches and the pains and the figure change may not seem worth it. One mother had finally shed the weight she gained from her first pregnancy. It had been a hard, three-year struggle to lose it all. When she unexpectedly learned she was pregnant again, her thoughts turned first to her figure. "I was upset about getting heavy again. During my first pregnancy, I hadn't minded wearing maternity clothes. But after all my dieting, I didn't want to show up at the beach in a junky maternity bathing suit."

If the pregnancy is enthusiastically planned by one parent and reluctantly agreed to by the other, a serene pregnancy is not in store for either. The wife may be annoyed that her husband isn't eager to feel the kicking of a baby he doesn't really want. Or a husband may not understand why his wife isn't peppy and perky, just because she would rather be doing something else, anything else, than being pregnant.

FIRST CHILD, SECOND PREGNANCY

But even all else being equal (which it never is), your second pregnancy will not be a replay of your first. The main reason is that your first pregnancy produced something which changed your life dramatically and forever—your first child. You can't just wish that child away when your stomach is turning inside out. You still have to fix her breakfast, as nauseating as it may seem to you, or make up her lunch pail, even if it sends you staggering into the bathroom for yet another losing round with morning sickness. Feel too tired to move? Do your legs, etched with varicose veins, feel they cannot remain upright for one more moment? Just then your galloping child may try to lasso you for a game of cowboys and Indians, or your more modern child may try to snare you in Spiderman's web. Even if your child sometimes responds to your pleas for mercy and goes off alone to tease the dog or fingerpaint the walls, you are still stuck with the essentials—providing food and clothing, perhaps some diapering, and a generous helping of hugs and kisses.

As a consequence of those activities, more women are more tired during their second pregnancy than they were during their first. During a first pregnancy, it is more common for a woman to be working outside the home, but even a full-time paid job is rarely as rigorous as child-rearing. During my second pregnancy, I worked as a medical writer three days a week and was home the other four, so I was in a good position to make a direct comparison. At the office I was able to sit down when I wanted to. No one asked me to tie his shoelaces or fetch him orange juice or help him look for a lost fire engine. I often took just a short break for lunch and then spent a good hour dozing on the couch in the first-aid room. The time when I wasn't napping, I was so engrossed in my work I didn't have time to think about being tired. I arrived at home relaxed and refreshed, a condition that would be undone in no time by dirty dishes and dirty diapers.

Your first child may make you sick as well as tired. The nasty colds she brings home from nursery school will undoubtedly start you sneezing, too. And while you can give her medicine to relieve her sniffles, you may be unable to help yourself because of the possible risk of medication to the fetus.

But having a child to care for during a pregnancy isn't all bad, particularly if the child isn't too young and you're not too out-of-sorts. If you enjoy being a parent, your feelings of fulfillment can enhance your pregnancy. You may find you have a lot of fun with your child, and that his antics help keep your mind off any physical discomfort. If he is away at school or play group part of the day, giving you some time off, you can really appreciate the time you spend together. If he is too young for a program away from home, he is probably still young enough for an afternoon nap. So you can use that time to catch up on your own rest, leaving the housework for another time or another person. Hiring a childcare helper a few mornings or afternoons a week can also afford you some much needed sleep time, and a much more pleasant pregnancy.

WHO'S MINDING THE BABY?

Being a mother while you are having a baby has yet another effect. Most parents focus much more on the existing child than on the one who is growing inside. "What does Joey think about all this?" they wonder. "When should we tell him? How should we tell him?'' they discuss with friends and each other. ''Should we move Jessica out of her crib? Should we toilet-train her? Wean her? Warn her?'' ''How can we prepare her for what we are doing to her—moving her out of the center of the universe?''

Many parents have a second child primarily for the benefit of the first. Yet during the pregnancy, they may feel saddened at the adjustment she will have to make, guilty for their part in ''dethroning'' her from her special position, and apprehensive about the sibling rivalry they have heard so much about. So a lot of their thoughts and actions are involved in trying to ease the transition for their first child from being an ''only'' to being ''one of two.'' (That is an important task of a second pregnancy, one discussed in detail in the next chapter.) Parents may also try to be extra-good at parenting during a pregnancy, perhaps fearing that they won't have the time to be so attentive after the birth. One study rated maternal behavior before, during, and after pregnancy. It found that during pregnancy, mothers are more understanding of their children, and make fewer suggestions to them. In short, they are more mellow.

Where does all this focus on child number one leave child number two? Usually, a distant second. ''During a second pregnancy, the growing baby is not the shining light,'' said Gene Cranch, assistant director of the Maternity Center Association in New York City. The pregnant women I spoke to all admitted to thinking a lot less about this baby than they had about their first, and being less involved in the pregnancy. Generally, second-timers are not as conscientious about their diet, don't read up as much on the month-by-month development of the growing fetus, don't exercise as much in preparation for the birth, and aren't as likely to take a natural childbirth course or to practice the breathing. Why? No time, no energy, and sometimes, no interest.

Some parents feel guilty about their current lack of involvement with the growing baby, and scared that it might continue into the future. A very common fear expressed to me by pregnant women and expectant fathers: Will I be able to love my second child? Dr. Joel Sambursky, clinical psychologist at Brooklyn Jewish Hospital's Developmental Clinic, has a seven-year-old daughter and a four-year-old son. He told me some of the feelings he and his wife had during her second pregnancy. ''We felt we loved our daughter so much, and were so attached to her, we were afraid we wouldn't be able to give the same amount of love to the second child. How could we share this love? Was there enough to go around? We really didn't know how that would work out, we were so involved with our first. But it did work out.''

OLD NEWS, OLD CLOTHES

A second pregnancy is also different than a first just because it is second. Do you remember your *second* kiss? Do you recall how you felt when your baby spoke her *second* word? A second experience rarely surpasses a first for excitement or thrills. The novelty, simply, is no longer there. "I loved every minute of my first pregnancy," recalled Wendy, just four weeks after she had her second baby. "It was terrific. I didn't believe what was happening to me. My second pregnancy? Eh! I could take it or leave it." To Diane, a woman pregnant with her second child, "The joy of pregnancy is not such a joy anymore."

The differences begin at the beginning—the initial news of the pregnancy. Some couples report feelings of disbelief the first time they got the news. "Maybe the doctor's wrong," thought Lydia, who has since had her second child. "I couldn't believe it. I was in a daze for days. I remember giggling and acting stupid. I was giddy for a long time, and very happy." Another woman told me she called her husband at work with the news of her first pregnancy. "His secretary told me he laughed for ten straight minutes." Another common feeling is relief. For both mother- and father-to-be, a first pregnancy confirms fertility. For some women, it signals the fulfillment of "womanly destiny"; for some men, it provides visible confirmation of their masculinity and sexual prowess.

In contrast, some parents have trouble even recalling their reaction to the news of a second pregnancy. Those who do remember generally describe their emotional state as "happy"— but no laughs or giggles or even chuckles. One woman recalls going over to her husband, shaking his hand, and saying, "You did it again." His reaction: "That's nice."

The spacing between births appears to influence the way in which the news is received. A study of New England women showed that only one of ten mothers was "delighted" at the new pregnancy if the interval between children was less than twenty-one months. But if it was twenty-two to thirty-one months, about three out of ten mothers recalled being "delighted." The proportion of happy mothers continued to go up as the spacing increased: up to four out of ten mothers when the spacing was thirty-two to fifty-four months, and five out of ten mothers when the baby was due fifty-five or more months after the last.

First-time parents have a unique style of giving the news as well as getting it. They may tie up their doctor's phone as long as the nurse allows them, spreading the glad tidings to family, friends, and anyone else whose number appears in their address book, even if it is a grammar school buddy who hasn't been seen since grammar school. Or there is the opposite approach—keeping the pregnancy private for a time, just between mother-to-be and father-to-be, a secret to be whispered about in bed at night and smiled at over morning coffee and prenatal vitamin. The expectant couple may carefully plan how they will break the news to overanxious parents and unsuspecting friends for greatest dramatic impact.

The second time around, the intrigue is gone. The news is usually delivered in a matter-of-fact way to family and close friends. Some women wait until their friends call them, and then casually mention the pregnancy right along with the price of groceries and their progress in bridge. One woman learned of her second pregnancy at about the same time many of her friends were starting their first. She didn't let on about her condition until her secret was too big to hide. She didn't want to steal any of the glory from the first-timers.

The feeling of uniqueness follows the expectant couple through the first pregnancy. Many women can't wait until they begin to "show," and many men are proud of their wives' widening waistlines. One of the milestones of a first pregnancy is the first visit to a maternity shop. Maternity clothes are often purchased, and worn, long before regular clothes become uncomfortably tight. "I really went wild shopping for maternity clothes," said Annette, the pregnant mother of a two-year-old boy. "I bought a whole new wardrobe." This time, she is more interested in saving money than in looking stunningly pregnant. "I'm begging and I'm borrowing. In addition to my own leftovers, I'm wearing my friend Pat's tops and my friend Barbara's bottoms."

Annette had a whole different outlook on this pregnancy. "My first was much more exciting. I felt special. I looked good. When I walked into a room I thought, 'Everyone's eyes are on me.' I wanted the pregnancy to last so I could hold onto that feeling. This time I just want to get it over with. I feel fat and uncomfortable. I want to get out of maternity clothes and back into tight pants."

Another common feeling during a first pregnancy is one of awe —awe at the idea of carrying a real live baby. The reality of new life may first be felt at quickening, the earliest sensation of fetal movement. Some parents are enraptured at the fetal heartbeat— further evidence that they have actually produced life. The excitement of those moments may be repeated during a second pregnancy, but probably not equaled in intensity. As one second-time father-to-be described it, "The sense of wonder is never the same after the first pregnancy because the experience is no longer new."

COUNTING YOUR KICKS

Some people spend most of their second pregnancy comparing it with their first. When they notice their zippers getting hard to pull up, they may recall, "Wow, last time I didn't have this trouble for another three weeks." If they are carrying the baby lower this time than the first, they wonder why. If they are carrying more in the back than in the front, they wish they weren't. It is common to compare the month when life was first felt, and how lively that life got toward the end. "My first baby kicked a lot harder than this one," some expectant mothers may recall. It is also common to compare weight gains. Some pregnant women I spoke with remembered exactly how much weight they gained each month of their first pregnancy, and were able to compare it, month by month and pound by pound, with their current increase. Some women were proud they were doing "better" this time, others a bit embarrassed by being ahead of their previous timetable.

Why all the comparison? For some people, it is just the natural thing to do. It gives them something to think about, something to talk about. Other people think it will provide a clue to the sex of the baby. If a woman was carrying high the first time and had a boy, her lowered abdomen this time may mean a girl is on the way—at least that's her hope. If the kicks are harder this time, the parents of a daughter might conclude that an athletic little boy is responsible. "A little girl would never kick me so hard," the pregnant mother of a three-year-old girl confided in me. One couple, who already had a boy, very much wanted a daughter. They started off by comparing every possible aspect of the second pregnancy, hoping it would be as different as possible from the first. But when amniocentesis was performed for other reasons, they learned that the baby was, alas, a boy. They stopped comparing, and started accepting.

Another couple, the parents of a very active two-year-old boy, are paying close attention to fetal movements for another reason. They are not so interested in the sex of the baby, but they are interested in having a less active child. They don't think they could cope with two whirlwinds. So for them, the quieter the baby is inside, the more hopeful they are for a peaceful future.

PAMPERED NO MORE

You are not the only one who will feel differently about this pregnancy. Most everyone else will, too. You will find that out as soon as you tell them the news. Of course, some people will be excited, especially your pregnant friends who can welcome one more member into the club. But you may be disappointed in the reaction of your parents, in-laws, and other relatives. If they are happy about this pregnancy, they are probably not as happy as they were about the first one. They already have their grandchild, and the family line has been carried on. They may quickly shift the conversation to your current child. "What does Michael think of all this?" "How will Meredith react to the baby?" Their tempered joy may turn to disapproval if they think you didn't wait long enough between children. One woman, who spaced her babies' births two years apart, recalls the reaction of her mother-in-law. "We were alone in my house when I told her. She didn't say anything, but her eyes said it all 'Oh no, you did it again!' "

Some couples are grateful to be out of the limelight, but others resent the lack of enthusiasm. Many women miss the pampering that is lavished on first-timers. "Last time, people couldn't do enough for me," one woman, just a month away from her second delivery, recalled. "This time, I could be carrying three shopping bags and no one would make a move to help." During a second pregnancy, a pregnant woman is a pregnant mother, with the emphasis on mother. She is expected to play the part, to fulfill her responsibilities, to carry her burden gracefully and alone.

The lack of support may extend to her physician's care as well. I asked a number of obstetricians about the emotional state of their patients who were experiencing second pregnancies. About half the doctors thought they were more stable, more at ease, and less stressed than first-timers. They noted that complaints of emotional difficulties were rare. So the doctors focused on the physical aspects of the pregnancy, not the psychological. Yet, research shows that women having a second (or subsequent) baby have more emotional problems and are more irritable and depressed than women having a first. According to one study, a full 50 percent more "repeaters" than first-timers had pregnancy-connected emotional difficulties.

Why is the perception different than the reality? Apparently, most people, including doctors, assume that pregnancy is a snap for old-timers. After all, they have already been through it, they "know the ropes," they should be able to handle it without help. The pregnant women themselves don't do much to elicit support. Perhaps they are embarrassed at not doing as "well" the second time as the first. Perhaps they are too caught up in their child's emotions to notice their own. Whatever the reason, they are not talking. Most obstetricians can suggest a counselor to help expectant parents sort out any problems that may come up during a second pregnancy. Some pregnant women get together in groups to talk about their feelings and fears. By facing their emotions and dealing with them, the women can be more relaxed in their pregnancy and prepare more confidently for the future.

THE SUNNY SIDE OF THE SECOND

Things are not all doom and gloom for parents approaching a second pregnancy. They know, more or less, what physical changes to expect. The woman's figure has blown up before, so it is not such a shock to her body image when it happens again. She may have already experienced nausea, heartburn, or swollen ankles, so she is not surprised when they make a return appearance. She knows that a mild contraction during the middle of the pregnancy does not necessitate a frantic cab ride to the hospital. There may be less ecstasy during a second pregnancy, but there is also less anxiety. Several studies indicate that women are less dependent during a second pregnancy than a first, and less insecure.

The attitude toward labor and delivery is also quite different. The first time, childbirth is a great unknown to the mother-to-be. Her mother may warn her of "excruciating pain." Her childbirth instructor may call it, simply, "discomfort." She knows some women go through it with comparative ease, while others yell deliriously for anesthetic relief. What is the pain really like? Will she be able to handle it?

Some women fear the very worst. "I thought I would die," said Denise, recalling her feelings during her first pregnancy. "I knew everything about childbirth. I read all the books. Intellectually, I knew I'd be okay. But emotionally, I was terrified I wouldn't live though it."

Most women approach a second labor and delivery with less fear than a first. If they had a good experience the first time, they are usually confident it will be as good or better the next. If they underwent a long and painful labor, they may dread going through it again. But some women don't remember the pain even a few days after they felt it, and are not haunted by the fear of more of the same. For women who were given pain-relieving drugs the first time, there is often the comforting knowledge that if the pain becomes too much, they can always rely on the drugs again. Some women may have heard that a second labor is usually shorter than a first, and hope they are not an exception to the rule (more about comparative lengths of labor on page 73).

Denise is now pregnant for her second time. Her first experience was about average—not easy, but not long and complicated. She is still around to talk about it. "I really don't remember it too well. When I think of it, it's not like I lived through it, but like I read it in a book. I'm not scared at all about the coming birth. I know I'll survive it and feel fine after."

Anxiety over the baby's health is also less during a second pregnancy (if the first baby was healthy). The parents realize that they are capable of producing a normal, perfectly formed baby —as miraculous as it may seem—and that they can do it again. So they may not be as likely to count the baby's fingers and toes and eyes and ears while the doctor is waiting to cut the cord.

One of the biggest worries during a first pregnancy is the ability to parent. "How will I ever be able to take care of a helpless baby?" the first-timer wonders. "Will I survive it? Will the baby survive it?" If everyone is alive and well by the second pregnancy, there is less concern over child-caring ability. Indeed, research indicates that after the birth, second-timers report fewer sleeping, feeding, and crying problems with their infants than do new mothers.

Some expectant parents are not sure they will like their new role in life. That can be a particular problem for men or women who are temporarily foregoing a professional career for full-time parenthood. Eve, an attorney, was haunted during her first pregnancy by the fear of losing her personal and professional identity. She did find the first year of motherhood a rough time, but through counseling and group meetings with other mothers she was finally able to accept and even embrace her new role. Now she is pregnant with her second child and looking forward to the birth. "I have a much better mental attitude during this pregnancy. I am finally comfortable with being a mother. Some people are born to it, but I found it the hardest thing I ever had to learn. I had to grow up and learn a lot about myself. My second child will benefit from my new self-knowledge."

Parents going through a second pregnancy are certainly more experienced than they were the first time, and often more mature.

They know how a child will affect their style of living; they have adjusted to any loss of freedom that parenthood entails. So the pregnancy can be a more relaxed experience, a prelude to the new life awaiting the entire family.

THE PREGNANT FATHER

Certainly, the father-to-be is not actually pregnant, but he may experience emotional and even physical symptoms similar to his wife's. Like his wife, he often has ambivalent and changing feelings, ranging from euphoria to anxiety or depression. Expectant fathers often fear for the health of mother and child, and fear the responsibilities of fatherhood. At least one in ten experiences such symptoms as nausea, strange food cravings, and more rarely, abdominal bloating. Sound familiar? Those reactions disappear, like magic, after the birth of the baby.

A second pregnancy is as different for the father as it is for the mother. Because it is second, some of the luster is gone for the father, too. He has already established his virility. He has already gotten the handshakes and given the cigars. He has already felt the kicking. Many women report that their husbands are not as involved with the second pregnancy as with the first. If the expectant father brought home a flood of toys and gifts during a first pregnancy, there may be just a trickle the second, or none at all. If the first-time father-to-be has spent hours with hands on his wife's abdomen, the second time he may barely manage a touch, and then only when he is asked.

But some things are better the second time around. The "pregnant" father has lived with a pregnant woman before, and knows what to expect. "My husband is much more understanding this time," says Rita, five months into her second pregnancy. "He realizes I get moody when I'm pregnant, that little things bother me. We don't fight this time, and we're a lot closer." Some men also feel sexually closer to their wives during a second pregnancy. They are used to her pregnant body, they may have overcome their fear of harming the baby, and they may be quite practiced in the new sexual variations they discovered with their wives toward the end of the first pregnancy.

One of the main concerns during a first pregnancy is financial. The family's paychecks may dwindle from two to one. Even if income does remain the same, expenses will be going up, what with Pampers and playpens and Port-A-Cribs. But by the time of a second pregnancy, the family is generally settled into the new financial pattern. Either they have found ways to cut costs, or ways to make more money. Often, earning power has increased during the interlude, easing financial worries.

During a first pregnancy, some fathers worry about their role in a three-member family. Will they still be as important to their wives? Or will they somehow be shut out of the mother-child couple, and made to feel the odd man out? But during a second pregnancy, they are generally quite confident they will be needed more than ever. In fact, their increased value to the family is already quite apparent. Many second-timers do more work around the house and spend more time with their first child than before the pregnancy. They may become very close to their child during this period, making up for any lost opportunities. And they are cementing a bond that will be important for the future, when there is another child around to claim some of mother's time.

As the pregnancy nears an end, there is generally less fear of the labor and delivery process for a second-time father. He may actually look forward to the "preparation for childbirth" classes, sometimes in a dramatic departure from his original balky attitude. "The classes were a lot more pleasant during the second go-round," recalls Marty, the father of four-year-old Noah and ten-month-old Danielle. "We felt like old pros. They didn't have to teach us anything." He also remembers being a better coach during the second labor. "I knew what I was doing and what to expect. I was more at ease. The whole thing went better."

Ron and his wife are currently expecting their second child. He vividly remembers his fears of the first labor. "I was afraid of failing. I thought I might faint during labor or fall asleep. If I managed to stay awake, I was afraid I'd forget to count, or to say 'Breathe in, breathe out.' I felt I had so much to do—watching the clock, putting a washcloth on Miriam's forehead. I was afraid I would screw it up." He didn't. He remembers the birth as a terrific experience, and is looking eagerly ahead to the next.

Looking even farther ahead, to the arrival of the new baby in the home, the experience of prior fatherhood can ease the way. Fathers who are proud of how they have handled parenthood can anticipate another fulfilling experience, without the fear of failure. Fathers who realize they have made mistakes can look forward to the chance to do a better job. Eric recalls the difficulties he experienced with his first child. "Parenthood was harder than I had anticipated. I thought I'd be good at it, but I wasn't. I was annoyed by the baby. He didn't let us sleep. He took all our time. I didn't treat him like a person. I just wanted him to shut up." Eric plans to act differently when his second child is born in the spring. "I'm sure I won't be a perfect father, but I'll try a lot harder. This time, I'll be attuned to treating the baby like a person right from the beginning."

THE PHYSICAL FACTS

If you are surprised at the emotional differences between a first and second pregnancy, you will be stunned by the physical ones. You may assume that your body is going through the same physical processes, and will react in the same way. But your body is not the same body you started out with. During your first pregnancy, you went through remarkable changes from top to bottom. Dr. Steven Meltzer, a Long Island, New York, obstetrician, calls pregnancy "a structural and chemical metamorphosis of the human body." Those changes don't all just go away when the pregnancy is over. Some of them linger, and affect the course of future pregnancies.

One of the changes you will probably notice first is in your figure. Many women find that they "pop" earlier on in the second pregnancy than they did in the first. (One woman swears she started to show the day after conception.) So even if women are not as enthusiastic about maternity clothes during the second pregnancy, they may find they have to wear them sooner than they would like. And the reason goes back to the first pregnancy. Your abdominal muscles were stretched at that time, and unless you worked hard at building them up again, their tone is just not the same as it used to be. Also, your skin was stretched, so it is a little laxer and less elastic than it was prepregnancy. All of that adds up to a bigger belly. Some second-timers mistakenly conclude that twins are on the way.

Later on in the pregnancy, you may notice that you are carrying lower this time, that your abdomen feels like it is sinking fast. To me, the difference was clear. I carried my first baby high and compactly. My second felt as if he would fall out at any moment. I couldn't believe he would stay put until his June due date.

Why the sinking feeling? The culprit, again, is the abdominal musculature, weakened by a first pregnancy. In addition, the ligaments that support the uterus have been stretched by the heavy burden of pregnancy, and have not returned completely to normal. "Gravity plays more of a role during a second pregnancy," points out Dr. Roger Gittelson, New York obstetrician. "Everything is lower down, causing more vaginal pressure."

Your body may have a different shape this time for another reason—your breasts may not get quite as large and as sore. During your first pregnancy, your body was undergoing the tremendous hormonal changes of pregnancy for the first time, and changes in your breasts may have been especially marked. Some pregnant women told me their breasts did not enlarge as quickly, or as much, during their second pregnancy. In fact, they found they often needed maternity bottoms earlier than they needed maternity tops—a situation reversed from their first pregnancy.

How about your overall weight? Can you expect to gain even more this time, or will you put less of a load on your doctor's scale? Of course, that is largely up to you. If you can resist your child's half-eaten macaroni salad, and the cupcake stripped of its frosting, you may keep yourself from gaining much more. Some women find they are so active chasing their little one around, they burn up a lot of extra calories. In general, women gain about the same amount of weight—within five pounds—each pregnancy because of their particular body metabolism. The recommended weight gain during pregnancy has changed in recent years. It may be higher now than it was during your first pregnancy. Check with your obstetrician for the latest guidelines.

One of the most exciting moments of your pregnancy will probably happen earlier this time than it did last time. Quickening, the first feeling of life, usually occurs during the fourth month of a second pregnancy. (Most first-timers don't feel movement until the fifth month.) The reason for the difference is not known for sure. It may simply be that you will know what to expect this time, and won't mistake your baby's motions for indigestion. Or perhaps the wall of your uterus will stretch slightly thinner during this pregnancy, making you more sensitive to what is happening inside.

Another memorable moment of pregnancy, the first time you hear the fetal heartbeat, also occurs earlier with a second baby. With the use of a stethoscope, the heartbeat can be discerned at about the sixteenth week of a second pregnancy. That's about two weeks earlier than in a first-time mother.

A sensation you remember from your first pregnancy, that you may not feel again, is "lightening." It probably occurred about two weeks before you gave birth. The baby's head "dropped" into your pelvis, making your waistline seem lower and your breathing seem easier. But in this pregnancy, your abdominal wall is probably so lax that the fetus will move forward, not down, for any extra room it needs. Your baby may not descend until you are already in labor.

If you think you will have less trouble recognizing labor this time, you may be in for a surprise. "False labor" is more common for a woman who has already had a child. Regular contractions at fairly close intervals can begin weeks before real labor commences. So you may be making more trips to the hospital than you anticipate.

If you expect your baby to come about as "early" or "late" as it did last time, you may be in for another surprise. If your first baby was born prematurely—two to twelve weeks ahead of schedule—you have a 70 percent chance of having a full-term baby this time. If your first baby was a week or so early, and you are assuming the second will be as speedy, you may find yourself still at home a week after your due date fielding a lot of curious phone callers. If your first baby took an extra week or two on the inside, and you are planning on another procrastinator, you may be caught with suitcase unpacked and goody bag unfilled. There is no telling from your first experience when your second baby will emerge. In general, however, more second babies come out sooner. According to government statistics, about 36 percent of first babies are "late," born forty-one or more weeks into the pregnancy. (The average pregnancy lasts forty weeks.) That late figure declines to 31 percent for second babies. But those statistics are based on large populations of pregnant women. They don't say what will happen to you. Be prepared ahead of time, but also be prepared for a long wait.

SYMPTOMS, SENSATIONS, AND STRETCH MARKS

Some women go through pregnancy feeling physically fit, even glowing with good health. Others are plagued by one ailment after another, and wish their nine months of suffering could be compressed into one. Will your current pregnancy be a medical rerun of your first? Here is a look at some common complaints of pregnancy you may, or may not, experience during your second pregnancy.

Nausea and Vomiting

About one in two women have periods of nausea during the first few months of pregnancy. About one in three have periodic bouts of vomiting, most often in the morning. If you missed out on this "morning sickness" during your first pregnancy, and assumed it is more in the mind than the body, you may come to a different conclusion during this pregnancy. Morning sickness can strike for the first time in a second pregnancy. Or, once having struck, it can ease off or even disappear in subsequent pregnancies. So your first experience is not a good gauge for your second.

The treatment for morning sickness is quite simple: Eat a couple of dry crackers before you get out of bed in the morning; during the day, eat frequent, small snacks of dry foods, such as graham crackers; don't eat foods you don't like. If those dietary measures are not helping, ask your doctor about the availability of safe medications for combating nausea (safe for you *and* your baby). Don't take pills your doctor has not prescribed.

Heartburn

This fiery, burning sensation in the lower chest is quite common during pregnancy. The growing uterus compresses the stomach and pushes it up; that acts to open the sphincter muscle between the stomach and esophagus (the tube running from the mouth to the stomach). Gastric juices and gases can then be regurgitated up through the opening, producing the burning feeling. If you missed it the first time, you may miss it again. But if you had it, it may be worse this time. The acids coming up from the stomach may have produced scarring. The scarred area is easier to irritate than normal layers of cells. A bland diet can give you some relief from heartburn. If that doesn't help you enough, consult your physician. Be sure not to take sodium bicarbonate because it promotes water retention, and may contribute to elevated blood pressure.

Varicose Veins

Enlarged veins in the rectal area (hemorrhoids) and in the legs are another common complaint of pregnancy. They are caused by the downward pressure of the fetus and uterus, and by the increased blood volume of pregnant women (it increases by about 40 percent during pregnancy). If you didn't have them the first time, don't count them out the second. Varicosities often appear for the first time during a second pregnancy. If you did experience them during your first pregnancy, they are likely to surface earlier and be more severe during this pregnancy. You can expect a worse case for two reasons. First, you are older. Your vessels are less able to accept the fluid load, and they may have more plaque—hardened deposits of fat—to impede fluid movement. Second, your vessels have been changed by the first pregnancy. They have withstood a large fluid load for the last four months of that pregnancy, and may not be able to withstand the pressure again without enlarging. The best way for you to cope is to stay off your feet as much as possible, prop your legs up as often as possible, and ask your doctor which stockings would offer you the most relief. Sitz baths may help soothe the pain of hemorrhoids. If the pain remains severe, discuss it with your doctor. It may help to know that the veins usually return to normal size after the delivery.

Backache

Many women who suffer backache in late pregnancy attribute it to their new and awkward posture. That is one of the reasons for pain in the lower back, but there is another reason they may not be aware of. "Relaxin," a hormone produced by the placenta, softens the joints of the pelvis and hips of a pregnant woman, making them looser and more mobile. A feeling of fatigue and backache, as well as difficulty in walking toward the end of a pregnancy, may result. The aches and pains are often worse during a second pregnancy, according to Dr. Louise Tyrer, vice-president for medical affairs of Planned Parenthood. "The joints were firm before a first pregnancy. Now they're stretched and loosened. They don't hold a woman together as tightly." She suggests a well-fitted, light girdle to keep everything in place and to ease the pain. Massage and heat may also help relieve the aching back of a second pregnancy.

Swelling

The wedding band too tight to take off, and the shoes too tight to wear, may be your first clues that something other than your abdomen is swelling. Extra water is held by the tissues during pregnancy. The water accumulates in the extremities—hands, feet, and face. If you are waiting to hear that you will experience more swelling this pregnancy than last, relax. You won't, unless you gain more weight or consume more salt. A moderate weight gain and mildly restricted salt intake helps keep swelling to a minimum.

Stretch Marks

Some women call these red markings "badges of motherhood," but most women would rather not be so honored.

The marks result from the stretching of the skin of the abdomen and breasts, and little can be done to prevent them. After delivery, the markings become smaller, and eventually turn almost silver in color. Now, some more good news for second-timers. You probably will not develop any new stretch marks with this pregnancy. You have gotten all the badges you are going to get (unless you gain a lot more weight this time, or there is extra fluid around the baby).

COMPLICATIONS OF PREGNANCY

If you had anything go wrong with a previous pregnancy, you are probably anxious about the chances that it will happen again. Even if things have gone smoothly, you may wonder if your luck will run out this time. The following is a discussion of some possible complications, and the risks they pose during a second pregnancy.

Miscarriage

The chances of a miscarriage, or spontaneous abortion, are no greater with a second pregnancy than they are with a first. Most obstetricians I interviewed think the risks are about the same (about one in eight pregnancies end in miscarriage). But Dr. Louise Tyrer of Planned Parenthood feels that the risk may actually be less with a second pregnancy. "One common cause of miscarriage is that the uterus is not well-developed enough to carry a baby. But if a baby has already been borne, the uterus is tried and true. It's been through it already." A New York State study conducted in the 1950s looked at fetal mortality by the order of pregnancy. The death rate was lower for a second pregnancy than for any other.

If a woman has already had a miscarriage, her risks of having another are no greater than the average one in eight. Most miscarriages are due to random factors, such as a placenta that doesn't grow well, or a "blighted ovum"—an embryo that suddenly stops growing and dries up. A factor which produces repeated miscarriages is present in only four out of a thousand women. Only if a woman has had three miscarriages in a row, and no live births, is she a candidate for extensive medical examination of the problem.

Anemia

Pregnancy places a tremendous drain on a woman's reserves of iron. During the latter half of pregnancy, about 500 to 700 milligrams of iron are transferred to the fetus and placenta. But the average woman has only about 300 milligrams of iron stored up. The result, in about one of five pregnant women, is anemia, reduced levels of hemoglobin in the blood. Its earliest symptoms are fatigue, weakness, and lack of energy. Another signal is that the heart may seem to be beating faster. If a second pregnancy comes soon after a first, the iron stores may not have had a chance to build up again, and anemia may be more of a problem. Severe anemia can be harmful to the fetus as well as the mother. The National Research Council's Committee on Maternal Nutrition has recommended that all women take iron supplements during the last six months of pregnancy. Pregnant women should be sure to discuss this with their physicians. If iron pills are prescribed, keep them in a child-resistant container out of the reach of your older child. Each year, scores of children are hospitalized because of accidental iron poisoning.

High Blood Pressure

Most women have lower blood pressure than usual when they are pregnant. But for women who have a chronic problem of high blood pressure, it is likely to go even higher during pregnancy. It may go higher still during a second pregnancy simply because the woman is older, and her blood vessels less elastic. High blood pressure can pose a serious threat to the fetus, so pressure is monitored carefully throughout the pregnancy. If blood pressure suddenly spikes up, the woman is taken to the hospital for observation.

Toxemia

Toxemia is a disease that occurs only during pregnancy (usually in its last three months). It is characterized by puffiness around the ankles, hands, and face, high blood pressure, and protein in the urine. Most cases are mild, but more severe cases threaten the well-being of the fetus. Many theories have been advanced to explain the cause of toxemia. The most recent puts forth "angiotensin," a hormone produced in the kidney, as the culprit. This hormone is present in everyone, but is produced in larger quantities during the later stages of pregnancy. Most pregnant women build up a defense against the hormone, and so ward off a rise in blood pressure, according to this theory. Women who don't build up adequate defenses fall victim to toxemia.

What is known for sure about toxemia is that it is most common during a first pregnancy. If you didn't experience it then, there is very little chance you will experience it now. If you did experience it then, the odds are you won't have a recurrence. But adequate prenatal care is vital to protect you against even the slightest risk of developing this potentially dangerous disease.

Genetic Disease

If your first child has a genetic disease, you may be justifiably concerned that a second child will be similarly affected. If a couple has a child with cystic fibrosis, for example, the odds are one in four that a subsequent child will have the same disease. The incidence of Down's Syndrome is one in six hundred in the general population, but one in twenty if there is already a Down's child in the family. Tay-Sachs disease is rare in the population as a whole, but if a couple has had a Tay-Sachs child, the odds for each subsequent child having the disease are one in four. The story is the same for all genetic disorders: Once they occur in a family, the chances are increased they will occur again. Fortunately, there are now techniques for diagnosing genetic problems during pregnancy. An obstetrician can guide a concerned couple to genetic counseling services.

Rh Disease

Rh incompatibility occurs in one of eight marriages: The woman is Rh negative (she does not have a substance known as the Rh factor in her blood) and the man is Rh positive (his blood does contain the Rh factor). Even for those couples, there is no danger to the fetus until the second pregnancy. The reason is this: The mother's blood does not intermingle with the baby's during pregnancy itself, but after the placenta is delivered, some of the baby's blood cells may travel into the mother's bloodstream. If those cells contain the Rh factor, the mother reacts by producing antibodies to this foreign substance. Those antibodies remain in her blood, and during a subsequent pregnancy, can cross the placenta and destroy the fetus's red blood cells. Sometimes, a transfusion in the uterus or early delivery can minimize damage to the baby. But since 1965, a vaccine known as Rhogam has been available that prevents the problem from developing. Given within seventy-two hours after delivery (and after every miscarriage or abortion), the vaccine prevents the mother from developing antibodies. This vaccine has almost wiped out Rh disease—good news for second children and their younger siblings.

THE BIRTH EXPERIENCE

At this point, you may feel pretty discouraged. A second pregnancy has some advantages over a first, but overall, it sounds tiresome, tiring, and sometimes even hazardous to health. But the best news comes last: The culmination of your second pregnancy—the labor and delivery—will probably be a lot easier than your first experience, and every bit as exciting and rewarding.

The beginning of the labor process may not be as clear-cut as it was the first time. As I mentioned earlier, false labor is more common in a second pregnancy. But you can't ignore any regularly repeating contractions. Call your doctor to find out if you should go to the hospital. If you are in real labor it may go very fast, so prompt action is important to avoid a "taxicab" birth.

If, in your first experience, the membranes around your amniotic sac broke before your contractions began, don't be surprised if it happens again. Some women seem to have membranes that are relatively unstable, and break more easily than other women's. Some scientists suggest that a genetic factor may be responsible.

The most dramatic difference between a first and second birth experience is in the length of labor. If no unforeseen complications occur, you can expect your second labor to take just about half as long as your first. The only known reason for the quicker pace is a change in the cervix, the narrow outer end of the uterus. In a first pregnancy, the cervix has to first thin out (efface) and then dilate. But with a second baby, the cervix is already stretched and perhaps even torn. So it doesn't have to efface during labor, and dilation occurs more readily. Some obstetricians speculate that other bodily changes may also contribute to a faster labor. For example, the vagina and perineum (the area between the vagina and rectum) have been stretched by the first delivery. The tissues in the birth canal are not as resistant to the passage of something as large as a baby. In fact, according to New York's Dr. Roger Gittelson, the difference in the ease of passage is greatest between a first and second labor; it is not as marked between a second and third labor, or even between a second and fourth labor.

The contractions of the uterus are just as forceful during a second labor, and so the potential for pain is as great. But the knowledge that it probably won't last as long makes the pain more bearable for many women. Also, most second-timers find the going easier because they know what to expect. Just as they could anticipate the physical changes of the pregnancy, they know how the stages of labor will progress. And the environment of the hospital (if that's where they deliver) is familiar to them. They might not like it, but at least they are accustomed to it. Perhaps, most important, they can look ahead more easily this time to labor's end, to the birth of their baby, to the sight and sounds and sensations of their second child.

Speediness of labor is an advantage to the baby as well as the mother. Most important to the baby's well-being is the second stage of labor, the passage through the birth canal. During that period, the baby's head is subject to compression with every contraction. The second stage usually lasts about an hour or an hour and a half during a first pregnancy, and not uncommonly more than two hours. But in a second labor, it usually takes under an hour, and sometimes as short as five minutes. A long second stage—whether it occurs during a first, second, or later labor—may cause the baby to be "depressed" at birth, says Dr. Bruce Young, director of obstetrical services at New York's Bellevue Hospital. The baby may be less reactive than the average newborn, and have a lower Apgar score (a type of medical rating of newborns).

Just a word of caution here: Your second labor may be longer than your first. It may be more difficult than your first. It's not likely, but it's a possibility. Women who don't realize that can be bitterly disappointed when labor isn't the breeze they anticipated.

If your first baby was a breech—"buttocks first"—you are probably hoping this baby will lead with its head. That very well might happen. Not all women who have one breech have a second. But you are more likely to have a breech birth than someone who had a normally positioned baby the first time. Your uterus may be shaped in such a way that would encourage a breech position. For example, you might have what is known as a "septate" uterus, with a ridge on top. Or you may have a fibroid on your uterus that prevents the baby from settling in properly with head down. Perhaps, an abnormality in your pelvic structure will produce one breech baby after another.

If your first labor was a back labor, that is probably an experience you don't care to repeat. You may avoid it, depending on its original cause. Sometimes back labor is produced by unusual positioning of the baby. For example, the bones of his head may be pressing on the back of your uterus. Back labor won't be repeated if the position of the next baby is different. But some women simply feel any uterine contraction in the lower back area. That's how their uterus is constructed, and every labor will be a pain in the back.

One thing that makes front or back labor more bearable is the support and encouragement of a confident coach. Second-time coaches, now skilled at their craft, can generally do a better job of it. They are no longer terrified of witnessing a birth. They are no longer intimidated by sophisticated hospital equipment. They are not quite as unnerved by seeing their wives in pain. They can focus exclusively on the progress of labor, and on making their wives as comfortable as possible.

Because the second stage of labor can take just minutes, you may be wheeled into the delivery room as soon as your cervix is fully dilated. During your first labor, you may remember, you did your pushing in the labor room, and were not moved to the delivery room until your baby's scalp was already visible.

If you had an episiotomy before your first delivery, you may assume you will need one again. Actually, the need for this cut in your perineum may be less. There are two major medical reasons for an episiotomy: to prevent jagged rips in your perineum, and to protect the baby's head from bouncing against the perineum. But your perineum may be somewhat more flexible and yielding as a result of your first delivery, and an episiotomy not as imperative. But what about the episiotomy scar? Doesn't that create a weak point, susceptible to ripping? According to my obstetrical consultants, that scar does not increase the chances of tearing (though any tearing would occur along the scar). Some physicians perform episiotomies not only for medical indications, but to keep the vagina from stretching too much and becoming too lax. If you feel you don't want an episiotomy unless absolutely medically necessary, it is a good idea to let your obstetrician know your views before you go into labor. The final decision can't be made until you are near the end of labor, and your baby's head is on your perineum.

Although your second birth experience will be physically different than your first, you will probably reach the same emotional heights. Childbirth is a transcendent event, and even hardened parents experience it on a plane unequaled in daily living. The actual emergence of the baby, after months of gestation and hours of labor, is the high point of the drama. No amount of previous experience can dull its impact.

You may be pleasantly surprised by the appearance of your newly born second child. You probably expected the same funny-shaped head—like a melon with a point at the back—that your first baby had. That shape is the result of "molding," compression of the head to adjust to the shape of the birth canal. But because the head generally spends less time in contact with the bony pelvis during a second labor, less molding occurs.

Your second child may look a little bigger as well as a little better. On average, second babies are a few ounces heavier than their predecessors. You shouldn't expect a baby *too* much bigger or *too* much smaller than your first. You are not going to graduate from a five-pounder to a ten-pounder (unless the first was premature), or have a six-pound pixie after a nine-pound bruiser (unless the second is born early).

Despite their excitement at the birth, many parents are keenly disappointed with one particular aspect of their second-born baby—its sex. Sexual preference is usually much stronger for a second baby; for couples who want only two children, this is seen as the last chance to have that darling daughter or that all-American boy. Louise Schwartz, childbirth instructor, has witnessed many births, and many disappointments. "If a couple wanted a boy but had a girl, or vice versa, the excitement is still there, but it is a forced excitement. The parents feel they *should* be happy because the baby is healthy, that they *should* love the baby, despite its sex. But there is an undertone of great disappointment, and guilt at being disappointed. Those reactions are much more blatant with a second baby." Understanding that disappointment is a natural reaction may help alleviate some of the guilt. And understanding that love will come may aid in your acceptance of your second child, boy or girl.

A CAESAREAN BIRTH

If your first delivery was vaginal, you may assume your second will go the same route. You may find yourself skipping over the sections on Caesareans included in childbirth books, tuning out your childbirth instructor when she broaches the subject. Your lack of interest is somewhat justified. Most Caesareans are performed because the mother's pelvis is too small to allow the baby to pass into the vagina. Unless your second baby is much bigger than your first, that won't be a problem for you. Your pelvis (like your uterus) is "tried and true." Another common reason for Caesarean births is breech presentation of the baby. But if a woman has already given birth vaginally, a vaginal birth will usually be attempted. "We know what size baby got through the first time," says Bellevue Hospital's Dr. Bruce Young. "If a woman has already delivered a nine-pound baby vaginally, she could probably get a breech baby of that same weight through, though perhaps with some more difficulty."

There are still, however, a number of reasons why a Caesarean delivery may be performed the first time for a second baby. The placenta may separate prematurely; the labor may not be progressing well; the baby may be in danger. So even though the odds are against it, you should be prepared for a Caesarean by reading up and listening well.

If your first baby was born by Caesarean delivery, you are probably fully expecting another one. But you may secretly nurture the hope that it won't be necessary this time. Will it or won't it? It depends largely on two factors: why you had it the first time, and who your doctor is. Certain reasons for Caesareans are called "recurring." They will be present at each and every delivery. The major one, discussed above, is that the baby is too large for the pelvic opening. That same situation will almost surely repeat itself this time. Your pelvis hasn't gotten any bigger, and your baby probably has. Only if labor is premature, and the baby weighs only three or four pounds, will some doctors consider trying a vaginal delivery. Other "recurring" reasons involve your health. If you had your first Caesarean because of diabetes, heart disease, or chronic hypertension, you will probably need a surgical delivery again.

Other reasons, known as "nonrecurring," occur as isolated events in a particular pregnancy. Some were already mentioned, such as fetal distress and placental separation. Some others are multiple births, severe toxemia, and infection.

All physicians will perform a second Caesarean for a "recurring" reason (with the possible exception of a premature delivery, described above). But there is much less unanimity of opinion if the first Caesarean was due to a "nonrecurring" factor. Some obstetricians firmly believe in the adage, "Once a Caesarean, always a Caesarean." They point out that the scar from the first Caesarean will always be weaker than the rest of the uterine wall, and that subsequent pregnancies can lead to rupture of the scar. Rupture is most common, they say, during labor, when the scar is under stress. A ruptured uterus can be deadly for the baby as well as for the mother.

But late in 1980, a National Institutes of Health task force recommended that conventional delivery not be ruled out so long as doctors are prepared to perform surgery if an emergency arises. A growing number of obstetricians will now try for a vaginal delivery if the reason for the original Caesarean is not repeated. A major impetus for the change in philosophy and practice is the "low-flap" Caesarean, which involves a horizontal cut in the lower part of the uterus. That type of incision, popularized in the last twenty years, produces a much stronger scar than the previous "classical," or vertical, incision (performed through the upper part of the uterus). A "low-flap" scar is less likely to rupture because it isn't subject to the strongest uterine contractions. Currently, almost all Caesareans done in the United States are done in the lower uterine section.

Physicians who oppose the "once a Caesarean, always a Caesarean" edict say the risk of rupture of a "low-flap" scar is only one in two hundred births—and that the risk is the same whether or not labor occurs. Also, they point out, rupture usually means just a slight separation of the scar; only if abnormal labor is allowed to progress will the scar rupture in a dangerous way.

Why take any risk? You may not have loved your Caesarean or the pain you felt afterward, but what's so great about a vaginal birth? For one thing, it's not major surgery. It usually involves less anesthesia, or none at all, and requires a shorter recovery period (meaning less time away from your older child). It allows for more husband participation, and more of an opportunity to cuddle the baby right after the birth, the best time for parent-child bonding to take place. Also, the process of labor is beneficial to the baby, helping his bodily systems to function more readily outside of the uterus.

Either a vaginal or Caesarean delivery can be physically successful and emotionally satisfying. But if you would like the chance to experience a vaginal birth, discuss your feelings with your doctor. Some women, dissatisfied with the responses of their current obstetrician, look for one with more compatible views. If you do change doctors, be sure that your new physician sees your old hospital records. The details of your last delivery are vital to making the best decision now. If the decision is to try labor, be sure you will be delivered in a modern, fully equipped medical center ready for emergency surgery twenty-four hours a day. In case anything goes wrong during labor, an immediate Caesarean should be possible.

AFTERBIRTH PAINS AND PLEASURES

It's all over. You have given birth to a real live baby. Unless it was a delivery at home, or in a maternity center that whisks you away after twelve hours, you are now faced with several days in the hospital. Remember your last stay? The room full of flowers? The telephone that never stayed on the hook? The awful pain of your stitches, almost but not quite forgotten while you explored the wonders of your new baby? Will this time be like last time? Well, the hospital food will probably taste about the same, like it or leave it. Your newest new baby will probably be as delightful as your last. There, the similarity ends. Physically, you will experience pain again, but it will be in a higher locale. If you had an episiotomy, it was probably shorter than your first one, and done along the original scar. For both those reasons, it may not cause as much pain. But your afterpains, the contractions of your uterus to get back into shape, will probably be worse than you remember. Your uterus has been stretched twice now, and has a tougher time returning to normal. It will work harder, and you will feel it more. Incidentally, your uterus will never again be quite as small as it was preparenthood. Your first pregnancy left it slightly larger. Your second pregnancy may leave it a bit larger yet.

If you breast-feed, you'll be happy to know that your baby may be getting more milk sooner. In a recent study conducted at the Maternity Center Association of New York, some 380 women were asked how long it took for their milk to come in. Of the first-time mothers, 37 percent reported that it took two days or less. Of the mothers who had been mothers before, that figure was 47 percent. So if this baby seems more content than your last, and fonder of feeding, you know one of the reasons.

If flowers make you sneeze, you won't have to take an allergy pill this time. You probably won't have much to sneeze at. Most second-time mothers don't get many bouquets, or phone calls, or visits. Friends and relatives figure they will see you at home, but some don't even get around to it then. Your second birth is just not such a big deal to other people. If your second baby is a different sex than your first, there may be a slight flurry of interest; if the sexes are the same, you may as well be in the tuberculosis ward for all the attention you'll get.

But you may not mind the peace and quiet so much. In fact, you may welcome the chance to rest, and view your hospital stay as an oasis of calm in your otherwise hectic life. It will provide you the opportunity to reflect on the past and plan for the future. One woman, pregnant for the second time, knew she would be having a second Caesarean delivery. When a friend asked her where she was going for her vacation that year, she replied, "I'll be spending nine glorious days at North Shore Hospital. My reservations are already in." She was looking forward to the time away from household chores and family demands.

Some women spend time in the hospital savoring their non-pregnant condition. Janice had felt really draggy toward the end of her second pregnancy, exhausted by the combination of motherhood and expectant motherhood. She was ecstatic when the "expectant" part was over. "I remember looking at myself in the mirror in my hospital room. I looked so thin. My stomach was flat. I was so glad there was nothing moving inside. I felt a new lease on life, like I had been reborn. Finally, my body was my own."

In addition to thinking about yourself, you will also be thinking about your family, especially your first child. You will probably wonder how she is taking the news, how she is doing, how much she misses you. And you will probably be missing her, even if you are away only two or three days. You will look forward to phone conversations with her, and perhaps even a visit, if your hospital permits sibling visitation. And you will probably be thinking of how to arrange the homecoming so it will be a joyful event for the whole family.

Don't be surprised if you feel moments of sadness or even deep depression after the birth. "Postpartum blues" can occur after any pregnancy. If your depression persists for several weeks after you are settled at home, you might find it helpful to discuss your feelings with your doctor.

Your second pregnancy may be hard or easy, your second labor disappointingly difficult or surprisingly simple. But once you hold your baby in your arms, your thoughts will be on the future. You will look forward to bringing your newborn home, to including him or her in your circle of family, to nurturing this tiny creature from infancy to childhood to adulthood. And though you may not feel it yet, you can look ahead to developing a very special love for this, your second child.

3. Preparing Your First Child for Your Second Child

IT WAS A HOT SUMMER EVENING, just a month before the due date, and a preparation-for-childbirth class was under way. The participants saw a movie about newborns and practiced diapering dolls. Previous participants came by to share their experiences of childbirth and infant care. At the session's close, diplomas were awarded for successful completion of the course. That class may sound just like one you went through during your first pregnancy. But there is one major difference: The doll-diaperers and movie-goers in this class were children, from two to five years old. And they were being prepared for the birth of a sibling.

Not too long ago, childbirth was for women only. The physical facts have not changed, but social forces have. Fathers, no longer content to pace the waiting room and pass out cigars, have broken hospital traditions and gained entrance to labor and delivery. Some families wanted their children, too, to be involved, and have succeeded in bending hospital rules even further. Sibling preparation classes like the one described above are becoming more common, as is sibling visitation to mother and baby after the birth. Some hospitals and maternity centers even allow children to be present at the birth itself. A common aim of those innovations is to ease the baby into the first child's life, to mix the inevitable hostility with a little bit of love.

But most parents don't wait until delivery, or a month before, to concern themselves with the impact of their second child on their first. As I mentioned previously, one of the main preoccupations of a second pregnancy is preparing the first child for the new arrival. If the preparation is done right, it can help a child maintain a sense of self-worth, and give her the ability to accept her sibling's birth—or at least to accept her feelings about it. Ideally, preparation should begin even before you start trying for your second child.

STARTING EARLY

First children who are treated like so many first children are—like the king of the mountain, if not the center of the universe—don't make the best candidates for older siblings. They will be in for a rude shock when their demands are no longer always immediately met. "How dare you not pick up my toy as soon as I dropped it on the floor?" "How come, when I yell out 'Milk!' you're not already in the kitchen pouring it out?" It is hard for a child who has been catered to, to give it up. It is hard for a child who has had the beam of the spotlight always on him, to share center stage with another.

That's not to say a first child should be given the cold shoulder, or be forced to fend, totally, for himself. Dr. Bernice Berk, school psychologist for the Bank Street College of Education in New York City, rejects both those extremes. "A child shouldn't feel like he's the only thing of importance in the parents' lives. That doesn't prepare him well for changing his status to *not* being the only thing. But the child shouldn't be prepared by being deprived. That leads to anger and resentment in advance. The child feels he's not getting enough, and fears that later he'll get even less." What Dr. Berk suggests is that parents be attentive, caring, and available in a natural way. They should try going out at least a few hours a week on a regular basis, so the child realizes that other realities demand his parents' time. And they should introduce some other adults into the child's life—grandparents, a friendly neighbor, a trusted babysitter. "In that way, the child won't have a new sibling *and* new adults to deal with. But keep it down to a few adults, not lots and lots."

Even within the family, it is a good idea for mother and father to switch off jobs—to take turns making breakfast, giving the bath, performing the bedtime ritual. After the new baby is born, Mommy won't always be available, so it's helpful if a child has learned to know and accept Daddy's ways, too.

Just as a child will have to share attention, she will have to share some material objects, too. Her changing table may be handed down to her new little sister, her rocker moved into the nursery, her stored-away baby toys taken out and cleaned up for baby's use. Even if she gets a bigger chair and better toys, she may regret her losses. "Often, children hold onto things they don't need anymore," says Dr. Ilana Reich, a clinical psychologist and consultant to Head Start. She suggests having a friend or relative pass on her child's outgrown toys to your child. "That will introduce her to the idea of sharing and passing down, and may make it easier when her turn comes."

You may have seen or heard about books designed to prepare children for a new baby in the family. Some highlight the physical aspects of the growth and birth of a baby. Others emphasize the practical and emotional effects of the baby on family life—particularly on the life of the older child. Many parents seek out those books toward the end of pregnancy, and read them together with their child as their due date draws near. But you don't have to wait that long. Dr. Reich suggests buying some good preparation books even before pregnancy begins. "They should be part of a child's library. In that way, a child can read them and learn from them in a nonthreatening situation, when she's not worried about the effect of the new baby."

SAY IT SOON, SAY IT STRAIGHT

When you find out that you are pregnant, you may have some friends and relatives you are eager to tell, but you may also have one child you would like to keep in the dark. Do you really have to tell your child that another child is on the way? Could you claim you have a beer belly that just won't quit, or that you thoroughly enjoy walking around with a watermelon under your dress? Maybe you could just send him an embossed announcement when it's all over? Anything to spare you the anguish of delivering the news. Isn't it enough that you're delivering the baby?

Actually, you are doing your child no favor by putting the announcement off too long. "Your child should not be the last to know," says Bank Street's Dr. Berk. "An air of mystery will only create anxiety. So when you share the news with other people, you should share it with your child." One child overheard his parents talking about the pregnancy, walked in the room, and said, "Aha! You're trying to keep it from me!" If you wait too long, your child may hear the news from someone else, and really feel betrayed.

If your pregnancy makes you feel tired and act differently with your child, that's a good reason for telling her why. Otherwise, she may think you fall asleep during her bedtime story because you have lost interest in her. Or she may decide, if you spend half the day in the bathroom and the other half in bed, that you must be deathly sick. Instead of letting her wonder, or worry, tell her right away that you are sleepy because you are having a baby —not because you are ill or uninterested in her. Again, it is the mystery that does the harm, not the facts.

An early announcement gives children time to get used to the idea of a new baby, to work out their ambivalent feelings, to begin to master their anxieties. For very young children—two or three years old—the time period may seem very long to wait. (Some psychologists suggest that if your health has not been affected, you should hold off with the news until there is concrete evidence of the pregnancy—an enlarged abdomen to see or fetal movement to feel.) But a child's poor time sense is not a good reason for a long delay with the news. Even if your child tires as the months pass uneventfully by, boredom is not as bad as the secrecy of almost-heard whispers and behind-the-back plans. If your child gets very restless in the last months, you might try to key the timing of the birth to a familiar event. One mother told her daughter, "The baby will be born during your vacation from nursery school," another that the baby would arrive when the snow was gone from the ground.

You may be putting off telling your child about your pregnancy because you haven't figured out what you should say. You know the stork is passé, but what has taken its place? Nothing fancy, nothing flowery, just the simple, unadorned truth: There is going to be a new baby in the family. You may add that the baby is growing in your uterus (not your stomach), and that a doctor or midwife will help the baby be born. If your child asks questions, answer them specifically and honestly, without adding details she is not yet ready to understand. And be prepared to answer the same questions again, because your child may well ask them again.

Many parents find that pregnancy affords a good opportunity to talk about sex and body parts. Take advantage of that opportunity by using correct terms, not euphemisms, and by adapting your explanations to your child's interest and understanding. Too much information can be confusing to a very young child, but too little information can give an older child a distorted view of reality. Some parents find it easiest to broach this subject by reading a "sex-education" book together with their children. It tells them what to say and how to say it. But if your child has further questions—and she will—you're on your own.

HUGS AND KICKS FOR MOMMY

Despite their parents' misgivings, some children respond positively to the news of the pregnancy. One little girl hugged her mother excitedly, and spread the word to everyone she saw. She started making plans to teach the baby, to feed the baby, to diaper the baby, to share her room. Another little sister-to-be looked forward eagerly to having an instant playmate. Some children get so carried away, they fantasize they are pregnant themselves. One young boy already felt possessive of his unborn sibling. "I'm not going to let you touch the baby," he warned his friend, sounding as threatening as a two-year-old can. But some children have more tempered reactions. "Oh yeah, what else is new?" a four-year-old boy responded to the announcement. His mother didn't know whether to be upset he wasn't more joyful —or relieved he didn't kick her in the belly.

Some children do just that. They are jealous of the baby that is already tiring Mommy, and they strike out. The attack may be a bit less direct. Two-year-old Joey seemed generally positive about the family's future addition. If he saw a baby outside, he would say "Oh, a little baby! We hold baby. We take care of baby." So when his parents brought home a little reclining chair in a box with a baby's picture on it, they were unprepared for their son's reaction. Seemingly serene Joey took one look at the box and kicked it right in its smiling baby face. In case there was any confusion about his intention, he said loudly and clearly for all to hear, "Baby, kick!"

Jealousy may take a different form. Some children become clingy, others anxious or whiney. Their emotions are not hard to understand. They wonder why their parents wanted a new baby. "Is something wrong with me? Am I not good enough?" And they may fear the future. "Will the baby replace me? Will my parents still love me?"

Neither very young children, nor very "old" children, are immune to ambivalent feelings about the birth of a sibling. Janey wasn't doing much to prepare Alex, almost two, for the birth, though it was less than a month away. "I assumed he was too young to realize anything or to be prepared. He'll be so young when the baby's born, it won't make much difference in his life. I hope he won't notice it so much or make a big deal of it. I hope he'll just accept it." That's a lot of hoping.

Neil was expected to accept the birth happily, like an uncle would, because he was a mature thirteen. But he had been a content only child with just one regret. "I'm tired of throwing the ball and then having to run and catch it myself." The prospect of having a budding Johnny Bench in the house was not enough to lift his spirits about the pregnancy. When his mother started to show, he asked, "Will you keep looking like that—or like a regular person?" He was afraid he might be moved out of his room. His parents tried to reassure him by redecorating his room when they decorated the baby's. They also bought him an expensive pool table to help ease his mind, and theirs. "That's a disadvantage of this spacing," his mother noted. "With a three-year-old, you can get away with buying a teddy bear."

Actually, words can go farther than dollars in easing a child's fears. The most important words are those that assure him of your continued love. A child may find it hard to understand how you will love him as much if you will also love the baby. If you share a cookie, there is less for you. Isn't it the same with love? Some parents compare love to a flame. You can light many candles with the flame, they point out, but it still burns as brightly. One woman told her four-year-old daughter that the heart gets bigger and feelings larger—you can love more people and more things. "My daughter seemed to understand. She imagined her own heart getting bigger. She asked me if that was okay."

Children need to know they will be cared for, as well as loved, after the birth. "Reassure the first child that all his emotional needs will be satisfied," Dr. Berk suggests. "Make it clear that she will not be neglected or rejected." Reassure her that the good things you do together—the books you read, the shopping trips you make—will continue. A natural time to discuss it is during the activity itself, says Dr. Reich. As you are working on puzzles together, you might say, "Even after the baby is born, you and I will have time alone to do the puzzles. The baby won't know how. Only you and I will do them." Of course, you have to be prepared to follow through on your promises. Even if you are wrung out from a day of diaper-changing, bottle-washing, and carriage-rocking, you are going to have to find the red piece that fits next to the blue piece, and smile while you're doing it.

But your child's life *will* change after the baby's birth, and a lot of changes won't be welcomed. Should you give her some advance notice, or let her find out for herself? Some psychologists recommend not talking about the negative aspects unless the child brings them up. "If the child is looking forward to life with a sibling, let him!" Others recommend pointing out the negative, not just the positive. "I might not have as much time just alone with you," for example, or "There'll be times you'll want my attention, but I'll be with the baby and I won't be able to stop right away. You may have to wait." But won't those warnings just put unhappy ideas into a happy child's head? "Children may be thinking those things anyway, without verbalizing them," says Dr. Emily Rubinstein, clinical psychologist at Brooklyn Jewish Hospital's Developmental Clinic. "You're not telling them they *have* to feel angry or jealous. But should they feel that way later, they'll be prepared." They won't feel surprised, and they won't feel tricked.

But they will feel annoyed if they think they are the only one who will have to suffer. Are things going to be heavenly for their parents, but horrid for them? Where's the justice in that? They will be happy to hear *you are* going to suffer a bit, too. You might point out that waking in the middle of the night to feed the baby will be a real pain for you, that the fuss, and the bother, and the extra work won't be much fun. Your child may not feel so sorry for himself if he knows the grief will be spread around the family.

The general idea is not to paint too bright a picture of what is ahead, or too gloomy a picture, either. Rather it is to tell your child factually what you envision life will be like with the new baby, for him and for you, for better and for worse.

GETTING TEDDY READY

There are things you can do, as well as things you can say, to prepare your child for the new baby. Here are some ideas.

Reading Books, Making Books

The preparation books discussed earlier are available for children of all ages. Those for very young children are heavy on the illustrations, with just a word or two on a page. Others are complex enough for nine-year-olds. Try to pick out a few books at the right developmental level for your child. If you come across a book where everyone is always smiling, baby never cries, and big brother is as happy as a bear in a honey tree, leave it on the shelf. Just as your words should give your child a true picture of life with baby, so should the text and pictures in the book. Do your shopping early on in the pregnancy (if you haven't done it before your pregnancy, as I suggested previously). That will give you and your child a chance to read them together and discuss their message well in advance of the event. One woman was lucky enough to find a book with a child named Dana as the older sister. That book went over big with her own first child—Dana, of course.

I never did find a book with a big brother Brian in it. But the books I selected seemed to help, anyway. Brian chose them, every night, for bedtime reading, preferring them to *Cookie Monster and the Cookie Tree, Scuffy the Tugboat,* and even his superhero comic books. The first night I was home from the hospital, I asked him if he wanted me to read one of the preparation books to him. He said "no," and he never asked for them again. They had done their job.

If you can't find a book you like, or if you feel creative and have some spare time, you may want to prepare your own book. At a special prenatal class for "repeaters," parents were shown a sample of a homemade book. It included a simple sketch of an unborn baby inside his mother, as well as photos of the mother during her first pregnancy, the hospital where the first child was born, and the first child from babyhood to toddlerhood. The text described how his parents took care of him as a baby, how he has grown, how many things he can do now, and what the new baby will do. Several of the participants decided to make books for their own children, geared to their age, personality, and needs.

Providing Pets: Lessons in Love

Some parents have found their family pet helpful in preparation for the new sibling, according to a University of Michigan Medical Center report (based on a survey of the literature on sibling births and on interviews of twenty-one families). One young boy learned to play with small fragile kittens before the birth of his sister. He had witnessed their birth, and related it immediately to the forthcoming baby. When his sister was born, he knew how to touch her gently, as he had been taught to handle the kittens. In another family, one that included three daughters and no sons, a male puppy had spurred on discussions of anatomical sex differences. So when the fourth child, a boy, was born, the element of surprise was reduced. Michigan researchers suggest another benefit: "The introduction of a pet can also provide some vicarious satisfaction for the young child, who may be jealous of mother's childbearing; the pet can serve as a substitute for the envied baby." A word of warning: After the baby is born, your older child may displace his feelings of anger onto the pet and abuse it. If you have introduced a pet, protect it. Provide your child with a punching bag to express his hostility, and make it clear that a pet, like a baby, is not for hurting.

Meeting Mother's Doctor

Should you bring your child along on your visits to the obstetrician? Some mothers have no choice. There is no one to watch the child, so along she comes. One woman tried to liven the event up by bringing along some cookies and picnicking on the doctor's floor. Another made each monthly trip an "outing" by following it with lunch at Burger King and a romp in the park. Some women intentionally bring along their older children to alleviate any fear they have about doctors and hospitals, and to acquaint them with just who, exactly, will help bring the baby into the world. For four-year-old Stuart, who was especially afraid of doctors, the visit was a big success. The doctor talked a lot to him, and asked him how Mommy'd been. When the doctor put the monitor on the mother's abdomen to amplify the baby's heartbeat, Stuart and the doctor decided it sounded like a train. Stuart had just been given some model trains, so he was intrigued by the comparison. But the would-be conductors couldn't quite decide whether the heartbeat sounded more like a steam locomotive or a diesel. After that visit, Stuart's mother found him much more relaxed about the doctor's part in the pregnancy and birth.

My son Brian was also intrigued by the sound of the baby's heartbeat during his one visit to the obstetrician. "The baby's talking to me," he said, in his first demonstration of sibling pride.

Whether your child will benefit from a visit to your obstetrician's office depends mainly on what the doctor, and the office, are like. If the waits are customarily an hour or two, he will probably become bored and unruly, and you will become embarrassed and angry. If your doctor doesn't welcome little children or spend time explaining things to them, your child's view of doctors may be worse than before. But in some offices waiting times are fairly short, and toys and books are provided for children. And some doctors are willing to spend a little extra time talking to children and answering their questions. You might decide to drop by the office when you don't have an appointment; in that way your child can see the surroundings and be introduced to your doctor without a long wait.

The Invasion of the Port-A-Crib

You may dread bringing out any of the baby's things for fear of your child's reactions, but it may be better to do it sooner than later. That was the conclusion reached by Stephanie and Reed Welson. Stephanie, an occupational therapist specializing in pediatrics, and Reed, a psychologist at the Queens Children's Psychiatric Center, were both "only" children themselves. So when they learned that their second child was on the way, they made a special effort to prepare their first, a little girl not yet two. One of their main strategies was to introduce tangible symbols of the coming baby. They established a corner for the baby, complete with Port-A-Crib, sheets, and baby toys. "We told Jenni the baby would sleep there," said Mrs. Welson. "We felt it was better for her to work out her feelings ahead of time." Dr. Welson added that children that age are unable to conceptualize, so words aren't enough for them. "They need concrete objects to hang onto." As part of that same strategy, they took Jenni to meet the doctor so she wouldn't think of him as "an unknown perpetrator." And they showed her the front of the hospital where the baby would be born. "We gave her all the pieces of information so she could make a picture in her mind, on her own level, of what was going on."

Many parents encourage their children to feel the baby move. That is another way to get them in touch with the coming reality, as well as to satisfy their curiosity. Some children use the navel as a microphone and introduce themselves to their unseen sibling. "Hi! This is your big brother. When are you coming out of there?"

The Baby Parade

Another obvious way to make the future more real is to show your child real live babies. Point them out around the neighborhood, or at a friend's house. Your child will notice how tiny they are and, incidentally, what poor playmates they make in the beginning. But don't focus his attention on just one baby. An example given by the University of Michigan Medical Center's investigators shows why. A nursery school teacher brought an eight-month-old baby to her class one day. The children seemed delighted. But several weeks later one little girl came to class looking sad. She told the teacher that "my new baby does not look at all like the baby here." Apparently, young children have trouble imagining a sibling similar to—but not identical with—a specific baby. So try referring to several babies—the younger, the better.

One pregnant mother has tried to instill in her child a positive attitude about babies. Whenever they see babies being walked outside, she says how cute and lovable they are. "That way, I hope my son won't be so overwhelmed when he sees one in his own home." Dr. Leonard Reich, a child psychologist at the mental health clinic of the Health Insurance Plan (HIP) of Greater New York considers that a good strategy. "Children pick up their parents' joy. If the mother looks at a new baby and acts happy, the child identifies with her happiness. That's a very good kind of role modeling."

If you plan to breast-feed your new baby, it might be helpful if your child sees another mother breast-feeding her baby first. That will familiarize him with the idea. He might not *like* what you'll be doing, but at least he will *know* what you'll be doing.

You might even try babysitting with a young baby, and observe your child's reaction. How does he respond when you hold the baby, feed the baby, change the baby? How well does he accept your divided time? That experience will help your child work out some of his emotions in advance, and it will give you an idea of what you will be dealing with when your child's real "rival" comes on the scene.

The Family Planners

Some parents include their first child in preparations for the new baby. They take her along on shopping trips, and may even let her select the baby's furniture. She may help set up the baby's room, and perhaps sort out the baby's clothes and put them in drawers. If your child is old enough and eager enough to take part in the decision-making and planning, there is no reason not to accept her help. But it certainly shouldn't be pushed. And you should not feel obligated to accept her choices of crib or high chair. A young child is not mature enough to make such decisions. Besides, she won't love the new baby any more, or hate it any less, for sleeping in the crib that she selected. Allowing the first child to help select the baby's name may also be a good idea —but it, too, may get you in trouble. One boy wanted his new sister to be named "Jillian," just like his neighborhood friend. His parents liked that name, too, and so there was a new little Jillian in the neighborhood. But another boy chose the name Muttley, McGee and Mopsey for his expected sibling. His parents plan to explain to him that that will be the baby's nickname, not his official name, and they hope he will understand. But if he insists, and they accede, there may one day be a lot of sibling violence in that household, and the older sibling will be on the receiving end.

Lifting with Love

"I can't lift you up. It may hurt the baby." Many women have said that many times to many children. But they should have done less talking and more lifting. "It's a myth that a pregnant woman can't pick up her child," says Dr. Louis Lissak, an obstetrician at The New York Hospital. "That myth has been terrible for the first child. Only if there's been a change in the cervix should heavy lifting be avoided." So ask your doctor, not your relatives, if it is okay to lift your child. Some women may find the lifting hard on their back, not on the baby. If you are in that category, you might try giving your child a stepladder for climbing onto his changing table or bed. And do most of your hugging while you are sitting down.

Life with Father

Many fathers draw closer to their older child during a second pregnancy, as I mentioned earlier. While mother is resting her swollen, aching legs, or doing her prenatal exercises, father and child may be exploring the worms in the backyard, or trying to expand the vocabulary of their still speechless parakeet. Don't discourage this delightful development. Their strengthened ties will help them make it through the hospital stay, when they are on their own, and through the first few hectic months with the baby, when mother will often be busy with the infant.

Don't be frightened off by the numerous ideas I have listed above. They are just that—ideas. They are not rules that must be followed to assure harmony in your household. There will probably be more havoc than harmony for a while, no matter what you do. The best approach is to try out the ideas that are appropriate to your child's developmental stage, and that fit into your way of doing things. "Each parent has his own style, consistent with his personality make-up," points out Dr. Leonard Reich of HIP. "There's room for a variety of styles. Most people respond creatively and positively to the challenge of preparing the older child. Trust your own creativity."

THE WRONG THING, THE WRONG TIME

What you don't do may be more important than what you do. Just a few ill-chosen words can undermine all you have tried to accomplish. "Don't worry," some well-meaning parents say. "We'll love you and the baby just as much." Already, they are comparing their older child with their younger, and setting the stage for sibling hostility. "You're going to love the new baby," is another common refrain of anxious parents. But the first child may not even like his new sibling, a competitor introduced against his will, and he shouldn't be deceived. Some parents emphasize the child's changed status. "You'll be the *big* brother. Won't it be wonderful?" Dr. Berk doesn't think so. "Those parents are fearful of the first child's reaction and are setting up ways to prevent hostility. But it doesn't work, and it's destructive." The Bank Street College psychologist also warns against showering a child with gifts or other special treats all during pregnancy—other tactics for preventing anger. "Those are guilt-laden messages. They tell the child that something dreadful is about to happen."

Another common mistake is to change the child's routine toward the end of the pregnancy—to move her into a new room to "make room" for baby, or to get her out of the way, and into a nursery school, when the baby is due. A child's life should be upset as little as possible in connection with the pregnancy and birth. Any necessary changes—a new room, a new babysitter, a new school—should be made as early as possible in the pregnancy so the child doesn't feel displaced by the baby.

If you are going to move your first child from crib to bed, that also should be done at least a month or two before baby's arrival. It is best not to simply move the crib from child's to baby's room, but to take it apart first and keep it apart until it is needed. The crib is such a personal object, "it needs some defusing time," the Welsons point out. Some parents repaint the crib for their second child so it doesn't stir up memories, or jealousy, in their first.

A second pregnancy doesn't mean, however, that a bed must be introduced. Some children are just not ready for it yet, and it would only provoke conflict. We took out the crib, and brought in the bed, when Brian was just two years and three months old. He didn't seem to object to it, but a slight problem did arise. He didn't want to be alone in it until he had fallen asleep. And he wouldn't fall asleep until I had done puzzles with him, read books to him, told him stories, and sang him songs. Each night I staggered, an exhausted wreck, straight from his bed to my bed. It took just a few weeks to reduce the ritual to an off-key rendition of "My Blue Heaven," but it was a grueling few weeks.

Some children may be ready for a bed even before they are two. But it is a decision that should be based on the child's readiness to give up the crib, not on your eagerness to claim it. If you can't borrow another crib, and don't want to buy one, you can try putting the new baby in a bassinette for a few months or in a portable crib for a year or so. Perhaps when he is so big he really needs a full-sized crib, your older child will be big enough for a bed.

Some parents push their children ahead in other areas, as well. They don't want two children in diapers, so they make potty-sitting a required after-dinner activity. They don't want two children on bottles, so they try glasses with straws and cups with spouts—anything without a nipple. But if the child is not ready for those steps, they may spell trouble. "To overemphasize acceleration is a mistake," says Dr. Ilana Reich. "It puts too much pressure on the older child." On the other hand, if a child is chronologically and emotionally ready, developmental progress should not be withheld during the pregnancy. "You should stick to what you would have done if the baby wasn't coming. If your child is four and on the bottle, it's okay to take it away, because you would have anyway."

Toilet training is a little trickier because of the emotional responses it triggers, combined with the common regression in that area after the birth. "If the child was trained just before, and a big fuss was made about his success, he feels it's a defeat when he regresses," says Dr. Reich. So if you decide to do it, and the child is ready for it, you might start toilet training at the beginning of the pregnancy. But keep in mind that "there should be no pressure to give up anything or to perform anything because of the pregnancy," the New York psychologist emphasizes.

Some parents attempt acceleration in less sensitive areas. One mother taught her four-year-old daughter to dress and bathe herself so she would be more self-reliant when the baby came. The mother of a two-year-old encouraged her son to do a lot of walking outdoors, so it would be easier for them all to get around when the baby was around, too. In general, such independence training is good preparation for the changes ahead, but again, a child should not be pressured beyond his capacities or emotional resources.

What do you do if your child demands a baby brother, or insists on a sister? Again, there is opportunity for error. Marta had promised Travis, almost three, a baby brother. "He was looking forward to it. When I brought home a girl from the hospital, that's the last thing he wanted. Now he wants me to have another child so he'll have a brother." A better way of handling it is to point out that there is no way of knowing, or guaranteeing, the baby's sex. It's purely by chance. You might add that a child of either sex can do the same things. "A sister can play baseball, too."

You may wonder at your child's preference in gender. It just could be that you, as parents, have a preference, and communicate it to your child. In general, a child who asks for a baby of the same sex wants a playmate, Dr. Berk points out. A child who wants a baby of the opposite sex may fear competition. "A little boy may be nervous that if you have another boy, the baby will replace him in your affection. He assumes the opposite sex would be less competition. He's anxious about his own security. You should reassure him that no matter what sex the baby is, he won't be replaced, and you'll love him as much as before." The reason for a boy to want a girl baby, or a girl to want a boy, may be more prosaic. Perhaps someone down the block just had a kid brother, and your child thinks it is pretty nice and wants one, too —or pretty awful, and will take a sister, thank you. One little boy wanted a sister so she wouldn't "bother" his trucks.

The last big mistake in preparation is too much preparation. It can be overdone. Dr. Leonard Reich's friends are now expecting their second child. "They're overly preparing their first. They're telling him 'You will feel this, you will feel that.' He's become nuts. He's parodying his mother's concerns, and trying to match up his feelings with what he's being told. But that's not what he's really experiencing." Your pregnancy may be uppermost in your mind, but there are other things going on in your child's life. He's making friends, learning, growing. Devote some of your attention to his interests and activities, and not all to your pregnancy, or he will be sick of the baby before it's even born.

COMING CLOSER

As your due date approaches, preparation should take a somewhat different form. You may consider signing your child up for a sibling preparation class if one is available in your community. If your hospital or maternity center doesn't offer one, perhaps a private childbirth instructor does. The class described at the beginning of this chapter took place at New York City's Maternity Center Association (MCA). In addition to the activities already outlined, the children were given crayons and coloring books relating to the baby and the visit to the hospital. At the end of the session, children and parents had a "birthday party" for the baby-to-be, complete with cupcakes, candles, and birthday napkins.

A class at the University of Minnesota Hospitals in Minneapolis has the same goals—making the child feel involved and reducing anxiety—but uses different tools. Most of the children are fascinated by a series of life-size models depicting a fetus at various stages of development. The children take the models apart, and put them back together again, while they learn all about the growth and birth of a baby. The umbilical cord, shown in the model, raises a lot of questions: What is it? What does it do? Will cutting the cord hurt the baby? Is that how *I* was connected?

That class also includes a tour of the postpartum unit and nursery, so the child will know just where mother and baby will be. Even if you can't find or don't want a sibling preparation class, you might ask your maternity facility whether such tours are allowed. In some hospitals they are not publicized but they may be conducted on an individual basis. If your child does get an advance look, be sure to point out a telephone in a hallway or room. "There's where Mommy will be calling you from," you might say. Also, write down the telephone number of the hospital and tape it next to your home phone. Your child will be relieved to know he will be able to reach you while you're away. If he is not used to your telephone voice, try talking with him over the phone a few times before the birth. That will make your calls from the hospital all the more exciting and reassuring.

Your hospital stay can be a difficult ordeal for your child, so he should be well prepared for it. Just as he should know where you will be staying, he should know where he will be staying, too. Tell him all the plans—what house he will be in, who will be with him, what he will be doing. It's best if you can arrange it so he will be in his own home with someone he trusts and loves, and if his routine can be maintained. Many fathers want to be that special someone, and take a vacation from work during the hospital period. A father's involvement during that time is very important, according to the University of Michigan study. It helps a child adjust to separation from his mother, and helps him accept the new baby. Most important, your child should be told that Mommy won't be gone forever—she will be coming back.

Some parents buy gifts ahead of time to be given to the child in the hospital or sent home with Daddy. Some prepare postcards to be mailed from the hospital. One woman took her son's picture shortly before the birth, and told him she would show it to the doctors and nurses. He was quite pleased that he would be the focus of at least some attention. Another mother didn't know quite how to prepare her eighteen-month-old son. She finally decided to make a tape with both voices. She said, "Hi! How are you doing? I'll see you soon." Her son jumped the gun a bit, and played it for a few weeks before the delivery. "He really thought it was great."

If your child is old enough, you might ask if she would like to help pack your suitcase for the hospital, or select the baby's homecoming clothes. You might also look ahead to the time when you are away, and together prepare food for the freezer, or review any special chores she will have, like watering the plants. That will make the event seem real to her, and give her the sense that life will go on while you are away.

Some parents are faced with an extra challenge: Their older child's birthday comes shortly before their due date. No matter how preoccupied or uncomfortable you are, don't let that important day go by without a celebration. It doesn't have to be an extravaganza, but it should have the basics: a couple of kids, a couple of goodies, and a gift. One woman in that predicament is determined to celebrate, no matter what. "Even if there's just a pizza with a candle in the middle, Sandy is going to have a real birthday party."

SIBLING PARTICIPATION IN THE BIRTH

Preparation becomes more complex if you plan to have your first child attend the birth of your second. The notion of sibling participation may seem bizarre to you, or it may seem beautiful. Since 1976, when the practice began in California, more hospitals are allowing sibling participation (as many as a hundred nationwide) and more parents are choosing it. Should you consider it for your family?

If you are totally turned off by the idea, you've got a lot of professional company. Many psychologists believe it can be a frightening, traumatic experience for a child. "Children are simply not emotionally prepared to deal with that kind of experience, or to understand what they're seeing," Dr. Welson points out.

"It's cruel to put a child through that, even though the idea is to be loving." Dr. Berk agrees, calling birth an "overwhelming experience" that can be scary if it is not understood. "Blood can be scary. The whole process can be scary. If you know it will be a normal delivery, that's one thing, but you can never know that for sure."

Dr. Berk points out yet another potential drawback. "The mother may be thinking of her child, and not yell because she doesn't want to scare him. But her total focus should be on the birth."

There is another side to the story. Proponents argue that birth is only frightening if that emotion is conveyed to the child. "Children can quickly pick up the atmosphere," says Janet Reinbrecht, education director of the Maternity Center Association in New York, a facility that has allowed children at births since it opened in 1976. "The setting here is homelike, not at all frightening, like hospitals often are." The center's director, Ruth Watson Lubic, also defends the practice. "Obstetricians assume that childbirth is an X-rated experience, with children gaping at the mother's genitalia, but that's not the case. I feel strongly that children will accept whatever their parents accept."

Proponents also emphasize the positive value of sibling participation. "It provides a real feeling of family, of doing something together," Miss Reinbrecht maintains. "The child doesn't feel his mother went off and got another child to replace him while she was out. It eliminates the separation, and decreases the initial shock of going from only child to oldest child."

Mrs. Ruth Newman, a family therapist in New York City, is not exactly an advocate of siblings being present at birth, but she does see a certain value in it for a girl. "It can help her self-esteem to see what she'll be able to do as an adult. It can be thrilling to know 'I can do that. My body will produce a baby.' By watching her mother, she will know her own body better."

What do the parents who choose it say? Ira and Maria had their first child almost four years ago at the MCA. They are due to have their second child there in three months, and are leaning toward their son's participation. "It will give him a sense of what it means to give birth," Ira explained. "We have no pets. We don't live on a farm. It's important for him to know how it physically works. It must be as remarkable an experience for a child as for an adult to see. And it will be a nice memory for him to share with his sibling.'' But Ira does not think his children will get along any better for it. "It won't necessarily improve their relationship. He'll react badly to his sibling no matter what happens. It's more important for our relationship with him than for the relationship of the children.''

Some parents and professionals feel, however, that it strengthens the bond between the children, and may even reduce sibling rivalry. In a study of fifty-five home births in Salt Lake City, Utah, almost a third of the women felt that sibling rivalry was reduced because the children had immediate contact with the newborn. In a more recent study of eighteen families, who had had a total of twenty-two children present at the birth of a sibling (at the Mt. Zion Hospital and Medical Center's Alternative Birth Center, San Francisco), overt sibling rivalry was reported in every family. Parents, however, uniformly felt that presence at birth had increased sibling attachment.

At that same California birth center, researchers looked at the behavior of forty children during the actual labor and birth process. The reactions of the children, aged three to fourteen, varied widely. Two of them slept through the whole thing. (Those births took place late at night.) Some children didn't seem too happy to be where they were. One ten-year-old girl had told her mother she would rather go to Disneyland. An eight-year-old boy was sorry there wasn't a TV to watch during the "boring" parts. But some children were actively involved. They asked questions, timed contractions, watched the baby's delivery. Some even watched the delivery of the placenta, and picked it up to examine it. No child in the study showed extreme distress, "but some parts of labor and delivery did seem to be somewhat distressing to some children," the researchers noted. They concluded that "childbirth is primarily an adult event. When children are present, it appears to be a wish of their parents that they be there."

Dr. Roberta Ballard, one of the investigators, told me that their published research was meant to be precautionary, not negative. "For some families, sibling participation is valid. For others, it's not. What's marvelous for all siblings is to come in immediately after the baby's born. Separation after the birth is totally unnecessary.''

At the MCA, most parents choose that last option, and bring in the child right after the birth. Some children hold their new sibling, some touch and kiss this newest member of the family. At another maternity center, one new brother was still holding the baby while the five-minute Apgar scoring was done. Another child was eager to be the first person to diaper the newborn. It has been suggested that such early contacts help siblings ''bond'' to each other.

So, have you changed your mind about sibling attendance at births? Do you think it is less bizarre—or less beautiful—than you thought before? Are you thinking about it for yourself? If you are, there are some factors you should consider. One is the age of your child. At the MCA, even two-year-olds are welcomed. ''Their experiences have been good,'' director Lubic reports. ''Even with the young children, there have been no negative reactions.'' But at Mount Zion Hospital and Medical Center, children under four have been discouraged. ''They can't assimilate it,'' says Dr. Ballard. ''Unless their mother is especially attuned, they don't understand what's going on. They don't know what their mother's noises are all about.'' In making up your mind, you should also try to anticipate your reaction to your child's presence. Will you be ''performing'' for your child? Will you be able to relax? Will his presence interfere with your dealing with the birth process? Those answers are important to your decision. But the decision is not yours alone. Both mother and father should agree that sibling participation is right for their family. And the child should have the option of participating, or of going to Disneyland (or at least watching TV) instead. Some parents put subtle pressure on their child to attend the birth, or they even turn on the hard sell. Dr. Ballard remembers asking a little girl how she felt about seeing the birth. ''I'm scared,'' the girl told her. Just then her mother chimed in, ''Oh no you're not!''

If you, and the rest of your family, decide to go ahead with it, you will have some additional preparation to do. Your maternity facility may have classes to ready children for the experience. At the MCA, children are shown a fifteen-minute videotape of a birth to familiarize them with the sights and sounds. Children who have been at births share their experiences and feelings with the others. The instructor suggests that mothers practice the breathing, and make the noises, in front of the child. "That way, the child will understand the noise," explains Miss Reinbrecht. "He'll know that labor is work, like jogging, and requires special breathing." (During actual labor, some children do the breathing along with their mothers.) A teaching tool you may find helpful is a rag doll that "gives birth" and then delivers the placenta. Such dolls are available in human or monkey form, and can even have a "Caesarean delivery." After the birth, the baby dolls can be "nursed" by their rag doll mommies. These dolls make wonderful birth educators for all siblings-to-be, not just siblings at birth. (For ordering information, see the bibliography.) Try to make sure your child understands all aspects of the birth—the contractions, the stages of labor, the episiotomy, the blood. And prepare him for the possibility of a complication, including the fact that he will have to leave if one should occur. His childbirth education should also include the appearance of a newborn baby. You would be surprised at how much some children don't know. A five-year-old girl was upset that the baby was born without clothes. In *her* baby pictures *she* had clothes on. So be sure to alert your child ahead of time to the baby's state of undress.

When it comes time to go to the maternity facility for the birth, it would be helpful to bring along some books and games and snacks for your older child. Otherwise, there may be lots of "boring" times for him, not to mention one very hungry stomach. It is important also to bring along a support person, someone other than Daddy whom he can be with and talk to during the labor. The father should feel free to be with his mate at this time, and not obligated to entertain his child.

If your child wants to participate in the event in some way, let him. Some children bring ice chips to their mother, or rub her back, or even help walk her around the room. But if your child ever wants out, either for a short time or the whole time, he should feel free to leave. When it's all over, remember to reassure him that everything is okay—and remember not to make the mistake of one enraptured, but thoughtless, mother. Right in front of her first child, she said of her new child, "This is the most beautiful baby I ever had!"

GONE BUT NOT FORGOTTEN

Even if you decide against sibling participation, there are ways you can minimize the anxiety of mother-child separation. One way is to minimize the separation period. Some maternity facilities allow the mother to go home twelve hours after the birth, if all is well. You might compare the minimum stays in your local hospitals and maternity centers, and use that information to help decide the facility you will use.

When it's time for you to leave for the hospital, you should tell your child exactly where it is you're going. Don't rush off secretly, or pretend you are going off to cruise the Bahamas. If you do, she will be very confused when you come back home without a tan but with a baby. What if your child is sleeping when your labor pains tell you it's time to get going? There is no harm in waking her to tell her, but you may be disappointed in her reaction. When the Welsons tried it, their daughter said "Leave me alone," rolled over, and went right back to sleep.

While you are in the hospital, you should try to keep in touch as often as possible. Ask if you can call your child right after the birth, so you can personally deliver the news. (If you can *see* her right after the birth, that's even better.) Call her at least once a day, at a set time, if possible. Some mothers call every night right before their child's bedtime to assure their child Mommy hasn't forgotten her. You might suggest that your child call you. Most children find that an exciting adventure.

But what should you say during those numerous phone calls? You don't want to rave about the new baby, so what's left to talk about? You can, certainly, talk about the baby—what he looks like, his name, the color of his eyes. It would seem strange if you ignored the baby, since he is the reason you are away. But what your child wants to hear, most of all, is that you love her, and miss her, and will be coming home to see her.

Another way to keep in touch is to write your child letters that Daddy can read to her. Some parents take instant pictures of the baby to show their older child. Those photos let the child know that something really is going on. You haven't fled to the Bahamas to soak up the sun, after all. This is also the time to send home those presents you bought ahead of time. If you have chosen them thoughtfully, and they are something your child really wants, she will treasure them as a reminder of you, and as a sign you are thinking of her. One or two presents are sufficient. Dr. Berk warns parents against "trying to buy off hostility by over-giving and overindulging." She also warns against the common practice of saying that the present is from the baby. "That's nonsense. It's just an attempt to say that baby loves you, and so you should be nice to him. It's a kind of bribery." It is also an insult to the child's intelligence. Here you have been telling her all along how helpless a newborn is, how can that helpless little baby possibly buy a present and wrap it up, not to mention count the change?

A VERY IMPORTANT VISITOR

The best way to keep in touch is by a personal visit. The battle for sibling visitation was long and difficult—hospitals argued that the children would infect the babies, that they would cause chaos in the corridors, that they would be traumatized when it came time to leave. But some hospitals tried it anyway, and proved those fears unfounded. Then consumer demand took over. Some parents began to select hospitals with their sibling visitation policies in mind. One hospital bucked the trend until the hospital closest to it allowed it. "That's what turned it for us," the hospital's childbirth educator told me. "The administrators were afraid of losing patients." Now, the question is not only whether a hospital has sibling visitation, but how liberal its visitation is. Some allow only one visit a stay; others allow one or more a day. Some have mother and child meet in a waiting room; others allow the child to visit in the mother's room.

So now, it is pretty much up to you. Before you decide for or against, you may want to know how it has worked out for other people. At least two studies have addressed that point. In one, twelve "visitors" and twenty "nonvisitors" to a maternity hospital in Cleveland were compared. The two groups of children, aged one to three and a half, responded differently when it was time for their mothers to come home from the hospital. The non-visitors were more likely to ignore their mothers and refuse a request for a kiss or hug. They were also more likely to ignore their parents' question of whether they liked their new sibling, or to give a resounding "no." The New York Hospital began a sibling visitation program in 1977. The next year, it sent a questionnaire to patients who had taken advantage of it. Most mothers (145 of 172) rated their children's reaction to the hospital environment as positive, and 18 rated it as mixed. The rest reported such negative reactions as "clingy," "upset with wheelchairs," or "overpowered by other visitors." Most mothers (131) also felt their children reacted well to the new baby. A few children, however, seemed "indifferent" or "jealous," and one child said the baby "looks like a worm." Some of the mothers had been hospitalized previously without visits from their children. Of those 39 women, 29 said they felt the visit had made home adjustment easier for their children.

The main value the women saw in the visit was that it eased separation anxiety. Some said that it helped lessen their loneliness for the child, that it increased a "family feeling," that it gave a sense of reality to the baby and so helped their older child adjust. One woman said that "the visit was as exciting as giving birth."

Some parents decide against sibling visitation for fear their child will be upset when it is time to leave mother and go home. Some children do find the parting not-so-sweet sorrow. One two-year-old boy wept for hours after, and even cried himself to sleep that night. But the New York study showed that even when children had cried, their mothers felt the visit had been advantageous.

What if your child generally suffers from separation anxiety, and cries when you go out for an evening? Perhaps it would be better if he didn't see you at all, than have to be torn away? Even then, a bout of crying may be better than a long separation. According to Dorothy Metzger, the head of childbirth education at The New York Hospital, "Seeing Mom is important for all children, *especially* if there's a separation problem. It's less anxiety-provoking for them to see where Mother is."

Some parents don't think their child will be interested in the baby, and so they see little point in sibling visitation. "There'll just be rows of little bundles of babies," said Marilyn, an expectant second-time mother. "Oliver won't see that much, so he won't get a big kick out of it." But Marilyn is missing the point of the visit. Most children are much more interested in mother than in baby. Some fear she has been hurt in childbirth, and want to see for themselves that she is okay. They want to see where their mother is sleeping, what her room is like. Three-year-old Alison asked her mother, "Where do you eat, if you're always in bed?" One mother took her child to the bathroom to continue the habits of home. Some children actually have to be coaxed to look at the baby. One little boy, not even two, appeared totally uninterested in his new baby sister. His mother couldn't understand it. "You don't want to look at your sister?" she asked him, "What a no-good brother!" At that rate, her prophecy may well be self-fulfilling.

Some children have the opposite reaction. They say a cursory hello to their mothers, then spend the rest of the visit staring at the baby, marveling at its tiny size, incredulous that they, too, were once so small. One woman was so upset by her daughter's cold reaction to her, she was sorry the visit had taken place. "Molly was so angry at me, she hardly paid any attention to me. She was more interested in the baby and the other relatives. She was actually glad to leave." A reaction of anger or indifference is not uncommon. But it doesn't mean your child doesn't love you, and that she didn't benefit from seeing you.

The visit may provide parents with their first clue of how their child is taking the latest event. The Welsons' daughter had seemed quite happy during the pregnancy, but when she came for the visit, "Jenni looked shell-shocked to me," Mrs. Welson recalls. "She just looked different, totally freaked out. It's like an adult when somebody dies. She just seemed shocked." So the Welsons had time to prepare themselves for what life at home might be like during the initial adjustment period.

The visit can provide some unexpected benefits as well. When I was in the hospital with Michael, he was not the best eater the nurses had ever seen, and they didn't hesitate to let me know. But when sturdily built Brian came up for a visit, the nurses took one look at him and their complaints ceased immediately. They figured if I had done so well by Brian, Michael was in good hands. Another second-time mother, Betty, was visited by her very active two-year-old. He took the hospital by storm, running energetically up and down the hall. He even ran into the nursery to give his new brother a present. When he left, Betty was greeted by welcome words of sympathy. "We really feel sorry for you," her roommates said. "Here, you'll be going home with a new baby, and you'll have to contend with that dynamo, too!"

Sibling visitation is an important innovation that all children can benefit from. If you prepare yourself for the possibility of a cold shoulder from your child, or a crying jag at the end, you will benefit from it, too. There are ways you can make it even better for everyone involved. You should tell your child, in advance, exactly what will be happening—that he will be able to see you and touch you, that he will be able to see but not touch the baby (if that's the case), that he will have to leave the hospital without you but that you will be home soon. It's best if the same person brings your child to the hospital and takes him home again. Some children have been distressed when their father has brought them but another relative taken them home (while the father stays on for a longer visit). It must have seemed like a double desertion. It's also a good idea to limit the visit to the immediate family, so your child can have you all to himself during this special time.

Your child's visit is a good opportunity to give him that present you bought ahead of time. But don't be surprised if he doesn't pay much attention to it in front of you. Children have been known to seem indifferent at first, but then to clutch the gift all the way home and play with it to the exclusion of all other toys. It is a reminder of his visit, and of you. Another way to make the visit extra-special is to serve a birthday cake and have a little family party. But the best way to make it special is to remind him, again, how very much you love and miss him.

COMING HOME

Finally, the day has come for your family to reunite. It is a day that can truly bring your family together if you are sensitive to the needs of your older child. A good way to start the day is to have your child come to the hospital to greet you and the baby, and to help bring you home. He will see, right away, that he is still a valued member of the family, that he is not left behind when there are important things to be done. During the ride home, try to have someone else attend to the baby—a grandparent or baby nurse. And spend the time with your first child, catching up on your days apart.

Just as your child may have been cold to you during sibling visitation, he may act angry when he sees you now. "He may look at you like you're not there," Mrs. Newman points out. "After all, you've gone away and brought a baby home. Or he may act clingy and weepy. Don't get hysterical or try to change his behavior. Keep calm."

Once you arrive home, you will see, for real, what it is like to be a mother of two. Two screaming children; two hungry children; two needy children. Just for today, pay more personal attention to the needs of your older child (while a relative or nurse helps out with the baby). Your child has been waiting for you, so be there for him. Today is his introduction to the experience of being an older sibling. Don't spoil it for him, especially not this soon.

When you do tend to the baby, try to include your first child in the things you are doing. Talk to him as you are feeding the baby, as you are bathing the baby. "Don't closet yourself alone with the baby," Dr. Berk advises. "Show your older child, by example, that what's between you and the baby is not exclusive. He can share in it, too."

The Welsons put a twenty-four moratorium on visitors during that first day home with their baby son Grant. "We all just sat in bed together, so that Jenni and Grant could meet." Homecoming day is an important day for your children. It is probably the first day they can touch. It is certainly the first day they are living under the same roof as part of the same family. It is truly the first day of the rest of their lives together.

4. The Highlights and Hazards of Second-Time Parenthood

FIRST-TIME PARENTHOOD CAN BE A TRYING EXPERIENCE filled with insecurity, uncertainty, and a constant state of high anxiety. But by the time the second child rolls around, the parents can roll right along with him, confident, experienced, secure in their ability to hold the baby without dropping him and feed the baby without choking him. Besides, as the saying goes, "You've already made your mistakes on your first child." Presumably, you know exactly how you strayed from the proper path of enlightened child rearing, you have repented, and you won't do it again.

You have probably also heard that second children are easier than first children. Perhaps that's why you decided to stop the pill or discard the diaphragm and take your chances. *Surely* your second child won't cause you as many sleepless nights as your first did. *Certainly* the terrible two's won't be as terrible again. Or will they?

On the negative side of the ledger, second-time parents don't get high marks from the teaching profession. There is an educator's aphorism, "The first child is brought up; the others grow up." This saying suggests that parents may be too laid-back with their second children, allowing benign neglect to substitute for a firm parental hand.

So much for sayings. What is it really like to be a parent the second time around? For some people, it's better. For some, it's worse. For everyone, it's different. One difference is apparent from your very first glance at your second baby. This time you have a standard of comparison, and you use it. "Another Brian," my husband and I said, practically in the same breath, when we first saw newborn Michael. If the sex is the same and size and coloring similar, it is hard to believe a totally different human being has just been born. But if this little creature looks nothing like your last, it can be hard to believe that this baby is your baby, too. An "ugly" baby seems even uglier if the first was smooth and unblemished, a pretty baby even lovelier if the first looked battered and blue.

If the first baby looked decidedly more like its father or its mother, the genetically neglected parents may be relieved if that oversight is not repeated. "Brett, our first child, looked just like Glen," Fay recalls. "But Seth didn't. I liked that. It gave me the hope there'd be something of me physically in my second child." Glen, predictably, saw things in a different light. "Brett was beautiful. She looked just like me. But Seth, our second, was ugly and wrinkly. He didn't even look like he was mine."

Parents are also alert to differences in behavior as clues to the new baby's temperament. They pay close attention to how loud, and often, the baby squeals, how alert she is, how calm she is—always with the example of the first in mind. Many parents told me their second babies seemed easier even in the hospital. "Sean got very taut and tense," said Dina. "Brandon, my second, was laid-back and relaxed." But if the first was a "good" baby, the second had better be as good—or else. Edith and Harvey considered Russell, their first child, a very special child. "He was precocious, way ahead of himself. He did everything early," Edith recalls. "There wasn't a day that went by that he didn't amaze us. I thought when I had the second he'd be like the first. He wasn't. He's a different type of child, a difficult child." Edith noticed the differences right away. "Even in the hospital, Paul never ate. He couldn't hold his head up like Russell did. It was disappointing, because I had a yardstick to measure him by. If he was the first, I probably wouldn't have felt that way—but then I might not have had another child!"

Feelings of attachment sometimes come later with a second child than with a first. Your love has already been "staked out," and you may fear that a show of love to your second is a show of disloyalty to your first. But your new baby may break down your resistance and win you over early on. It hit one woman while she was feeding her two-day-old second child. She realized the baby was not just a toy brought in to be fed and then whisked away. She would be taking the baby home, and the baby would be part of her family. Another woman felt rather aloof from her newest offspring until she heard him scream during circumcision. "That's *my* son in there," she thought. "It's not someone else's baby." Even if you don't feel really close to your second child for several weeks, or even months, there is no cause for concern. Second children have the reputation of "growing" on you. If you just keep yourself open to your new baby's smiles and sounds and developing personality, you will be won over, too.

While you are still in the hospital, you will probably notice that your baby is not the only one who is different. You are different, too. This time, you actually know what you're doing. I vividly remember my feelings of helplessness during my first hospital stay. I prayed that Brian would be considerate enough to "hold it in" until a nurse was around to change his diaper, because I hadn't the faintest notion how to do it. I made several desperate attempts to swaddle him as securely as the nurses did, only to see my efforts unravel time after time. I was eager to breast-feed, but afraid of failure. I marveled at a third-time mother who was nursing her baby and eating her dinner at the same time. During my second hospital stay, I was the picture of poise. I had no trouble diapering Michael because I was still diapering Brian. I immediately accepted the fact that I wasn't a good swaddler, so Michael simply went unswaddled while in my care—I figured he would survive anyway. I attempted the "You breast-feed, I eat," maneuver—and it worked. My experiences were not unique— mother after mother told me of their ineptitude and fears with their first baby, and their cool, calm handling of their second.

FILLING UP FAST

Any doubt about the expertise of second-timers was dispelled by a series of studies conducted in California. The first study looked at twenty-two first-time mothers and twenty-two experienced mothers as they bottle-fed their two-day-old infants. The second-timers (and third-timers) spent less time feeding their infants, but got better results. Their children drank more formula, and drank it faster, than did the children of the new mothers. Why were they lapping it up? What did their mothers do differently? The researchers, headed by Dr. Evelyn Thoman of Stanford University Medical Center, observed that a typical first-time mother simply puts the bottle's nipple in the baby's mouth and holds it there for the baby to suck on. "She may verbally encourage the infant to eat, but she provides little of the stimulation that is most likely to elicit sucking." In contrast, the experienced mother stimulates the baby's lips and mouth with the nipple whenever he starts to suck slower, or strokes the baby's cheek or chin to encourage sucking. "If the infant is sleepy, she is more likely to supply vigorous general stimulation at appropriate times."

Does a nursing mother also act differently if she has been a mother before? To find out, Dr. Thoman and her associates compared twenty "new" and twenty "old" mothers as they breast-fed their two-day-old infants. As expected, the experienced mothers devoted less time to feeding. But during the feeding sessions, their infants spent more time attached to the nipple, and while they were attached, they sucked more. The scientists pointed to a better "interactive mesh" between the experienced mothers and their babies.

This study of nursing mothers looked at the sex of the infants, as well as their order of birth, and came up with some interesting findings. The first-time mothers who had sons spent more time breast-feeding than did first-time mothers who had daughters. But for experienced mothers, the opposite was true: Those with daughters spent more time breast-feeding than did those with sons.

The investigators also observed how much the mothers talked to their infant during feeding. First-time mothers were, on the whole, a much more verbal lot than the second- or third-timers. The new mothers did the most talking if they had a daughter to talk to. The experienced mothers seemed to open up a little if they had a son. The child who was smiled at the most was the daughter of a first-time mother.

FADED MEMORIES

If you are trying to remember your first hospital stay, and how you fed your infant, or couldn't, or how you diapered your infant, or wouldn't, every ecstatic and embarrassing moment probably comes right back to you. You may be able to remember the color of your night nurse's eyes, the names of your roommate's in-laws, the pattern of cracks in the ceiling. The parents I interviewed told me much more than I ever wanted to know about those first days with their first child. But many had little to say about their second hospital stay, though it was more recent. They just couldn't remember it as vividly. "I can recall every detail about those first few days with Oliver," his mother told me. "But with my second son, I only remember snatches." This memory failure follows many second-time parents out of the hospital and into their home. Ask a two-time parent when each child became the proud owner of his first tooth. Chances are she can tell you, without hesitation, the exact date child number one got incisor number one. To find out the same information for her second child, it's a mad dash to the baby book, and a fervent hope she even remembered to record that event for future generations. First smile? First step? First sneeze? Same story.

"I can pinpoint every single one of Paulette's milestones," Bette recalled with pride. "I know exactly when she first sat up, when she first smiled. But with our second child, Teddy, those events just blended into the background. His first year seemed to flow evenly along."

What is it about second parenthood that deadens the memory and tightens the tongue? The same malady that strikes many a second pregnancy—terminal boredom. Some parents just can't work up much enthusiasm about a situation they have been through before. They may not have been pros at diapering their first child, but they could approach it as a challenge. They could try out different brands of diapers, cloth or disposable, elasticized or not. They could experiment with the adhesive tabs. Better in front, or better in back? Which wipie will do a neater job of it? Which powder will keep diaper rash at bay? Which cream will soothe the rash if it breaks out anyway? There are so many possible combinations of diaper and wipie and powder and cream, the novice parent can turn routine diaper changing into an experimental workshop on baby's derrière. But, alas, most second-time parents have already figured all that out—or else they have collected so many coupons over the years there is no *way* they're going to change brands, diaper rash or no. With the excitement of experimentation gone, the less aesthetic aspects of changing baby's diapers come to the fore.

Dr. Virginia Pomeranz, New York City pediatrician, colorfully describes the effects of novelty on the first-time parent—and the effects of déjà-vu on the second-timer. "Your first child seems so much more interesting. Every time it has a bowel movement or passes gas, it's a big excitement because it's the first time. So you're content to feed it and change it and pat it on the head. By comparison, your second child seems really dull. This time you notice that a little baby doesn't do anything but take it in one end and put it out the other. It doesn't smile at you, it doesn't do a thing but squawk. It's all so uninteresting, parents seldom fuss over the second as much as they did the first."

THE CASE OF THE EMPTY ALBUM

Most second children don't know what happened to them as infants. There is usually little visible proof that they even were infants. The photographer that roams through hospital corridors, trying to make a living off babies because he didn't do so well with brides, usually has better luck with first children than with second. One new mother plunked down a hundred dollars for a composite portrait of her adorable newborn son. When the photographer came around during her second hospital stay, he could have gotten a really good shot of her finger pointing to the door. "There is no way I was going to spend that kind of money on pictures again. We realized we could save money and take them ourselves." Did they? Not many.

The very same parents who go through a frenzy of photography of their firstborn, panicky they will let a gesture go unrecorded or a smile unsnapped, have to remind themselves to get a

single shot of their youngest—after they have reminded themselves to buy some film—after they have reminded their oldest
to stay out of the picture for once, which is the biggest trick of
all. Some parents, second children themselves, remember looking through their own parents' albums and wondering about the
pictorial gap between that embarrassing picture of themselves
naked on the rug and that embarrassing picture of them out on
their first date. Were they so ugly, their parents wanted to spare
them the pain of looking back? Did the cat run away with the
camera? Some second children are amused by the oversight,
some are annoyed, but most of them repeat it with their own
second children.

Do your second child's first years have to be an unrecorded,
unremembered blur, a rerun without surprise or suspense? Only
if you don't appreciate the unique person your second child is.
This child certainly looks different than your first, if you look
hard enough. And this child has his own style of crying, laughing,
loving. It can be fascinating to observe how your children develop in different areas, how they handle the same situation in
different ways. If your first child was the kind of toddler who had
her toys snatched from her, you may secretly enjoy watching
your second child develop into the neighborhood snatcher. If
your first child didn't talk until she was two and your second
started earlier, you may enjoy hearing what's on a one-year-old's
mind. Even if your first was a "joy" and your second a "terror,"
you may be curious to find out if you can do a better job than
your sister, who had her "terror" first. Every child, first, second,
or tenth, is an individual. Every child opens up new vistas for his
parents, if they only take the time to look, listen, and love.

LESS TALK, MORE TELEVISION

If anyone is having a dull time of it, it may be your second child.
A number of researchers have actually gone into homes and
watched how mothers interact with their babies. As early as two
weeks of age, secondborn babies are treated differently. University of Washington investigators who observed the home life of

thirty-two young infants found that the secondborn babies were talked to less, touched less, looked at less, and played with less than were the firstborns. The only thing they got more of was noise, especially the noise of television.

Older infants are also treated differently based on their order of birth, several studies show. An especially enlightening study, conducted by Blanche Jacobs and Howard Moss of the National Institute of Mental Health, considered the gender of the infant as well. The investigators first made observations in the homes of thirty-two three-month-old infants; sixteen of the children were male, sixteen female. The observers returned again to those homes three months after the birth of a younger sibling. They were thus able to compare how the same mother treated her first and second child. Their findings: "The mothers spent less time in social, affectionate, and caretaking activities with their secondborns than they had with their firstborns." But some secondborns got less attention than others. A girl with an older sister experienced the biggest decline in maternal attention. But a boy with an older sister got virtually the same amount of attention as his sister had. The authors had no ready explanation for the differences based on sex. They speculated that perhaps having a child of the opposite sex is enough of a novelty to maintain parental attention. Also, secondborn boys may elicit attention because of the "preferred status" of males in our culture.

You may not be interested now, but in the future you may wonder how secondborns are treated differently by their mothers than thirdborns, or (heaven forbid, you say?) fourthborns. Yes, there is a study on that, too, looking at the home life of 193 three-month-old infants. The major differences found by Michael Lewis and Valerie Kreitzberg of the Educational Testing Service were between firstborn babies and "others." Firstborns were talked to more, looked at more, smiled at more, played with more, rocked more, and given more time with toys and pacifiers than babies born later. But second children had one distinction: They were held more than babies of any other birth order. On the other hand, they were smiled at less, and played with less, than first-, third-, or fourthborn babies.

What about Dad? Is he also more attentive to number one?

Most definitely, according to this same study. Fathers did the most vocalizing to firstborn babies. Sex also made a difference. Fathers talked more to girl babies than to boy babies.

But as a first baby grows even older, and becomes less of a novelty, will attention begin to even out? Not by eight months, it doesn't. At that age, mothers do more to intellectually stimulate their firstborn babies. They more often praise them, instruct them, label and highlight objects for them, according to a University of California study. In fact, additional research indicates, such intellectual "acceleration" persists at least until the age of two, and recurs again at the five-year mark, when the first child is being prepared for school. Second children, generally, do not experience the same intense efforts to speed up development, especially during the first two years.

The parents I spoke with gave me no reason to doubt the research findings. Interview after interview, the same story: Parents talked to their second children less, read to them less, played with them less. Some parents who had never propped a bottle for their first child, and swore they would never prop a bottle for their second child, propped anyway. Those with a housekeeper often assigned their second child to her care.

Some parents made a special effort to plan activities for both children, to read books to them at the same time, to find a board game they could all play together. But in many cases, the parents admitted, the activities were more oriented to the needs of the older. A study done almost forty years ago clearly illustrates that point. Transcripts were made of conversations around the dinner table of thirty-five families, and the age level of the language was analyzed. "The family seems to adjust its age level to the older children, and to ignore the younger ones, especially if the age differential is not large," James Bossard of the University of Pennsylvania found. "Questions on word meanings raised by younger children are given less consideration, even in our most intelligent families."

Parents offer varying explanations for the fall-off in attention. Some purposely withhold attention from the second to prevent jealousy in the first (a ploy that doesn't work, as I point out in chapter six). Others explain that they just don't have the time anymore. They may have moved into bigger quarters, with more banisters to dust and more windows to wash. And, of course, all second-timers have one more child to care for than they did with their first. Many parents try to convert that "liability" into an "asset," encouraging their older child to entertain their younger, and to provide the attention that the parents don't.

Does the first child get too much parental attention? Does the second child get too little? There is no known "optimum" amount of attention. Certainly, neglect can damage a child, and bottle-propping is a bad idea. But overbearing, anxious attention can do its own brand of harm. (In the next chapter, the relation between attention and intellectual development will be discussed.)

WORKING LESS BUT ENJOYING IT MORE

Some second-time parents may be weak in the attention area, and flunk at photography, but most have a lot else going for them. They offer a confident, relaxed style of child care, secure in the knowledge they know what they are doing, finally comfortable in their role as parent. Parenthood is often easier, and more fun, the second time around.

For one thing, second-time parents can recognize when their baby is doing what babies usually do. "You don't even hear the hiccoughs, you don't even see the twitching," notes Dr. Pomeranz. "The first time, you're flapped about those things. The second time, they just don't register."

First-time parents can be just as flapped when they don't hear anything as when they do. Remember putting your first child in for a nap? Remember not hearing any sounds from the crib? Remember tip-toeing in, and looking for the rise and fall of her chest, or feeling for her heartbeat? Don't be embarrassed. We all did it. But we don't do it with our seconds. It's toss them in, shut the door, and pray for peace and quiet.

This relaxed attitude of second-timers may not be financially rewarding to pediatricians, but is a lot easier on the kids. They are not dragged to doctors as often for ailments that don't need doctoring. "If I saw a rash on Drew, I whisked him off to the doctor's office," Barbara recalls with some amusement. "But now I know what prickly heat looks like, so if I see it on Mitchell, I just say, 'Ah, that's nothing.' ''

"Ah, that's nothing" can be heard all across the country from second-time parents. In Milwaukee, Wisconsin, it's a common refrain, a recent study of 1,665 children from 587 families revealed. Second children were less likely than firsts to be taken to the doctor for a check-up or for a specific health problem. The researcher, Dr. Richard Tessler of the National Institute of Mental Health, summarized the study's results: "Parents appear especially quick to consult pediatricians about the health of their firstborns, even as these children mature and other children are born into the family." Why do doctor visits go down as birth order goes up? Dr. Tessler attributes the stay-at-home trend to the "parents' increasing knowledgeability in regard to child care as well as their growing understanding of the uses and limitations of physician visits."

Many first-timers feel totally dependent on their doctor's advice and follow it to the letter. Phyllis, the mother of ten-year-old Nicholas and seven-year-old Aimee, remembers how she was ten years ago. "My doctor told me I should feed Nicholas every three or four hours. I listened to him. Nicholas would sometimes start screaming after two and a half hours, but I wouldn't feed him. I was afraid something terrible would happen if I did. With Aimee, if she was hungry, I fed her. I realized that if the baby cried she needed something. I was more attuned to how I felt and how the baby felt. I was older and wiser."

Experienced parents are also more relaxed about physical safety. They are not as apt to trail their crawling baby around the house, horrified if she flops too hard on her fanny. In the playground, second-timers are easy to spot. They are the ones busy needlepointing, or leafing through a stack of magazines they hope is high enough to last the morning. The new mother is the one standing poised under the monkey bars, ready to catch the child she is sure will need catching, or sitting in the sandbox ready to protect her precious from the sandbox bully.

Some parents are sure their second children are easier and more relaxed because of their own relaxed attitude. Even the physical aspects of baby care seem easier the second time. If you had told me that before I had Michael, I wouldn't have believed it. During my second pregnancy my mind kept flashing back to the early days with Brian. As a new mother I had been in such a state I sometimes forgot to eat lunch until I realized it was dinnertime, and neglected to get dressed until I realized it was time to get undressed. I often collapsed in tears, looking around me at the mess I had neither time nor energy to clean up. Whenever I thought I had a free moment, my "master" would let out a wail. What would life be like with two "masters" and twice the mess?

Fortunately, I found the baby care part of it easier the second time, and so did the parents I interviewed. An obvious reason is that they knew how to do the things that had to be done—the diapering and the bathing and the baby-food grinding—and they could do them quickly and efficiently. More importantly, they knew how to get away with doing less. They didn't always have their hands down their baby's diapers, dashing off to the changing table at the first drop of moisture. This time, they went strictly by the nose. If the odor became too oppressive, off came the diaper. Some first-time parents check clothes and sheets if their baby wakes up crying. If they are wet, it means stripping the baby and the bed, putting on fresh nighty and clean linens, and waiting to see if it happens again. Second-time parents? Forget the middle-of-the-night maneuvers. Just move the baby over to a dry spot on the sheet. Second-time parents are also less likely to sterilize bottle and nipple if they land on the carpet. If the dog starts licking them, well, then, maybe. (And if their mother-in-law is visiting, well, then, of course.) Certainly, second-time children don't go unwashed, but their ears may not be cleaned as often, or their nails groomed as meticulously. And if a slight rip appears on the knee of their trousers, it doesn't mean a quick change to another perfectly pressed pair. Most second-time parents are less fussy about clothes, less fussy about everything, in fact, than are new parents. That leaves them with more time to appreciate the enjoyable aspects of child rearing.

The relaxed attitude of second-timers also extends to weaning and to toilet training. Some research indicates that experienced parents wean their children less severely than new parents, presenting less frustration to the child. I'm not a good example myself, since both my children weaned me. But some parents I spoke with did wean their two children differently. "I weaned

Tara too soon," Susan told me. "I didn't know what I was doing. I had nursed her eight and a half months. Somehow, everyone around me thought it was such a long time. I figured, 'Well, it's time to stop.' She was still enjoying her morning feeding, but I ended it. In retrospect, I feel bad about it." Susan nursed her second child for a longer time. "Kevin gave it up himself when he was thirteen months old. I was a little disappointed. I wanted him to continue more. But I liked the idea that he initiated giving up the nursing. It wasn't that I had enough. It was that *he* had enough. It's much more natural that way."

Second children are often given more of a role in toilet training as well. Many parents learn from unhappy experiences with their first child, and from friends and *their* first children, that toilet training cannot be forced. They may be more willing to wait for a child's signals of readiness, and more alert to those signals when they come. Also, they may have discarded the idea of an arbitrary age limit. "I felt that Bryan had to be trained by the age of three, or there was something wrong with him," Karen recalls. "It was like a magic number. But since then, I've learned from my friends that toilet training can be a long, ugly, upsetting experience if a child is not ready. I started my daughter later than I did Bryan. It just wasn't such a big thing. And if it didn't happen by age three, that was okay."

Some second-time parents are just as happy if their children are trained later. "It's easier on us if he's in diapers," one father confided. "We're not in a hurry. We know he'll be trained some day." That sounds pretty obvious—there aren't too many twenty-year-olds running around in diapers—but it can still be hard for new parents to really believe. It is hard for first-timers to believe their helpless little baby will ever learn to do much of anything. Sit up? Not likely. Walk? Impossible. Their doubting makes them perfect prey for the local playground predator. Remember her? "Can your child hold a bottle as well as mine can?" Or remember the proud-as-a-peacock papa? "My boy can say three consonants—how about yours?"

I was the perfect victim. When my friend mentioned, as casually as she could, that her baby flipped from stomach to back, I panicked—and spent the next month standing watch over Brian's crib until I saw him flip, too. When I heard a neighbor's baby say a sentence before mine could speak a syllable, I started imagining words of wisdom in Brian's every chortle and gurgle. Each month, I turned to the "Your baby should be doing this" chart in a child-development handbook. If my child lagged in any area of development, be it motor, language, mental, or social, I became despondent. I needed to *know* he would one day walk and talk and multiply fractions and conjugate verbs. But with a first child, you don't really *know* it until you see it for yourself.

Second-time parents have already seen it, and assume they will see it again. They have also seen that the timing of those early infant skills doesn't matter much. By age four or so, all the kids on the block are running and jumping and saying some very obnoxious things—no matter when they first started to walk and to talk. So with the pressure gone, experienced parents can enjoy each stage of their second child's development. Instead of waiting anxiously for each accomplishment, they can be taken by "surprise" by their child's progress. "Peter is constantly amazing me," Eileen said of her second child. "I don't get to spend that much time alone with him, but when I do, I'm surprised at how grown up he is, at how good he is at things." Second children seem to grow up almost behind their parents' backs.

Second-time parents are often more relaxed about behavior as well as accomplishments. If their child's latest hobby is stuffing all the toilet paper down the toilet, they realize that by next week he will move on to another creative pursuit—perhaps just as disgusting, but at least the plumber may get a breathing spell. Children change so quickly, these parents have learned, there is simply no point going crazy about today's antics. The terrible two's will eventually give way to the slightly less turbulent three's, and even twelve-year-old behavior, hopefully, will not last forever.

THE HANDS-OFF POLICY

Second-time parents feel differently and act differently, and those differences persist past infancy. Not only are parents more relaxed about their second children, they apparently interfere with them less and direct them less—in short, they're less bossy.

In a classic study, Irma Hilton of New York University observed the interactions of mothers and their four-year-olds as the children worked on puzzles. During the first part of the experiment, the mothers were told not to interfere with their child's performance. Yet, thirty-eight percent of the mothers of firstborns and only children disregarded those instructions and interfered anyway. They signaled the child to begin work on the puzzle, they made suggestions, and they gave direct help. Only 15 percent of the mothers of secondborn children provided that same type of "help."

The researchers then made things a bit more interesting. They took the mothers aside and told them how their children were "doing." In some cases, they reported the child was doing "extremely well," in others, the child "was much slower than the other children." (These reports had no real relationship to the child's performance.) When the mothers were placed back with their children, some more differences emerged. The mothers of firstborn and only children became more supportive of their children if they thought they were doing well, but more critical if they thought they were doing poorly. The mothers of secondborn children were more even-keeled. It didn't seem to matter as much to them how their children were performing. They didn't pour on the love when the child was "doing well," but they didn't withdraw it when their child was "failing." Their reactions were low-keyed, but consistent.

In a Stanford University study, mothers were watched as they supervised their five-year-old children on a variety of tasks, such as memorizing the names of twenty zoo animals from a picture, solving a difficult geometric puzzle, and learning the workings of a water tap. The mothers of the firstborn children gave more complex technical explanations, applied more pressure to achieve, and showed greater "anxious intrusiveness" than the mothers of the secondborn, according to researcher Mary Rothbart. The *most* pressure and "intrusiveness" were directed to firstborn girls. (As an aside, secondborn boys were the least likely children to help clean up after the experiment. So if your newest son is already gleefully scattering his toys and your clothes all over the house, you may be in for a rough time!)

Even with adolescents, parents seem to be more involved and

interfering with their firstborns. In a Swedish study, 820 children aged ten years, twelve years, and fourteen years were questioned about parental control. At each of those ages, firstborn children saw their parents as more controlling than did later-born children. The researcher, Joseph Schaller, speculated that new parents may use a higher degree of control to compensate for their inexperience. Another possible reason for the fall-off in control was suggested by one of the fathers I interviewed: Parents gradually learn from their firstborn that control doesn't work so well. "We really felt we could mold our first child," said Don, the father of four-year-old Andrea and two-year-old Michael. "But it hasn't worked out that way. She's developing quite independently of our efforts. It will be the same for Michael. We finally realize the limitations of our control."

Second-time parents are more likely to relinquish some of the control to other people. Dana didn't leave her older son with a babysitter until he was two and a half. With her second son, she didn't wait quite as long. He met his first sitter the day after he came home from the hospital. Many parents told me similar stories. Not only were they more willing to share control with other adults, they shared it with the child as well. They let their secondborn do more things alone and at a younger age than their first child, and allowed him more weight in deciding how he would be treated.

LOWER EXPECTATIONS

Apparently, there is a certain quality to the relationship between parent and first child that is not repeated with later children. Parents tend to keep the first child closer, more under their control. At the same time, they expect greater things from him. Studies show that parents expect him to act "adult-like" because they are accustomed to dealing with adults, not children. But by the time child number two is on the scene, they have been educated by their first child in how much—or how little—young children can do.

Marian, the mother of two, admits she expects more from her first child and is harder on her. "Naomi is only four, but when I look at her, I don't see a little child. Sometimes she seems so grown-up. When we're playing *Chutes and Ladders* and she counts wrong, I yell at her, 'Why can't you do it right?' I push her to read, too, because some of her friends can already sound out words. I don't think I'd be that way with Bobby. I'm not as pushy. I let nature take its course.''

Those differing expectations are not lost on the children, first, second, or otherwise. Charles, now in his thirties, is the younger brother of two. He recalls his parents' reactions at report card time. "I always got mediocre grades. When I'd bring home a 75, they'd simply say, 'You're not trying as hard as you could. We don't expect a 90, but we'd like you to do your best.' But even when my brother got marks in the 90s, they told him he'd have to do better. They were really unhappy if he didn't get excellent grades. They set higher standards for him, and were more intolerant of his failures.''

THE DISCIPLINE DIFFERENCE

Many parents seem to expect better behavior as well as better grades from their first child, and if they don't get it, watch out number one. Research indicates there is more likely to be "disciplinary friction" between parents and first children than between parents and their later-born, and that first children are more likely to be punished for transgressions. A study conducted about three decades ago, when spanking was more in vogue, found that first children were physically punished about 50 percent more frequently than second children. Also, thumb-sucking was permitted twice as frequently in the secondborn. Other research reveals that fathers often participate in the disciplining of their first child, but with later children, they spare the rod or hand it over to mother.

Second children would seem to have little to complain about. They are generally more indulged than their older sibling and are treated more warmly and with more consistency. But not all are happy about the dual standard. As adults, some of them remember with sadness how an older sister or brother was punished. "My parents sometimes would hold my sister up and hang her by her heels when she got on their nerves," Marsha, a thirty-three-year-old newspaper reporter, recalls. "She bore the brunt of a strict upbringing. But it wore off. They let down to some extent with me, and treated me more permissively."

Some second children remember, with embarrassment, their own contribution to their sibling's woes. "My sister got blamed for lots of my mischief," recalls Carol, a teacher and mother of three. "I was the cause of the argument, but she took the fall. I felt guilty and cried when she was punished—but I never told my parents that I was the culprit." Carol is determined to be fair and consistent with her own children, and to punish the guilty party. "One person is not the fall guy here. If I catch you, you get it, no matter who you are."

THE SCHEDULE'S THE THING

Childhood experience, or experience with a first child, molds the behavior and the expectations of a second-time parent. But there are also practical factors that make parents different the second time around. The main practical factor is their first child. With an older baby, or a toddler, or even a schoolchild around, a new baby can't be treated as the prince of the palace. "The family fits in with the first child, but the second child has to fit in with the family," points out Dr. Ruth Lesser, New York psychoanalyst and Clinical Professor of Psychology at New York University. The family's schedule has already been set, and it usually revolves around the older child's activities. The baby's mealtimes fit in with his sister's school times, the baby's nap times are determined by his brother's play times. Second children are dragged out on many a frigid day when a first child would have been kept inside, because it's mother's turn for car pool or brother's afternoon for midget football.

A second child's social life may also be limited by his sibling's schedule. If his older sister is home in the morning, he may miss out on the weekly toddler play group—the other parents may not feel that a fresh four-year-old is proper company for their winsome "ones." And if his mother has the choice between inviting over a preschool playmate for big sister or a pint-sized partner for him, big sister usually wins out because she complains louder if she doesn't.

Actually, this abbreviated social life may not be totally un-planned. Some parents have learned from their first experience that a six-month-old does not have to be in the company of other six-month-olds. During my first hospital stay, I made the rounds of the maternity ward, getting names and addresses of other new mothers living in my area. I wanted to assure my newborn son of a full social calendar. During those early visits my new-found friends and I would place our babies' carriages side by side, hoping our sleeping children would somehow sense the presence of a kindred spirit. By the time they were six or seven months old we placed them shoulder to shoulder, diaper to diaper in a playpen. We waited for some meaningful social interchange be-tween these identically aged infants; what we witnessed was a lot of yanked hair.

Second-timers usually realize that children don't play well to-gether until they are about two years old. And while it is impor-tant that they be around other children before that time (even babies may benefit from it), those other children don't have to be, within a month, the same age. Children gain special skills from older and younger playmates, too. Many second children actually prefer older friends to age mates because of the fun they have had with their sibling's friends.

DOING IT YOUR WAY

Don't get the idea, however, that everything you did last time you won't do again. That's not quite true. Scientists who have observed parental behavior have found certain consistencies from one child to the next. For example, the National Institute of Mental Health study discussed earlier uncovered a "style of mothering" that remained unchanged, regardless of the baby's birth order or sex. A mother who enjoyed kissing her first baby usually showered her second baby with kisses, too. A mother who used a pacifier with baby number one usually pacified baby number two the same way. And a mother who kept within close range of her first baby didn't stray too far from her second baby, either.

With older children, too, mothers tend to do certain things the same. Joan Lasko of Ohio State University compared mothers' behavior toward their first and second children up to the age of ten. She found that mothers had similar policies and techniques of managing their two children. If a mother was "democratic" with one child she was probably also "democratic" with the other; if she was "arbitrary" with one, she tended to be "arbitrary" with the other. Where mothers more often differed from child to child was in their emotional relationships. Some mothers who were quite affectionate and accepting of one child were much colder and less approving of the other. And some mothers who experienced "disciplinary friction" with one child got along quite smoothly with the other.

Parents who intend to do things differently the second time may find themselves falling into their old ways. Jay and Terry were unhappy about their older daughter's messiness. "She never put her toys away, and we never made an issue of it," Jay told me. "We decided we'd be more involved when it came to Tommy. We'd only let him have two toys out at a time. Terry and I talked about that—but we never did anything about it."

Even parents who follow through on their intentions may come up with the same results. "I've tried to do some things differently, but it hasn't helped," complained Estelle. "My older child is not a sleeper. Any little noise wakes her. So when I had my son, I let him sleep in the living room with the television on, and lots of noise. But by his fourth month, he developed the same idiosyncrasy. He hates sleeping. He hates naps. I haven't had a full night's sleep since my first child was born."

If you try to do things differently, your second child may resist. And if you try to do things the same, your second child may resist, too. Edie assumed Matthew would like the same kind of activities his older brother Adam did. She always enjoyed her reading sessions with Adam. But whenever she whipped out a book to read to Matthew, he'd turn tail and head straight for his Star Wars X-wing fighter plane. Edie had also loved taking long walks with Adam in his carriage. To her dismay, Matthew wouldn't even get into the carriage when he was old enough to refuse. He just liked to go outdoors and run, causing his exasperated mother to sit right down and cry. Parents do learn things from their old successes and failures—but they also learn things from their new child.

LIKE BROTHER, LIKE SON?

If you are still not sure how you will act toward your second child, it may be instructive to look even further back in time, to your own childhood. If you were a first child, do you remember wishing your twerp of a younger sister would simply disappear? If you were born second, did you hope your big-shot big brother would take a permanent vacation? Some psychologists stress the importance of the parents' birth order. "We replay with our children our own sibling relations," according to analyst Ruth Lesser. "If a parent is a first child, and had problems with his next younger sibling, he may identify with his own first child. He'll tend to treat his second child as he would have *liked* to treat his own sibling. As a result, the second child may suffer." Likewise, if a parent was a resentful second child, his first child may bear the resentment. But parents who can face their past, and figure out what their birth order meant to them, can free themselves to be better parents to both their children.

5. The Second-Child Syndrome: Slow but Steady?

BEFORE YOU EVEN MEET YOUR SECOND CHILD, you may try to imagine what she will be like when she is all grown up. You haven't got a lot to go on. If you consider heredity, you may picture her with your mate's good looks and your good mind, or if you are the one who has got it all, you may hope your genes are of the persuasive variety. If you consider astrology, you may think you know all about your second child's future vices and virtues, friends and lovers (though you'd better be sure your timing was perfect and delivery on schedule). If you consider birth order, you may be despondent or delighted, depending on what you have read, and what kind of grown-up you would like your secondborn to be.

For more than a century now, scientists have tried to figure out whether, why, and how a person's order of birth affects his development. Even Freud took a brief time out from his studies of sexuality and superego to ponder the point. He came to the conclusion that "a child's position in the sequence of brothers and sisters is of very great significance for the course of his later life." Alfred Adler, a psychiatrist generally credited as the father of birth-order theory, pointed out that a second child is born into a different psychological situation than a first. The main difference: "Throughout his childhood he has a pacemaker. There is always a child ahead of him in age and development and he is stimulated to exert himself and catch up." But his start-from-behind position may also make him feel slighted and neglected, according to Adler, and he may develop an attitude "similar to the envy of the poor classes."

But don't get Adler wrong. He never claimed that a child's fate is sealed, firmly and forever, by his position in the family. There are too many other important and influential aspects of family life—the personality of the parents, their marital relationship, child-rearing practices, the family's health and wealth, to name but a few. In every family, certain aspects change unpredictably from child to child, so every child faces a unique situation. The first child may experience the trauma of parental divorce at a vulnerable age—while the second child is too young to know what's going on. The first may have left home before a family windfall or financial wipe-out—and the second remains behind to learn to drive a Ferrari or to learn to use food stamps. But many psychiatrists and psychologists, including Adler's followers, believe that second children from all different kinds of families and circumstances experience common challenges, and so develop similar attitudes, needs, and ways of behaving.

Birth-order research began in 1874 when Sir Francis Galton found that a surprisingly large number of eminent English scientists were only sons and firstborn sons. Since then, birth order has been studied in relation to a multitude of characteristics, including intelligence, size, conformity, popularity, alcoholism, mental illness, even sexual orientation. Some of the studies contradict each other, and some of the earlier ones have been criticized as scientifically flawed. Also, the research has paid undue attention to child number one at the expense of those born after. Second children have rarely been singled out for study, but instead have been lumped with the "later-born," mixed with the "middles," or blended with the "babies." But in the past decade, birth-order research has taken new and exciting directions and a more scientifically sound approach. The findings, both new and old, provide interesting insights into the future of secondborn babies.

HORMONES IN HIDING

The easiest birth-order differences to measure have been the physical ones. Some of those differences are apparent right from the start. As I noted in chapter two, second babies are typically slightly larger than their older siblings. They also tend to breathe faster and be more active in the hospital nursery (perhaps because they have usually experienced a shorter labor). A few years ago, an interesting and unexpected difference was discovered by researchers at Stanford University and the Long Island Research Institute: Secondborn babies have different hormonal levels than firstborns. When the scientists collected samples of blood from the umbilical cords of 256 infants, they found that firstborn and only children have the highest levels of progesterone and estrogen. In addition, firstborn boys have higher levels of testosterone than do later-born boys. The hormonal differences are greatest if births are closely spaced.

Just what does that signify for your second child? Testosterone levels may be related to aggressive behavior, according to some research, and progesterone levels may be linked to social and intellectual development. But don't take your secondborn for hormone shots just yet. The Stanford team has been following up the babies for several years now, looking for a relationship between their early hormonal levels and their childhood behavior. So far, they have drawn a blank. But they may look again when the children are adolescents.

BIGGER, BROADER, BRAVER

Size differences do seem to last at least into adolescence. Research on children and teen-agers has found that secondborns are, on the average, taller than firstborns. Even within the same family, a child tends to be taller than siblings of the same sex born before (although this is, of course, not true in every family). One researcher speculates that the addition of each child to a family acts as a check on the growth of the older siblings. So even if your second child has to look up to your first child now, and endures the epithet of "pipsqueak," it may be your first child who resorts to elevator shoes later on—especially if he is dating a secondborn girl.

Your second child may be larger from side to side as well as from top to bottom. A recent study of almost 300,000 young men from the Netherlands found a slightly higher obesity rate among second children than first children in two-child families. But the men most likely, by far, to be obese were only children. (Some psychologists trace that tendency to "overprotective" parents, who seem to literally stuff their one and only with food. Others suggest that because only children bear the brunt of parental "hang-ups," they may seek solace in eating.)

If your second child is of different proportions than your first, you may be disappointed that all the clothes you had planned to hand her down won't fit her right, and you will have to hand them down to someone else. If you also hoped to hand down some sports equipment, such as your first child's baseball glove or beginner golf clubs, you may be equally disappointed. Some studies show that secondborn children are less likely than firstborns to be left-handed. (Some scientists attribute that alleged difference to a greater likelihood of complications during a first pregnancy and birth.) But you may find some advantages to the lefty-righty situation if it occurs in your family. You will find it easier to figure out who should sit where around the dinner table to minimize elbow jabbing and milk spilling. And if you find a chocolate-frosting handprint on the refrigerator door, you will know which of your kids just couldn't wait.

Another physical fact about second children is that they tend to get sick sooner. It's not that they have weaker constitutions; it's just that they have older siblings. The bacteria and viruses floating around the neighborhood nursery school or kindergarten often make their way, through big brother, into little brother's nursery. But those early bouts of illness may help build up his resistance so by the time he enters nursery school, his body can battle back some of the bacteria and viruses that laid him low as a baby.

Despite their more frequent early illness, second children rarely arouse the same parental anxieties as do first children. As I discussed earlier, experienced parents are more likely to recognize when a symptom will go away on its own, and how to treat it if it doesn't. That relaxed attitude directly affects the second child's future attitude toward illness. At Western Carolina University, 152 students answered a questionnaire to determine under what circumstances they would seek medical care. The firstborn students had a greater tendency than latter-born students, including secondborns, to turn to a doctor for treatment. So although second children may start out sickly, if you can take it in stride, you won't be receiving budget-breaking medical bills from their college infirmary.

Second children seem less fearful about safety as well as sickness. They participate more often than first children in dangerous sports, scientists report, and are less frightened by physical danger. As adults, later-borns make better aquanauts—undersea explorers—than do firstborns. One study looked at the effectiveness of fighter pilots, another occupation not for the faint-hearted or lily-livered. The "aces," those with more awards for destroying enemy planes, were more likely to be later-born than firstborn. So on land, sea, and air, your second child may one day take risks your first child wouldn't dare attempt—and you wouldn't dare watch.

In discussing disease and danger, and the fears they provoke, we are moving from the physical realm into that of the emotions. Emotional differences are harder to measure than variations in pounds, inches, and estrogen, but they are more revealing to parents and more intriguing to investigators. Some scientists have drawn up elaborate psychological portraits of "typical" firstborn and secondborn children. Firstborns are generally viewed as serious, shy, sensitive, conscientious, conservative, and dependent. In sharp contrast, secondborns are perceived as relaxed, cheerful, easy-going, diplomatic, friendly, and independent. Will your children be all those things—and none of the same things? It's hard to say from the studies. There is no "portrait" that paints a true picture of every secondborn child. Birthorder research is generally based on populations of children, not on children of the same family. Spacing also plays a role. If your children are more than five years apart, they are both likely to have certain firstborn characteristics. But if they are closer in age, their birth order may influence them in different and predictable ways.

PEOPLE WHO NEED PEOPLE

Do you remember how pitifully your first baby cried when you left the room even for a moment? His tears may have made you so miserable, you took him with you wherever you went. This time, your exits may not be greeted with such hysteria. Research on sixteen- to nineteen-month-old toddlers shows that firstborns are the most likely to cry, and to seek out their mother when she leaves the room. But don't be insulted at your second child's indifferent reaction. It's not that your secondborn loves you any less. It's just that your first child probably depends on you, emotionally, more.

Even as your children grow older, you may find that your firstborn remains more emotionally attached to you. Remember the study of puzzles mentioned in the last chapter, and the first-time mothers who were more interfering and inconsistent with their four-year-old children? Well, the mothers weren't the only ones who behaved differently. The children of the first-timers were rated as significantly more dependent than secondborn children. During intermission, all the children had been told to remain at their tables, away from their mothers. Yet many firstborn children ran to their mothers' sides; even when they were told to go back to their table, they kept returning to Mommy. Also, during work on the puzzle, the firstborn children more often asked their mothers for help and reassurance.

The investigator Irma Hilton noted a direct link between the parents' actions and the children's reactions. "Inconsistency and interference lead directly to dependency," she suggests, in the case of the firstborns. Those children learn to rely heavily on other people for support and guidance. In contrast, the moderate and consistent responses of experienced parents help to foster true independence in their secondborn children.

That seems to be the case in real life, too, not just in the laboratory. Heather, a secondborn daughter, thinks of herself as more independent-minded and strong-willed than her older sister, Elaine. She considers herself favored by her birth position. "My mother paid a lot of attention to Elaine—too much. She was always interfering with her, wanting to know where she was going and what she was doing. But she relaxed somewhat with me, and let me do things on my own. I didn't have to tell my mother where I was in the afternoon. That freedom was important to me, and helped me develop as an independent person."

Second children are relatively independent of their teachers as well as their parents. When teachers from the University of Iowa preschool were asked to "rate" their students on independence, the highest grades went to students born second and later.

In college, too, second children seem to show an independent streak. In a classic study conducted by Stanley Schachter of Columbia University, college women were put into a stressful situation; they were told they would be given a series of painful electrical shocks as part of a medical experiment. They were then asked whether they would like to spend the waiting time before the experiment alone or with others. The firstborn women showed a stronger desire to wait with others than did the later-born students. Professor Schachter termed this desire for company, when stressed, the need to "affiliate," and it became a popular concept in birth-order research.

Although Professor Schachter's findings seem to apply only to women, not to their male counterparts, his work has inspired other research, applicable to both sexes: Later-born children, males and females, have been found to be less susceptible than firstborns to social pressure, less easily influenced, and less conforming. But sex still plays a part. A study of high school students from one- and two-child families showed that firstborn males were by far the most conforming. The least conforming of all were secondborn males who had older sisters. Of the girls, the least conforming were the only children; then came secondborn girls with older brothers. That study also looked at the need to affiliate when feeling stressed. Again, sex of sibling was important. Second children with older brothers had a lower need to affiliate than did second children with older sisters.

MOST LIKELY TO BE LIKED

If you remember the hysterical wails of your first child when you left the room, you probably also remember his fearful sobs when your Uncle Alvin—or some other tall, forbidding stranger—walked in. You felt embarrassed for your uncle and bad for your child, and may have wished it was you, not your little one, hiding behind your skirt. But with your second child, you can comfortably wear the shorter fashions of the day. Your second child will probably leap, straightaway, into his uncle's arms, with his little hands readied for hair-pulling and nose-poking. Fearful of tall, forbidding strangers? Not him. If he has survived the murderous looks and well-placed jabs of his jealous big sister, what's to be afraid of?

The friendliness and playfulness of many second children is apparent even in infancy, and is documented by psychological research (though in this controversial field, not all research is in agreement). One study found that later-born children, thirty-eight to fifty-six weeks old, smiled more and cried less than firstborn children when a stranger was in the room. When that stranger presented them with a new toy, later-born children picked it up quicker and played with it more, mouthing it, banging it, and waving it in the air. The researcher Roberta Collard, of the University of California at Davis, attributes the friendliness and fearlessness of secondborns, and other later-borns, to their exposure to a variety of people.

Even in a roomful of strangers, secondborns often seem to be friendlier than firsts. Phyllis, the mother of Daniel, ten, and Melanie, seven, noticed that clearly with her own two children. "My daughter is much more outgoing. Put her in a crowded room and she lights up. She goes over to people she doesn't know and makes friends. But Daniel would never do that. If he finds one child he knows, he just stays with him."

Of course, every rule has its exceptions. My older sister and I proved that in our formative years. Put us in a room with relatives and other strangers, and my sister would waltz away with half a dozen. I, on the other hand, could always be found near the olive bowl, steadying my nerves by downing dozens of the green and black variety. Pitted or unpitted would do. If another olive-lover lurked nearby, we might strike up a friendship.

But most seconds do like being sociable. Not only do they like it, they're good at it, too. In a Riverside, California, grade school, teachers were asked to rate 1,750 students, from kindergarten to sixth grade, on social skills. Later-born children came out well ahead of their firstborn classmates. They were described as friendlier, more sociable, less demanding, and less jealous.

Those qualities weren't lost on the other children. As part of this same study, conducted by Norman Miller and Geoffrey Maruyama of the University of Southern California, the students were asked which classmates they would like to play ball with, sit next to, and work with. The last-born children were most popular as play choices and seating choices. Middle children were next in popularity, with firstborn and only children trailing behind. (Work choices were not related to birth order.)

In college, too, being second can be a social asset. In a number of studies, students born second and later have been rated as "better mixers," more sociable and well-liked, and more open in their relationships than their firstborn schoolmates. In another well-known study by Columbia University's Stanley Schachter, the members of fifteen fraternities and sororities at the University of Minnesota were asked to name the students they socialize with the most, and the ones they would most like to room with. The later-borns came out ahead in popularity on both those counts.

As you watch your second child in action, winning over the baker and the grocer and even dour Aunt Isabelle, you may wonder why second children are typically more socially skilled than firstborns. One possibility, put forth by Norman Miller and Geoffrey Maruyama, is that second children must learn those skills in order to deal successfully with their more powerful older sibling. They then use those skills with children their own age. Another explanation was offered by sibling researcher Brian Sutton-Smith. He points out that firstborn children have only parents as "models," but later-born children have more people, both parents and siblings, to observe and to please. By reacting to those people in different ways, they develop a versatile social style. On campus or at the country club, that flexibility will serve them well.

LIKE FATHER? LIKE FRIEND? LIKE FOE?

One Sunday, while your family is getting ready for its weekly outing, your youngest child may bolt off to his friend Bobby's instead. It may suddenly dawn on you that your secondborn is not all that fascinated with your company, and not especially eager to hear your explanations about the wanderings of the planets or the workings of a clock. Is it your imagination, or did you score more points with your first child? If your children are like the children some psychologists have studied, your first child may well appreciate you more. Firstborns have been found to be more adult-oriented, and actually to want to be like their parents. Exposed chiefly to adults in their earliest years, they often develop such adult-like attributes as a serious personality, a conservative philosophy, and a strong conscience. As one outcome, firstborn men tend to marry at an earlier age than do men born later. Second children, on the other hand, grow up in a more mixed environment, surrounded by children their own age and older, as well as by adults. They tend to identify more closely with their friends than with their parents, and to develop a more revolutionary outlook and gregarious manner.

The free-and-easy ways typical of second children were recently documented by research at the University of Tulsa in Oklahoma. Women students born second and later were found less likely than firstborns to take sensible contraceptive measures: They were less likely to have seen a gynecologist, to have received a pelvic examination, and to have used prescribed oral contraceptives. The reckless behavior of seconds extended from bedroom to highway. Of 138 male and female college students polled, only 25.4 percent of firsts and onlies had received a moving violation ticket during the past five years. That figure was 48.1 percent for seconds and later-borns.

If you are a second-time parent, it's not a bad idea sometimes to steer clear of your second child. Second children tend to be quicker on the attack than are first children. At least that's what mothers have reported when asked which of their two children is more physically aggressive. Second children, themselves, claim more often to be the "boss" when playing with their friends. Even before they hit school age, their aggressive tendencies are apparent. In a study of three- to five-year-olds, each child was left in a room with doll furniture and dolls and told, "You can make them do anything you want. You go ahead and play with them any way you like." The examiner watched for acts of aggression, such as scolding and fighting. The main finding was that later-born children of both sexes showed more aggression than did older siblings. As adults, that aggression may sometimes be channeled into dangerous sports activities or occupations. As noted earlier, later-borns are superior as fighter pilots and aquanauts, perhaps because of their physical daring.

To find the cause of their aggressiveness, researchers have again turned to the early home environment. As they grow up, second children are confronted with a child who is superior in size and in strength. Outstripped in ability as well, the second child may react by striking out physically, if not at his stronger sibling, then at dolls, or furniture, or friends. Also, if a second child has served as a punching bag for his brother or his brother's friends, he may be quick to find his own punching bag. Actually, Dr. Sutton-Smith points out, second children may not be any more hostile than first children. They may simply express themselves in a more primitive and spontaneous way.

FEELING GOOD ABOUT THEMSELVES

As the "inferior" member of a two-child family, often teased and taunted by his older sibling, it may seem that a second child would develop a lifelong inferiority complex. In cases of "sibling abuse," that may certainly be the outcome. Bruce, an attorney with two children of his own, recalls vividly and painfully how his older brother treated him during his childhood. "When he was in a good mood, he belittled me. When he was under pressure, he threw things at me. He was constantly picking on me. Once, while I was asleep, he put a mixture of horseradish, catsup, and eggs in my nose. I couldn't fight him because he was so much stronger, I could have been physically dead. It took me a long time—and some professional help—to overcome my inferiority feelings."

But second children who grow up with a less sadistic sibling tend to think rather well of themselves. Some research suggests that later-born children develop higher levels of self-esteem than do firstborns. One study looked at 165 firefighters from twenty Los Angeles firehouses. The later-born firefighters scored higher on a test of self-confidence than did their firstborn colleagues.

The popular impression is that second children are, in general, psychologically sounder than their older siblings. They are thought to be cooler, calmer, and more together. But that theory doesn't quite hold together on closer examination. Yes, some research shows that firstborns tend to be more anxious than later-borns. But a recent study of six- to eight-year-old children suggests that family size is an important variable. Firstborns tended to be more anxious in small families of two or three children, but the last-borns were the anxious ones in large families of four or five children.

The fear of failure does not seem to be a firstborn phenomenon, either. A study of high school students showed that secondborns exhibit more test anxiety than do firstborns. The most nervous of all about an impending exam was the younger sister in a two-girl family. I was not at all surprised at that finding. It brought back to me memories of sleepless nights before my seventh-grade mid-terms and feigned illness to avoid taking my ninth-grade science final. I made sure to drink hot cocoa before my mother took my temperature, and sucked a cherry lozenge before she probed my throat with a finger and a flashlight. For years I felt guilty about my deception. Little did I know that my birth order made me do it.

So where did firstborns develop their reputation for mental maladjustment? Some studies of elementary-school children indicate that firstborns display more nervous symptoms than do middle or youngest children. Also, first children show up in "disproportionately large numbers" as patients in child guidance clinics. But the fact that they are getting more help does not necessarily mean that they need more help. According to one theory, their inexperienced parents may simply mistake normal childhood mischief-making for problem behavior. They "learn" from their firstborn what to expect, and make more accurate appraisals of their later children. So what if your second child greets his friends with a right hook and a stream of obscenities? So what if he likes to test the law of gravity on your most fragile china, and hides the pieces in your Jell-O mold? You've probably seen it all before, and if you are brave enough to have another child anyway, you may well see it again.

As with other personality factors, it is not enough to relate emotional problems to birth order alone. Again, there is that small matter of sex to consider. When several hundred college students from the University of Maine were tested on a scale of "neuroticism," their sex did affect their scores. An abundance of firstborn women and only men appeared in the "high neurotic" group. But surprisingly few firstborn men or middle-born women scored high in neuroticism. The sexual make-up of an individual family may also help determine the emotional health of its members. If the make-up of the children is all male, there just may be some problems. One recent study found that a "significant excess" of psychiatric patients, both in and out of hospitals, were men who had only brothers. But another finding was that boys with brothers, but no sisters, make it to the White House in unexpectedly large numbers. Ford is the oldest of four sons; Nixon is the second of five sons; Eisenhower was the third of six sons.

Anything may seem preferable to having an alcoholic for a child. That is one mental health problem that second children, and other later-born children, have taken the rap for. Stanley Schachter of Columbia University views alcoholism as a withdrawal response to stress; he suggests that later-born children are more likely than firstborn children to react in that way. But recent research, conducted by James Conley of Wesleyan University, showed that only in large families (of seven or more children) is alcoholism more common in the last-born. Single children, also, were overrepresented in an alcoholic population. But in two-child families, neither first nor second child was especially apt to become a problem drinker.

MY SIBLING, MYSELF?

As you ponder the personality of your second child, you may wonder how it will be affected by the personality of your first. If your oldest is obedient and respectful, will your second also learn to mumble "please" and murmur "thank you"? If your first loves to pull cats' tails, will your second also be decorated with feline scratches? It has generally been thought that siblings do "model" one another's behavior and characteristics: They want to be like one another, and they become more and more alike. The younger is especially influenced by the older, according to this theory, imitating him and idolizing him.

A Barnard College professor has recently challenged that point of view. Professor Frances Fuchs Schachter and her associates noticed how frequently parents would say, "My two children are as different as night and day," or students would comment, "My sister is entirely different from me." That didn't sound like modeling to them. They termed it "sibling deidentification"—the attempt to be *unlike* one's siblings—and they conducted several studies of it. In the first one, the investigators asked college students from two- and three-child families the following question: "Are you alike or different from your sibling?" In the two-child families, almost two-thirds of the students considered themselves different. (In the three-child families, judgments of being different were most common between the first two children.) In a later study, the Barnard College researchers asked mothers whether their children were alike or different. In two-child families, four out of five mothers chose the term "different" to describe their children. To make things tougher, the researchers also asked whether their children were the "same" or "opposite," Given that choice, seven of ten mothers termed their two children opposite.

Professor Schachter was struck by some other comments in everyday conversation, such as "My sister takes after my father and I take after my mother." Or parents would say, "This child is just like my side of the family, the other one is just like my husband's folks." Do children really tend to identify with opposite parents? To find out, Professor Schachter asked college students these two questions: "In general, are you more like your mother or your father?" and "In general, is your sibling more like your mother or your father?" Her suspicion was confirmed. In two-child families, about two-thirds of the students reported that they identified with the opposite parent.

What does all this mean? Why do children apparently want to be different from each other, and ally with different parents? Professor Schachter explains it as a defense against sibling rivalry. By taking on different interests and personality traits, she theorizes, siblings avoid clashing with each other. And by attaching themselves to different parents, they avoid competing for parental love.

"Deidentification keeps peace in the family," says Professor Schachter. "It keeps siblings loving each other. They're out of each other's way, so they're not constantly competing with each other. Parents don't have to compete for the kids, and the kids don't have to compete for the parents." The one possible drawback, she says, is that the children may feel restricted in their choices. "If one child is athletic, the other child may intentionally avoid sports and concentrate on academic work. That can narrow the child's possibilities."

GUNS OR DOLLS

If our children are influenced—for better or for worse—by each other's personality, how are they influenced by each other's sex? It had been thought that boys with an older sister were more "sissified" than boys with older brothers. Likewise, girls with older brothers were considered more "tomboyish" than girls with sisters. It was as if the sexual identity of one sibling rubbed off a bit on the other. But a recent study found the opposite to be true. Adolescent girls with sisters tended to develop less "feminine" interests than girls with brothers, according to Harold D. Grotevant of the University of Texas at Austin. (The boy's interests were unrelated to the sex of their siblings.) The author suggests, as does Professor Schachter, that children try to differentiate themselves from their siblings. "These girls may be carving out a niche in the family by trying to become different from their sisters in the same way that identical twins who look and dress alike may develop contrasting personality characteristics."

Dee, the younger sister of a sister, provides another explanation. "Because we were both girls, there wasn't much male-female role assignment in my family. I played softball with my father. If I had had a brother, my father would have played with him, not me. So I found it helpful not to have a brother. There were more avenues open to me. I was allowed to be strong."

The sexual make-up of a family has still other implications.

Siblings of different sexes are both more stimulating and more stressful to each other than same-sex siblings, according to psychological studies. They also show more interest in creative occupations, such as artist, author, and musician. The second child with an opposite-sex older sibling has been found to be more quarrelsome and competitive than one with a same-sex sibling.

"MONKEY" IN THE MIDDLE?

What if your second child won't be your last child? Will he be demanding, and excitable, and overly aggressive, and all those other awful things you have heard about middle children? Are you condemning your secondborn to a childhood of neglect and a lifetime of trying to get over it?

The middle child seems to be in a pretty precarious position. There is a first child in front of him, getting all that anxious attention that first children get. And there is a younger child behind him, getting all that doting attention that the "baby" of the family gets. And there he is, floating in between, trying to figure out just how he fits into this pretty family picture. How can he get the spotlight on *him?* Some middle children respond to that challenge, research shows, by becoming verbally aggressive and developing an "attention-getting" personality. One study shows they are the most "changeable" of children, another that they are the least popular.

But before you shelve your plans to have a third, read on. Being middle isn't all bad. "The middle child has to learn to relate to the top and the bottom, and so he tends to become extremely sensitive and adept in human relations," notes Dr. Robert Sherman, family counselor and associate professor at Queens College in New York City. Parents are generally less anxious about the development of their middle child, some psychologists speculate; instead of prodding him on to high levels of mastery, they emphasize the virtues of cooperation.

Alfred Adler has noted that the oldest and youngest members of a family develop the largest number of problems in personal adjustment. A recent study of college students bears him out. At

Florida State University and the University of New Mexico, 261 undergraduate and graduate students completed the MMPI, a popular psychological test. The firstborns and last-borns "were more likely to have scored in the direction of maladjustment" than the middle-borns, according to the researchers, James W. Croake and Terrance D. Olson. In another study done on fifty inner-city Hispanic boys, the middle-born children displayed less aggression than either firstborns or last-borns. So making your second child a middle child is nothing to be afraid of. He will probably turn out just fine, maybe even best of all, as long as you are willing to acknowledge his rightful place in the family.

PROFESSORS, PRESIDENTS, AND OTHER VIPS

Studies on personality and birth order make interesting reading. It's fun to see how well your children fit the profiles of their particular birth position. They will probably be a perfect fit in some ways, but off a bit in others. Birth-order research is not an exact science, especially when dealing with the mystery of personality. But it's more sophisticated in its other major area of study—achievement and intelligence. "We're on firmer ground because the studies of intelligence involve larger numbers," points out Dr. R. Zajonc, psychology professor at the University of Michigan. "Sometimes hundreds of thousands of subjects are tested, so it's easier to come to reliable conclusions." If you are as interested in your second child's mind as you are in his emotions, you may wonder how bright he will be, how good his grades will be, how far he will go in his professional life. Just because he is secondborn, will his intellect and accomplishments be second-rate?

The first wave of birth-order studies was in the area of "eminence," and firstborn children came out best. They are more likely than later-born siblings to become scientists, professors, physicians, composers, and Rhodes Scholars, and to appear in *Who's Who,* according to various reports. Almost 40 percent of the thirty-nine U.S. Presidents have been first borns (a considerably higher proportion than would be expected from population data). Most dramatically, twenty-one of the first twenty-three astronauts were only children or the oldest in their families.

The early studies of eminence have been termed "head counts," and some have been discounted as scientifically unsound. One major problem, according to critics, is that they have not taken into account fertility trends: When the birth rate is high, a large proportion of babies are firstborns. So it wouldn't be surprising, twenty-five or thirty years after a baby boom, to find a lot of firstborn scientists, or scholars, or anything else. In fact, a 1970 study found a strikingly high proportion of firstborn strippers. But despite the scientific flaws, the general findings of this research have rarely been questioned: Firstborns tend to be higher achievers than later-borns. What has been questioned is, "Why?"

Is it because they have greater educational opportunities? Firstborns do attend college in greater proportions than children born second or later. That is the most consistent finding in birth-order research. Studies have shown that from one-half to two-thirds of all college students are firstborns. In graduate and professional schools, the proportion of firstborns tends to be even greater. Interestingly enough, the rate of college attendance decreases regularly as birth order increases.

This phenomenon has been termed "academic primogeniture." Firstborns may no longer get a bigger piece of the estate, but they do tend to get more reading, 'riting, and 'rithmetic, not to mention theoretical physics and advanced anatomy. But is that the whole reason they make *Who's Who* and the White House? College attendance has not always been a prerequisite to professional advancement, yet firstborns have been shown to be more eminent in different cultures and at different times. Maybe there is "something else" at work. Maybe that "something else" helps firstborns both get into college and do well later on.

Some psychologists believe that the firstborn personality is the key to firstborn success. They point to some "typical" firstborn features discussed earlier: adult orientation, seriousness, a strong conscience, conformity, nonaggressiveness. If you think back to your school days, can you remember who had those exact qualities? Wasn't it the "teacher's pet," that sugary little girl or obedient little boy who brought the apples and got the As? Those are the qualities that help win teacher's approval, and turn an average student into an excellent student.

There is another personality trait even more directly related to achievement: that is the *motivation* to achieve, the burning desire to do well. "The major difference between first children and other children is motivation," says University of Pennsylvania's Brian Sutton-Smith. "Firstborns are more motivated to put out." The evidence supports his statement. When more than 3,000 adolescents were interviewed, the firstborns of both sexes exhibited strong drive and ambition. In short, they were achievement-oriented. In another interview study, this one of eleven- to fourteen-year-old boys and their mothers, oldest children and only children had achievement values most like those of the mother (though the birth-order difference was found only at the higher socio-economic levels). When 251 high school students were given a psychological test of achievement motivation, the results were the same: Firstborns scored higher than secondborns. The firstborns who scored the highest were those with a younger sister. The secondborns who scored the highest in their position were those with an older brother. Again, the booby prize went to younger sisters of older sisters.

What makes firstborns try harder? (Isn't that the job of number two?) Again, it's back to their beginnings to find out. Several studies indicate that firstborns generally get more "achievement training" than children born later. Their interaction with their parents is more frequent and more intense. Their parents expect more of them and tend to overestimate their abilities. With the birth of a younger sibling, they may try to push their oldest ahead even more.

THE INTELLIGENCE GAP

But maybe those pushy parents have a point. Maybe their first child is especially bright and capable, and destined for greatness. Could the reason for their eminence be as obvious as all that?

Are first children simply smarter and more able than second children?

We can start looking for some answers at the nursery level. A test of mental and motor ability was given to 1,409 babies, ranging in age from one to fifteen months. The results were not dramatic, but they were consistent. Firstborn babies scored significantly higher on the "mental" scale in four of the fifteen months, and on the "motor" scale in five of the fifteen months. Later-born babies didn't score significantly higher in any of the months. In a test of older babies, aged sixteen to nineteen months, the firstborns again showed superior motor ability. They were better than later-borns at such tasks as throwing a ball and climbing on a chair.

Another finding has gotten a lot more publicity. That involves language development. If your first child talked at a relatively early age, you probably expected it, because you had been told that first children do that. If your second child is slower to utter "mama" and "all gone," you are probably prepared for that, too, and won't rush to enroll her in a class for slow learners or to cancel her college fund. Secondborns do tend to talk later than firstborns. As young children, their vocalization patterns are generally not as complex nor their speech as articulate as the speech of firstborns, several studies indicate.

If your children follow the expected pattern, you may have something to be grateful for. Our younger child, Michael, surprised us all by speaking early and clearly—too clearly, in fact. Before he was two, he was enunciating perfectly and frequently the obscenities his brother brought home from the kindergarten children on his school bus. Michael never missed an opportunity to greet a stranger or his grandparents with his favorite foul words of the day.

The research findings on infant development and birth order are fairly consistent—first children come out first—but many more studies have been done on school-age children. Little wonder—experimenters don't have to barge into homes, asking nosy questions, scaring their tiny subjects half to death; they can just get hold of some test results. If you remember back to your own school days, you know they have plenty to choose from—schoolchildren are forever taking tests. It would be nice to tell you that all the results show the same thing. But they don't. Since the 1920s, when this kind of research started in earnest, some studies showed firstborn superiority, some showed that seconds are smarter, and still others indicated the utter irrelevance of birth order to intelligence. But recent research suggests that earlier-born children do have a slight intellectual edge.

Especially interesting is a Massachusetts study which compared first and second children from the same families. The 258 children, from grades four, five, seven, and eight, were given an Iowa Basic Skills test. That test rates vocabulary, reading comprehension, language skills, work-study skills, and arithmetic skills. In general, the firstborns got higher scores. Within the same family, the firstborn child did better than the younger sibling in about 60 percent of the cases. (They were tested at about the same point in their school careers.) In only about one-third of the sibling pairs did the secondborn child score higher.

Three larger-scale studies show that the birth-order difference does not disappear in the teen-age years. One study was based on the Project Talent intelligence test, a measure of reading comprehension, abstract reasoning, and mathematical aptitude. The scores of more than 43,000 high school seniors were calculated. The findings: Firstborns tended to score higher than secondborns, who scored higher than thirdborns, and so on. The average difference between firstborn and last-born was 3.28 IQ points. If 43,000 students aren't convincing enough, how about 794,000? Those are the number of high school students who took the National Merit Scholarship Qualification Test in 1965. When Hunter Breland of the Educational Testing Service looked at their scores, he found the same pattern: the higher the birth order, the lower the score. The main differences were in the verbal part of the test. Firstborns were generally better with words, but not with numbers, than secondborn students. To complete the picture, a study of almost 400,000 Dutch males, nineteen years old, found the same relationship between birth order and intelligence. But this time, firstborns excelled in every area tested: language, mathematics, mechanical understanding, even clerical aptitude. When the chief investigator of that study, Lillian Belmont of Columbia University's School of Public Health, looked at 535 pairs of brothers, she found that the older brother tended to do better than the younger. So even within families, she wrote, "the birth-order effect, though small, persisted."

But don't get discouraged now, you second-time parents who didn't get an Einstein the first time and hope to have another shot at it. The differences we are talking about are small differences, and they don't happen in every family. Your second child may have a better chance of being brighter if your first child is a boy. Some research shows that second children with an older brother receive higher grades than do second children with an older sister. If you can figure out why, you are one step ahead of the scientists who are making all those fascinating findings.

Even if your second child isn't a shoe-in for Mensa (the high-IQ society), there is a chance he will be too busy painting pictures or playing the piano to notice his exclusion. Your second child just may be the creative one in the family. You may notice that even his first scribbles show a certain flair. When the drawings of three-year-old Japanese children were judged for creativity, later-born children scored higher than firstborn children. Even in large families, there seems to be something special about the second child. In one U.S. study, nine sets of four brothers each were given a special creativity test. They were mostly middle-class children in the middle grades of school. On every single measure, the secondborns did better than brother number one, and better than brothers three and four, too. In college, also, secondborn (and other later-born) art students have been judged more original and artistically creative than firstborn art students. In a recent study of college women at the University of Wisconsin, secondborns were found to be far more creative than firstborns (from two-child families), scoring, on average, 2.5 times higher on a creativity test. In three-child families, also, the secondborns showed the highest creativity, surpassing both the oldest and the youngest. So if your second child is not another Einstein, will Rembrandt or Rubinstein do?

BEHIND THE GAP

In the discussion of intelligence, I have spoken more about results than about reasons. The reason for that is simple: Scientists have not found an easy explanation for the slight firstborn superiority. But that's not for lack of looking. One of the first places they have looked is in the genes. Are firstborns genetically programmed to be brighter? Do their genes have more of the stuff of which geniuses are made? Almost as soon as researchers considered that notion, they rejected it. "Within families, genetic differences are randomly distributed with respect to birth order," writes University of Minnesota's Harold Grotevant. A first child is no more likely than a second to inherit genes for blue eyes, or baldness, or brightness.

Another theory is that of the "tired uterus." If you are familiar with "tired blood," you may have some idea of what a tired uterus is. In scientific jargon, it is "uterine fatigue." Perhaps later-born children are not as bright as first children, this theory goes, because the uterus is worn out and can no longer supply proper nutrition to the fetus. Without that nourishment, "mental and other development is slightly stunted," speculates Dr. Breland of the Educational Testing Service. But as soon as Dr. Breland spells out that theory, he dismisses it, because it does not explain a lot of the findings. For example, the uterus carrying an only child can't be any more pooped than a uterus carrying a first child—but first children (with a younger sibling) generally score higher on intelligence tests than do only children. And it can't explain why first children from small families generally score higher than first children from large families (unless the uterus gets tired just thinking about what's in store for it). So intelligence and the "tired uterus" have gone the way of iron and "tired blood."

Scientists have also looked at the birth process itself for an answer to the intelligence gap. They learned that labor is longer and forceps are more often used in first pregnancies. That was not the answer they were looking for! They also learned that nerve damage—resulting from lack of oxygen during delivery or the use of forceps—is more prevalent among firstborns. If anything, these birth experiences would suggest that first children grow up dull of mind, dim of wit. In most cases, that's definitely not true. Why?

The most likely explanation is that the social and psychological worlds of first and second chldren are worlds apart. In his earliest years, the first child is generally alone with his parents; they serve as his sole teachers and models. He may have playmates of his own age, but at home, he is the only child. Research has shown that language development is most advanced in children who associate mostly with adults. Young children use longer sentences, and ask more questions, when alone with an adult than when in a group of children. So the relative "isolation" of firstborns from other children may work in their favor. According to a theory put forth about forty years ago, children isolated from other children during early development may have an advantage in later achievement.

Second children are far from isolated. There is usually at least one other child around, and if that child is a popular one, there may be lots of little visitors coming and going. The parents' attention must be shared, and some of the "teaching" duties go, by default, to the older sibling.

Learning from a sibling is quite different than learning from an adult. Adults present an orderly world to the child. They answer his questions consistently and coherently. In contrast, an older child, being a child, may act impulsively and seem irrational at times. She answers questions as the mood strikes her. She may have three different responses for "How does grass grow?" and an astonishing variety for "Where do babies come from?" If my younger son had depended entirely on my older son for worldly wisdom, he still wouldn't know where his nose his. Brian took great delight in pointing out Michael's ear and labeling it "nose," touching his chin and calling it "foot," pulling on his nose and shouting out "belly button."

The child who may be benefiting the most from these sibling seminars is the tender-aged teacher. The older child learns to express himself, sharpens his language skills, practices breaking down complicated ideas and tasks into simpler components. The older child acts not only as teacher, but as the translator of messages between parents and younger child—a sort of go-between. According to Dr. Breland, this helps him develop his verbal abilities. "It's a great social mechanism for learning," he told me. "The others don't have that chance. If you're the youngest child, you just *receive* messages and instructions, you don't give them.

The verbal skills that the oldest child is developing can, in turn, lead to other knowledge."

If the oldest child does become interested in learning, and sends away for chemistry sets, miniature microscopes, and mountainous encyclopedias, the second child may be squeezed out of scholastics. The role of the family intellectual has already been taken, thank you; the second child may be encouraged to keep out of it and find something else to be good at. Of course, that is not said in so many words, but the message is clear, nonetheless. The second child may be more than happy to "find his own thing," and to carve out his own niche that everyone else better stay out of.

Another thing about being a second child, and youngest child, is never knowing the feeling of superiority in the family. You are not bigger than anyone, you are not a better Lego builder, you can't do more things, and you don't know more things. Sure, things may even out later on, but it can be pretty disheartening the first few years. As one grown-up secondborn brother put it, "There's always someone half a lap ahead of you." Some second children may be motivated to try to make up the distance. Others, tired of trying and failing, may simply drop out of the race.

THE FAMILY FORMULA

A recent theory has attempted to tie it all together—to explain why intelligence tends to decline with birth order, large family size, and small spacing between children. The theory is called the "confluence model" because it compares family life to the flow of a river with many different currents. It was proposed by Professors R. B. Zajonc and Gregory B. Markus of the University of Michigan. It goes like this:

Each family member contributes something to the "intellectual environment" of the home. The parents generally have the highest absolute intelligence (not to be confused with IQ). For this example, we will consider them each to be a 30. A newborn's absolute intelligence is 0, and increases with age. So when a first child is born, the family's intellectual environment is 30 + 30 + 0/ 3, or 20.

What happens when a second child is born? Let's assume the first child's absolute intelligence has increaed to 4. The intellectual environment is then the average of 30, 30, 4, and 0—which is 16. So, according to this model, the second child is born into a less rich intellectual atmosphere than the first child. And with each additional child the family's intellectual environment becomes more impoverished, affecting each family member for the worse. What happens, essentially, is that the intellectual capacity of the parents gets spread around too thin.

The confluence model has another prediction to make: Wider spacing improves the family's intellect. What if the second child is born when the first child is older, and developed an intellect of 12, not 4? That brings the family's intellectual environment up to 18—all the better for newborn number two. There even comes a point, if spacing is wide enough, that the second child is born into a richer environment than the first. According to Dr. Zajonc, "At a certain age spacing, the birth-order effect reverses itself and the second child has the intellectual advantage. In a two-child family, we've calculated, that happens when the gap is five or six years."

A wide spacing is a definite plus for a second child, according to this model, but a mixed blessing for a first. On one hand, he is around a long time before the family's intellect is "pulled down" by his sibling's birth. On the other, he has a long wait to become a tutor to his sibling and benefit from that activity.

The confluence model has gained great prominence in some scientific circles and considerable notoriety in others. Some investigators feel that it explains the research data well, and makes useful predictions; others believe it explains only a small part of the story. For parents, it is an interesting way of looking at things —but don't rush right out to buy a calculator to figure out how to time your children's births. Even Dr. Zajonc doesn't advise basing family planning decisions—including the spacing of children —on this model. "We don't know what the optimum gap between children is. This is theoretical work, not practical. I wouldn't use my theoretical information on my own children."

THE PARENTS' PART

If you are beginning to wonder how you fit into all of this—how you can help or hinder your second child's development—don't stop reading now. This section is all about you. Yes, you do have a role. How you interact with your second child, even when she is still an infant, will help determine how competent she will be as an adult.

Remember some of the studies we discussed in the last chapter —the ones that showed parents not talking to or stimulating their second children as much as their first? Such behavior, or lack of behavior, can affect the development of those second children. According to psychologists and educators, parents who play with, talk to, and smile at their babies, and who provide things for their infants to look at and explore, have babies who become advanced in attentiveness, visual pursuit, and coordination. And those advantages last into later life. Dr. Leon Yarrow, of the National Institute of Child Health and Human Development, has written, "Perhaps the most striking finding is the extent to which mother's stimulation influences developmental progress during the first six months. Its amount and quality are highly related to her baby's IQ."

One study looked at the attentiveness of forty-four mothers to their five-month-old infants, and at the exploratory behavior of those infants a month later. Not surprisingly, the most attentive mothers had the most explorative infants—those babies most likely to play with a new toy (a bell), and most likely to prefer handling a novel object to a familiar object. Also, the babies who had received the most attention vocalized nearly three times as much as did the babies who received the least attention. This study was not, primarily, a birth-order study, but it did sneak a peak anyway. Again, no surprises. Later-born babies received significantly less attention than did the firstborns.

In a longer-term study, researchers made home observations of thirty-six mothers and their infants from nine months of age up to eighteen months of age. They tried to identify what types of maternal behaviors fostered competency. The major finding: "The total amount of maternal stimulation was found to be highly related to infants' overall development," according to Alison Clarke-Stewart of the University of Chicago. The single behavior most highly related to children's competency was verbal stimulation. It was especially important in helping the child to understand and to express language.

Clearly, it is not just a coincidence that secondborns generally get less attention and verbal stimulation than do firstborns, and tend to be less academically successful. "Seconds just don't get as much put into them," says Dr. Virginia Pomeranz. Dr. Pomeranz is herself the older of two girls. "My family is a classic example. Before I was two, I was bilingual. I knew every nursery rhyme that Mother Goose ever wrote. I could count to a hundred in English, German, and Russian. But my sister didn't learn the nursery rhymes until she read them to her children. She didn't learn the alphabet until I taught it to her. When she was eighteen months, she only had one word, 'ga-ga.' Nobody put all that stuff into her. Nobody had the time."

Just what should you be putting into your second child? Should you be sitting her down for a lesson in square roots and Spanish? Should you buy those kits for teaching reading to babies who are still crawling? Should you try to treat your second child just the way you treated your first child? Before you do anything, you should do some thinking about your second child's future. Is it really important to you that she make her mark in the world, that her name go down in history or up in lights? "The world needs achievers, but it needs enjoyers, too," points out Dr. Dorothy Gross, director of the Program in Infant and Parent Development at the Bank Street College of Education in New York City. "Competency doesn't just mean attending Harvard, and then going on to have ulcerative colitis or a heart attack. It also means relating well to other people, going to a job and not being consumed by it, truly enjoying yourself and your family. It means taking pleasure in the world, not just in how much money you can make. In this broader sense, second children show a lot of competence."

So while second-time parents tend to fall short in some areas, they seem to do all right in others. As we discussed earlier in the chapter, second children tend to be socially skilled and confident and courageous and creative. But is there any way to help your second child have it all—social, emotional, and intellectual competency? Here's a summary of present thinking on early learning.*

Getting to Know You

Some second-time parents have established certain parenting patterns with their first child, and assume they will work well with their second child, too. But there certainly should be some changes made. Your second child will be different, and your job will be to find out how. Study your baby. Listen to what your baby has to tell you. Follow his cues, and relax. "It's like learning about a dinner guest," Dr. Gross says. "What kind of conversation does your guest like? What kind of dessert does he prefer? With your baby, you should try to find out what makes him cry, what makes him smile, whether he likes to be held close, or not close, whether he likes roughhouse play, what he likes to eat. It's not enough to go by your heart. You need your mind to study his cues, and then shape your behavior accordingly." It is also helpful to find out what kind of learner your second child is. How does he adapt to new things? How long is his attention span? How high is his activity level? Once you know his style of learning, you can help him build on his strengths and overcome his limitations. You can be most helpful if you are also attuned to your child's developmental level. There is no use in trying to teach him concepts and tasks far ahead of his ability to learn them. Nor is it wise to make things too easy for him because you don't want him to ever fail. A little challenge goes a long way.

The Cry of the Child

Some second-time parents pride themselves on their ability to hear their second baby cry hysterically—and to keep right on

*I am especially grateful to Dr. Dorothy Gross of the Bank Street College of Education, Dr. Irene Shigaki of New York University, and Carol Schapiro Kekst, a New York City educator in infant development, for their contributions in this area.

doing whatever they were doing. They say their "ears have grown deaf" to the crying, and their time too short to do anything about it. But if they knew how their hardened hearts and deafened ears were affecting their second child, perhaps they would manage to find the time. Psychologists and educators strongly suggest that parents pick up a crying child, and do it as quickly as possible. A prompt response helps a child to develop basic trust and a strong sense of self. "When a crying baby is picked up, he feels that he matters in the world, that he affects the world," says Carol Schapiro Kekst, an educator in infant development. "But if there's no response, he feels that what he does doesn't matter. He incorporates that feeling into his self-image. Later in life, it can show up in the attitude, 'Why try?' So even though it's fine for parents to be relaxed, they should know what's important and what's not. Crying *does* matter in the end. Picking up a crying baby is a very important principle." With a second child, a parent's response can't always be immediate. He may be rushing to send his older child off to school, or tending to a bruised knee after a playground fall. But a slightly delayed response is still better than no response at all.

Loving and Touching

An affectionate parent not only makes a baby feel good, but also helps him develop capabilities in many areas. Your kisses and hugs and loving words will help him develop social skills, play skills, and even help him cope with stress, research indicates. If you physically handle your child gently, firmly and frequently, he will have a head start in cognitive and motor development. As an extra bonus, he will be more attached and responsive to you. So you will get a little hugging, too.

Talk, Talk, but Take a Breath

Children need to hear language to learn language. Keeping the radio or television on all day is not sufficient (or wise), even if you can find something other than rock music or cartoons to tune to. Children with normal hearing, who have deaf parents, don't learn to speak by listening to radio or watching television.

If you think it's no use talking until your baby is old enough to laugh at your jokes, you are waiting too long. Infants respond to the human voice—and should begin to hear it—as early as the first day of life. But what do you say to a kid who would never even read a newspaper, who doesn't care much whether it's sunny or snowing, who doesn't realize what inflation is doing to the price of formula? Just try talking easily about what's going on. "Oh, did you have a burp?" "Now I'm washing your face, now I'm washing your belly button, now I'm washing your . . . Hey, couldn't you wait until I put your diaper back on?" Generally, a normal conversational tone is best, but a little baby talk is okay, too, when you are talking to a baby. That's their stage, and it helps the two of you establish emotional rapport.

If you sometimes get tired of all the talking, you can figure your baby's probably getting tired of hearing it. Nonstop talking can be deadening for all concerned. Your child will begin to tune you out. So if he is engrossed in something else, cut the chatter for a while. The sounds of silence are sometimes just the thing.

The Playpen Prison

Playpens can come in quite handy for a first child. They allow parents to relax their vigilance temporarily, to clean the house without someone dirtying it just as quickly, to cook a meal without having to scream "Keep your hands off the oven door!" and "Don't pour the pepper into the cake batter!" From what second-time parents tell me, they are even more useful for second children. They keep the baby away from big sister's block building, and at least one child out of mother's way. But that convenience comes at a high price for your second child. A playpen is generally used most when a baby begins to move around and get into things, to explore her surroundings with her body and her hands. But that is the worst time for restrictiveness, says Dr. Gross. "To prevent a crawling baby from getting into things is to prevent that child from thinking." Dr. Irene Shigaki, head of the Program in Infant and Toddler Development at New York University, agrees that playpens are overused. "The more environment a child can explore, the more potential there is for growth. Playpens restrict the environment that can be explored. If the parent puts two or three toys into the playpen and then walks away, and the child tosses them out, that's it!'' Research has shown that restrictive devices such as playpens and jump seats play a relatively prominent role in families where children are developing rather poorly.

But some parents point out how content their baby is in a playpen—the child never gives any indication he wants out, so it is easy and convenient to leave him in. But these "content" children are especially in need of the stimulation of a free environment. "The parents should offer that kind of child the opportunity for expansion," says Dr. Gross.

All this is not to say that playpens should never be used. There is no harm in placing a first or second child in a playpen for a short period, to protect her and the food from damage while you are cooking a meal, for example. "That's different than using it for an hour and a half in the morning, and an hour and a half in the afternoon, because a neat home is more important, or because you don't want to be bothered," Dr. Gross points out. If and when you do use a playpen, it is best to place it near the "action," where your child can see you and hear you. Add a little music and some toys, and it's not a bad place to spend a little time. (But for better long-range solutions to sibling rivalry, child safety, and terminal maternal exhaustion, turn to chapters six and nine.)

Toys Are for Tots

It's great to give a child a lot of your time and attention, but it's not quite enough. The things in her environment—the colors, the sounds, the textures—should be as stimulating as her parents are. Some of the most important things in her environment will be her toys. Toys (and other items she plays with) are important for learning. They are almost symbols of the world to her, and are used to try out developing concepts. But what kind are the best kind? Of course, toys should be sturdy and safe. That's easy to remember. But some parents forget, when they go shopping, that toys are for children, and should be purchased with the child's needs in mind. Students at New York University did a study of infant mobiles to find out which kinds babies responded to the most. Infants were most taken by "high contrast" mobiles —especially black and white—and they preferred mobiles with a face to identify with. When the students then visited toy stores, they saw a superabundance of pastel mobiles, but nary a black and white. Most had swans and ducks or fairy tale figures. Certainly such mobiles add a nice touch to the nursery decor. But what about the poor baby? He gets to see the underside of Cinderella or a swan—not exactly an inspiring sight. So when you walk into a toy store, try to think about what your child will enjoy and learn, not what Aunt Harriet will say about your decorating wizardry.

You should also think about what your child can do with the toy. Some toys, such as blocks and boxes and pots, can be used in many ways. Those are the best toys for very young children, says Dr. Gross, because "the child can invest the object with his purpose." But as the child gets older, she advises, parents should add some toys with only one use, such as puzzles. "The child will have to learn to bend, to do things a certain way."

Although toys are for tots, your tot will benefit the most from them if you sometimes play along, too. The best idea is to first let your child explore the toy—she may find ways to play with it you never dreamed of. Then sit down together, become involved, and have fun. For the most part, let your child take the lead. Do what she does. You may wish to name some of the parts of the toys, or to introduce a slightly different way to play with them. Your child may then take it further. In this way, toys don't become a substitute for your attention, but part of your total relationship with your child.

What about special "infant stimulating" programs, books and records that purportedly speed up development? As Carol Schapiro Kekst describes them, "You take out the record, plug your kid into the stimulator, and zoom along." But, she warns, "Some children may be overwhelmed, unable to sort out all the stimulation coming into them. Some of those children will go off to sleep to tune it out. Others will become too excited, and will fret and cry." She also points out that such programs are not tailored to the individual child.

You Live and You Learn

Even if you feel pressed for time, what with two kids to care for, a home to tend to, and your career or other interests to cultivate, you can help your second child to learn in the course of the everyday routine. He can learn from everything he does. All you have to do is set things up for him. For example, if you put his clothing in low drawers or in baskets or cubbies on the floor, he can learn to get his own outfit for the day. If you give him some extra time before an outing, he can begin to learn to dress himself (which will be a time-saver for you). At mealtime, provide him with lots of finger foods. As he develops more dexterity, give him some child-size utensils to use and a small pitcher he can learn to pour from. The opportunities for natural learning are all around, inside and outside. The challenge is to help your child take advantage of them.

The More Things Change . . .

Do you think children learn best in a very predictible environment, where they always know what to expect? (It's Tuesday, so supper's got to be tuna fish!) Or do you think it is best to keep them off their guard, to keep changing toys and times and even the menu? Actually, it is a combination of the two—constancy and change—that promotes learning, according to Dr. Shigaki. Certain things should be predictable in a child's day, she says. "Lunch should be around twelve, for example, not ten one day and four the next. There should be a certain pattern to the day. In that way, the child learns about time and the sequence of events." The child should also know he can always find things in a certain place, and that his parents have certain consistent expectations of his behavior. "Such constants lead to a sense of security and self-confidence." But for growth to occur, there must also be some change—new kinds of toys, new types of outings. Novelty helps to capture a child's interest and to motivate learning. "Don't always take your child to the same park on the corner," Dr. Shigaki suggests. "Try the park down the street.

Venture out to the supermarket. Do new things with him, always with sensitivity to what he can handle comfortably."

The Tag-along Kid

Once there are two children in the family, they are often simply referred to as "the kids," rather than by the individual names you struggled so hard to come up with. Unfortunately, some people don't just talk that way, they think that way, too. The second child becomes like an appendage to the family, one of "the kids." And more often than not, the family's activities are oriented around the older child because most parents are more interested in going to a museum than to the local Y's rendition of *The Three Little Pigs.* But, Dr. Gross advises, the needs of the younger child should be taken into account as much as those of the older. "Sometimes, make believe your second child is a first or only child, not just one of the crowd." Even if you hate pigs, don't panic. If wolves are more to your liking, you can try to convince your only second child to see *Little Red Riding Hood* instead.

Fathering Is Not a Sometime Thing

You may have noticed that a lot of the research cited in this book focuses on mother and child, with dear old daddy left out in the cold. But children are much better off with a warm-hearted father very nearby. Scientists have found that children brought up in families without fathers score lower on intelligence tests than do children from two-parent families. But even in two-parent families, father can be hard to find. Some studies have looked at the amount of time fathers spend in direct contact with their infants in the first year of life. Their estimates range from less than a minute a day to slightly more than an hour a day. So in some households, apparently, father and baby are little more than strangers in the night. Some fathers may be even stranger to their second child than to their first. One study looked at "affectional closeness" between parent and child. In two-child families, a higher proportion of second children than first chldren felt "close" to the mother, but a higher proportion of first children than second felt "close" to the father. Other studies suggest that fathers are more actively involved in child rearing with firstborns than with later-borns. Fathers who are warm, involved, and accepting with their children, firstborn or later-born, are richly rewarded; they are most likely to have children who develop to their fullest potential.

Mothers and fathers both have an important role in guiding their second child's development. That role is not to treat the second child just like a first child—or just like a second child, either. It is to treat her like the child she is. It is to learn everything you can about her and to do what you can to help her grow. Her birth order doesn't have to be her destiny. Certainly, even if you do a good job of it, she may not grow up to be everything you want her to be. But she will be everything *she* wants to be.

6. The Combat Zone: Children at War

ONE OF MICHAEL'S FIRST WORDS WAS "MINE." His very first sentence was "Brian did it." No mistaking the second child in him. Unlike his brother, he was not born into a "home, sweet home" where his pleasure was prime. Instead, there was someone out there who hated him as passionately as he loved him, who secretly delighted in his discomfort, who occasionally even desired his demise. Before too long, those feelings became mutual, and a once-peaceful household was transformed into a combat zone—the staging area for the war between the siblings.

Sibling rivalry is a great weapon for the proponents of a one-child family. And it is a great worry for the parents who closed their eyes and got pregnant a second time anyway. Despite the advance warning, some parents don't know what's hit them when their children start hitting each other. "Some people are very naïve and don't understand why two brothers should fight," says Dr. Joel Sambursky, clinical psychologist at Brooklyn Jewish Hospital. "They come here and ask, 'Why do my sons fight over each other's toys?' They don't realize what's causing it, and they think it's a problem."

If you have two children, you are almost sure to have sibling rivalry as well. Freud came right to the point when he wrote, "There is probably no nursery without violent conflicts between the inhabitants." Each inhabitant wants his parents' love, completely and exclusively. But he can't get it all to himself, and so resents the person he must share it with. Siblings must also share attention, and time, and toys, and Daddy's lap and Mommy's smile. Rivalrous feelings are not limited to the first child or to the second. The younger child may fear she will never catch up to

169

big brother; she will never be able to run as fast or stay up as late, and she will never, ever, be as old. But big brother fears that his advantage is fading, that his dominance is declining with every passing year. And so the battle is joined.

Sibling rivalry has a highly publicized, if sordid, past. It accounted for the very first murder recorded in the Old Testament: Cain's infamous killing of Abel. Jacob fled for his life after taking the birthright from his older brother, Esau. Joseph's brothers turned green at the sight of his "coat of many colors," threw him into a snake pit, and then sold him into slavery. If you prefer fairy tales to biblical stories, the same pattern emerges—a struggle for power between brothers and sisters. An analysis of Grimm's fairy tales tried to sort out the winners from the losers. In twenty-eight of the stories looked at, there were two children. In thirteen of those, the second child was judged the "winner"; in just five, the older came out ahead and the second child second; in the remaining ten stories, no one lost.

In real life, too, there need be no losers. If not too severe, sibling rivalry can play a positive role in the lives of the rivals. "It helps children to carve out their place in the family structure, and to develop their lifestyle," says Dr. Robert Sherman, family counselor and associate professor at Queens College in New York City. If one child is capable in one area, the other child may try to excel in other areas (echoes of deidentification). In that way, "Sibling rivalry helps children find their place in the sun." Dr. Benjamin Spock points out that rivalry can help children to grow up more tolerant, more independent, and more generous. If sibling rivalry is successfully resolved, the former rivals will be able to handle competition with other people, and won't feel compelled to dominate or to appease their future friends and lovers.

Just like nonrelated children, siblings who are rivals can be friends, too. In a study done more than forty years ago, the relationships of twenty pairs of young sisters were examined. Surprisingly, the pairs of sisters who seemed most rivalrous were just about as companionable as less rivalrous sisters. So competition can be just one part of a loving, cooperative relationship.

But if sibling rivalry becomes too extreme it can have devastating, lifelong effects. In its most extreme (and rare) form, it can be life-threatening, as Cain so dramatically demonstrated. In more recent times, there have been cases reported of attempted drownings, poisonings, and burnings. More commonly, there may be intense competition, less lethal physical abuse, and undeniable hatred. If one child is always on the receiving end, he may be seriously affected. In a study at the University of Michigan Medical Center, such an effect was found in three families. In each, an older sibling was jealous and aggressive toward a younger. One victimized younger brother found it extremely difficult to express himself with his peers. Another lacked assertiveness and had difficulty talking. In one family, a boy had started talking at around one year of age. At that time he also became more active, and his older sister responded with increased aggression. His attempts at speech abruptly stopped and didn't resume until he was nearly two years old.

If rivalry is intense inside the home, it is probably carried on outside as well. Children who bully and tease their siblings often use the same tactics with their peers, and find themselves without many friends. If childhood jealousy isn't worked out, it can be carried into adulthood, and take a variety of forms. It can be seen in people who resent other's good fortune, in drivers who never let anyone pass them on the road, in middle-aged tennis players who can never admit their service was long. It can also be seen in people who avoid all competition, who prefer solitaire to gin or bridge or backgammon, who never make a peep about taking out the garbage. Their sibling rivalry has left them unable and unwilling to stand up for their rights.

In its most obvious form, the sibling rivals remain rivals as adults. The brother and sister who slammed doors in each other's faces now slam the phone down on each other. Dr. Ilana Reich, psychologist and consultant to Head Start, notes an instance in her own family. "My husband has two aunts, eighty-nine and eighty-seven. They sit down and bicker like our daughters do. After all these years, after all their grandchildren and great-grandchildren, they're still at it."

Rivalry persists into adulthood if it was suppressed in childhood, according to Dr. Bernice Berk, school psychologist at the Bank Street College of Education. "Some children aren't allowed to work out their rivalry. They're made to be very polite.

So as adults, minor squabbles can lead to anger and to a feud lasting twenty-five years. Childhood things should be worked out in childhood. If siblings are forty years old and still angry about who had the larger cupcake, there's nowhere to go with that.''

But how can parents distinguish the healthy, character-building kind of rivalry from the kind that can distort personality and destroy self-confidence? A clear sign of the negative variety is the attempt really to hurt each other or even to cause permanent damage. If one child is always the tyrant and the other always the victim, that is another cause for concern. Contrary to expectation, the victim can be the older child, perpetually pestered by the younger without defending himself. If the rivalry becomes destructive to the whole family unit, as well as to the warriors, that is another reason for alarm, and perhaps a call for outside help.

SUGAR AND SPITE

If your first child is a sweet little girl, and your second the same, you may feel confident that all forms of rivalry will pass your family by. How can your two sugarplums utter an angry word, much less kick, bite, or scratch? When your ears turn red, and your Band-Aid supply dwindles, remember you read it here. Studies have shown that girls are more likely to be jealous than boys. In fact, there is more jealousy in a girl-girl combination than in a boy-boy pairing. If your children, boys or girls, are eighteen to forty-two months apart, keep your ear plugs handy and your first-aid kit well-stocked. Jealousy is thought to be most common with that age separation (give or take a few months).

While firstborn children are considered more likely to be jealous, there is evidence that secondborn children more readily admit to quarreling (and more readily confess defeat). First and seconds also use different tactics to exert power over each other. Research suggests that firstborns rely heavily on attacking, interfering, bribing, and ignoring to show that young upstart just who's boss. The young upstart tries to win his way by pleading, reasoning, and attacking property (perhaps because property can't hit back).

But a child is not the sum of his sex, spacing, and sequence in the family. Even a boy who comes a comfortable decade after his older brother may burn with jealousy, while a girl followed closely by another girl may barely feel a flicker. A child's individual temperament may outweigh her family position. Some youngsters are more demanding and possessive than others, more likely to want everything for themselves. The green-eyed monster would find them easy prey. Other children, even when very young, find it easier to share. They are less likely to fall victim to consuming jealousy.

WHAT THEY SEE IS WHAT THEY DO

But it is not enough to look at the children for the roots of jealousy. Parents play a major role in helping or hindering the sibling relationship. That's not just something psychiatrists tell patients to heap yet more blame on the ever-vilified parents. It is scientific fact. Research reveals a greater frequency of jealousy in homes in which parents are inconsistent and oversolicitous. Another study found that in families rated as poorly adjusted, 63 percent of the children were jealous, as compared with only 10 percent in families rated as well adjusted. Parents are powerful models for their children. However, some parents don't act according to their words. "A woman will say to her older child, 'Don't hit your brother!' and then she'll give the offender a whack," Dr. Robert Sherman of Queens College relates. "So it becomes very clear to the child that you get what you want by whacking." And younger brother is likely to bear the painful brunt of that lesson.

Anne, the mother of Justine, three, and Ivan, two, has begun to understand how her own behavior has contributed to her children's behavior. "In the beginning, Justine would hurt Ivan a lot. She would bite him, or she would push him down. To put it plain, she was a little bit mean. Now, he doesn't take any more abuse from her. He's hurting her more than she's hurting him. He comes up and bites her. She's got teeth marks on her shoulder and on her back. He grabs her dolls and runs away with them. He likes to tease her and make her mad. I don't know where they get this aggression from, this violence toward each other." After some reflection, Anne was able to provide part of the answer herself. "I feel sometimes it's my fault they're so violent toward each other. When they fight, it makes me very nervous. I lose control sometimes, and yell and scream at them too much. I don't hit them that often, but sometimes I hit them if things get out of hand. I lose my temper and hit them. Not on the face, but on the arm or something. Maybe that's why they're violent toward each other. Maybe I shouldn't hit them."

Fighting parents often breed fighting children. Dr. Leonard Reich, psychologist at the Health Insurance Plan of Greater New York, recalls a couple who requested his help with their warring offspring. "Our kids are killing each other," they told him. But when he looked at the parents, "I saw they were angry as hell at each other." Dr. Reich, father of four, notes a similar phenomenon in his own family. "When my wife and I fight, our children fight more. Even if we're just tense, our children fight more. Very often, fighting between siblings is a reflection of what goes on between adults."

The children may actually become caught in the parents' conflict, and each becomes a satellite to one of the parents. "They become like warring couples, parent and child versus parent and child," says Dr. Tess Forrest, a family analyst. "The parents need help, and so do the children. The children have to be cut loose as satellites. They have to be freed to develop an alliance, to identify with each other as siblings."

HOME FROM THE HOSPITAL

Even if you provide a good model for your children, you are not home free, and your home won't be free of conflict. On a day-to-day basis, how should you handle it? How can you encourage the healthy aspects of sibling rivalry and discourage the elements of hatred and consuming jealousy that can poison your children and your family? The first task is to set a good foundation during the early months when your children are first learning about each other. "What's important is how the parents react right from the beginning," says New York pediatrician Dr. Virginia Pomeranz.

"That can kill the sibling relationship or make it lovely." (For parents who have already survived those first few months, you might wish to skip this section and turn to page 185, "The Peace Will Pass.")

As you prepare to leave the hospital with your second child, you may wonder what manner of child will be awaiting you in the lobby or at home. Will she be that same sweet, or same mischievous, or same easy-going child you kissed good-bye a few short days ago? Or will she have turned mean, or sullen, or more mischievous than ever? You may not notice it at first, it may not even happen at first, but there will be some changes made. No child can fail to react to such a major upheaval in her living situation and family structure. Some children are very obvious about their feelings. They become aggressive and hostile, biting their parents, painting the walls, even smearing feces on the hated newcomer. If their actions don't tell it, their words may. They request that the baby be disposed of with all deliberate speed. Down the toilet, into the garbage, back to the hospital, no matter, as long as she is gone without a trace.

Some children react in subtler ways, retreating into silence to hide their anger, or becoming overly affectionate to the baby, hugging her and warning her parents, "Don't drop her!" Other children may really, honestly, be happy about the new baby, and proud of their new status—until they realize what it's all about. Dr. Joel Sambursky of Brooklyn Jewish Hospital traces a typical progression from joy to jealousy. "Often there's excitement and anticipation at first, because the baby's like a toy. The child's fantasies are 'I'll have a playmate to live with me.' But then the reality sets in. The children start to realize, 'It's not really my playmate. It's someone who's going to take my mother's attention from me. And while everyone's coming to the house to kitchy-koo the kid, I'm sitting here like a moron and nobody's paying attention to me.' I think that's the point when the jealousy starts."

Many enlightened parents and other relatives try very hard to avoid that scenario. With every gift for the baby comes a gift for big brother. One mother says her older son actually got *more* gifts than the baby at the baby's *Brith*. "Some people who brought presents for Dustin said they'd send me gifts for the baby, but I haven't received them yet." One well-meaning grandmother kept reassuring her first grandson after her second was born, "You're still my number-one boy." In another household, visiting relatives wouldn't even step into the baby's room without first asking the older child, "Can I see your sister?" As part of that protective attitude, some parents pay little attention to the baby while the older child's around. They fear that a kiss on the cheek of their second child would be like a knife in the heart of their first.

Is that the way to go? Should you try to convince your older child he is still king of the castle, and the new baby but a lackey? Not unless you want a lot of trouble down the road. "If you tell your older child he's number one, then what's that other thing lying there?" asks Dr. Emily Rubinstein, Brooklyn Jewish Hospital psychologist. "And how can that continue later? Something will have to change. It's best if you use other language from the start, like 'You're very special and important.' " Dr. Rubinstein also emphasizes that ignoring the younger for the benefit of the older is not good for either. "Expressing affection to both children is important. Otherwise, you're denying your feelings and the importance of the baby to you. If you kiss your younger child only when the older isn't looking, it would seem strange. If you want to kiss the younger, fine. If you want to kiss the older, that's fine, too."

If you withhold affection from the baby, you may actually be making your older child more insecure and anxious, not less. He may fear that if you can ignore a permanent member of the family like that, maybe one day you will do it to him. Displays of affection are helpful to everyone in the family, as long as one member isn't doted upon at the expense of the others.

How about that closetful of toys? Should you make sure to dole one out whenever a relative turns up one present short? If the child is feeling particularly shortchanged, it's helpful to have a present handy. But it's not a good idea to make it a ritual, or the child will ask, "What's for me?" whenever anyone brings a baby gift. You might show him some of the gifts he received as a newborn so he realizes he hasn't been overlooked.

TO NURSE OR NOT?

A recent survey revealed that later-born babies are slightly less likely than firstborns to be breast-fed. Apparently, some mothers "protect" their older child from hurt by denying their breasts to the baby. They fear that the intimacy of nursing may be too much for their older child to bear. And they may have heard some scare stories from their friends. Nadine had a hard time with three-year-old Todd while she nursed little Natalie. "From the time she was born, he was jealous and carried on during each and every nursing. He'd bother the baby. He'd bother me. He'd jump on the bed. He'd do anything to get our attention. The nursing period was never peaceful. The only relaxing feeding she ever had was at five A.M. when he was asleep."

But how would Todd have behaved if Natalie was on the bottle instead? "It probably would have been the same," Nadine admitted. Experts are somewhat divided on that point. Some believe that breast-feeding arouses more jealousy than bottle-feeding. Others feel that feeding can be a difficult time, whether done by breast or bottle, simply because mother is so taken up by baby. A recent study conducted by Carol Kendrick and Judy Dunn of the University of Cambridge helps to clarify the picture. They observed forty mothers and their firstborn children during a feeding session with a new baby. There were more incidents of "deliberate naughtiness" if the feeding was done by bottle, and more confrontations between mother and child. In contrast, the breast-feeding mothers were less likely to issue stern prohibitions to their older children, and more likely to play with them during the feeding. The researchers concluded that "mothers who are expecting a second child should not feel that the choice of breast feeding rather than bottle feeding will involve subjecting their first child to added stress."

If you decide to breast-feed your second child, even though you bottle-fed your first, you may run into some difficult questions. What do you tell a child who feels that the rubber nipples and artificial formula he got were no match for the real thing?

One mother decided to pretend that her older daughter had, indeed, been breast-fed, and to admit the truth at a later date. But the best course is to be honest from the start. Tell your child that you have learned new things since she was born. Or if you had tried and failed to breast-feed her, tell her about it. Make it clear, however, that her feeding experience was a good one. "You liked your bottle. I held you in my arms close to me, like I hold the baby." If you really did nurse your first, she will be eager to hear about it. And if you captured her feedings on three-by-five glossies, now's the time to get out her baby album so she can see for herself.

Some mothers hide themselves away during nursing to avoid arousing jealousy. That strategy can only backfire. The older child will certainly sense his mother's embarrassment and guilt, will feel left out because he *is* left out, and will feel confused and perhaps betrayed when he makes the inevitable discovery. It is far better to nurse, comfortably and naturally, in front of your child. If you feel confident, your child will accept it. Four-year-old Danielle actually looks forward to breast-feeding sessions. She piles up two or three pillows next to her mother and enjoys a close-up view of her two-week-old sister being fed. Mandy, a second-time mother, had a special concern about the nursing. The concern was her older son, thirteen-year-old Neil. Dare she nurse in front of him? Would he dare stay in the room, or would he dart out in a fit of adolescent embarrassment? She dared, and he dared. "When I nursed Zach, Neil had no reaction that he expressed. He would just sit down and talk to me, as if nothing at all were going on."

For the more typical sibling, of two or three or four, you can make nursing a special time. Cuddle her with your free hand, read her a book, put on a record, give her a special doll or toy to play with. During some of the sessions you can give of yourself to both of your children. But you should try to reserve some nursing time for just you and the baby as a time of intimacy and developing love. Perhaps your husband, or a friend or relative, can entertain your older child, or you can time one session to coincide with your first child's nap or school.

Once parents have made the feeding decision, some are faced with yet another decision. Should they let their older child take a taste? Here, professional opinion is once again divided. Some experts feel that if the mother's not embarrassed about it, there is no harm done. The child will try it, probably won't know what to do, and then won't ask again. Meanwhile, his curiosity would have been satisfied. But other psychologists point out that suckling at the breast may arouse sexual fantasies in preschoolers and older children. In another negative vote, Dr. Leonard Reich points out that nursing is an expression of bonding between mother and baby. "If you feel it will intrude in the bonding, you should stand pat and say no. Just because your older child feels he wants to experiment, you shouldn't be his pawn. That's not setting appropriate limits." The decision, of course, is an individual one, and depends largely on what you are comfortable with. If you do decide to refuse your child's request, you might tell her, "I know how you feel, but that's not the way you get your food anymore." As an alternative, you might express some milk and let your older child taste it from a cup.

MOTHER'S LITTLE HELPER

Some parents don't even realize they are overprotecting their oldest child when they are doing just that. They have read that you are supposed to enlist his help with baby care as a way to immunize him from the ravages of rivalry. So they have him folding the diapers and holding the bottle and burping the baby and pushing the stroller, when all he really wants to do is stretch out with a good comic book, or stare at the ceiling and think about twiddle-bugs. Of course, a child should be allowed to help out if he wants. It can help him feel important, and proud that he is able to do things for the baby. But it should not be a responsibility or a burden. "He shouldn't be involved as an assistant parent as a way of suppressing his anger," Dr. Bernice Berk maintains. "The idea is that he'll begin to identify with his parents, and because they don't get angry, he won't, either. But his anger will come out in hundreds of ways, like squeezing the baby too tight, or even dropping her." Dr. Berk emphasizes that a child should be free to be a child. If he wants to help, okay. If not, okay.

Randi found that her four-year-old son B.J. was more help than she bargained for. In fact, he wouldn't leave his new sister alone. He told his mother, "I want to feed her, kiss her, bathe her. You better go in and check on that little girl." When his grandmother came over to babysit, he was really in his glory. "Oh Grandma, baby made a doody," he said, solemnly. "I'll have to get you a dry and wet paper towel." Later, "She had half a bottle of milk, Grandma. Try to belch her now."

His motives may have been pure, but some overeager helpers may simply be trying to get attention for themselves. They are forever spilling things, asking how to do things, trying to reclaim the spotlight. If helping is done out of jealousy, it is not a good idea to encourage it. Instead, tell your child you will spend time with him later, and make sure that you do.

HOLDING WITHOUT HURTING

Just as you shouldn't overprotect your first child, you shouldn't overprotect your second, either. To fall at her feet like the Messiah has come isn't good for anyone in the family. To keep her always out of reach of your first child will only make your eldest feel hurt and excluded. New babies aren't as fragile as they look. Let your older child touch the baby and hold her while he is securely seated on an armchair or couch. Whether and when it is safe to leave them alone together, only you can judge. But make it clear, from the start, that the baby is not to be hurt in any way. Your older child will feel relieved to know you won't let him carry out any hostile impulses he may have.

To a new parent of a first child, a cry from the nursery signifies the baby is hungry, or wet, or just plain ornery. To a second-time parent, the first thought may be, "I bet that little stinker of a big sister is letting her 'drink and wet' doll wet all over the baby's face," or "My son the sadist is probably practicing his drum rolls on the baby's bare bottom." Dr. Pomeranz remembers her parents' thinking taking that very turn. "When they heard my baby sister cry, they wouldn't even get up half the time. They'd just yell, 'Virginia!' from the next room, and I resented it bitterly."

She advises the parents of her patients not to repeat that mistake. "A lot of the trouble begins with the misguided notion of protecting the baby from the ravages of the older one. So they say, 'Don't touch, don't do this, don't do that.' When the baby cries, it's automatically 'You did it,' always the blame. I tell parents to get up and see what is happening. It isn't going to kill you. If the older one *is* molesting the baby, just break it up."

So far, this section has been stressing actions to avoid, behaviors that would botch things up right from the beginning. But there are also positive ways to keep the damage to a minimum and get sibling rivalry off to a good and healthy start. The most positive way is to give each of your children the love and attention they crave. If the baby is fretful and colicky, you may find you have little energy left for your older child. But you have to manage to provide for his needs anyway, or he will become fretful, too. If it means cajoling a relative to help out, don't be shy about it. Cajole loudly and clearly. If it means hiring a babysitter because your cajoling didn't work, try to find it in your budget to do so. And don't assign the babysitter only to your older child while you are occupied only with the baby. Hire someone you trust with an infant so you can free yourself to do all those things with your first child you promised to do way back when you were pregnant. It is important that he has time alone with each parent. If he feels the love of his parents, he won't begrudge it so when he must share it with his sibling.

During the first summer after Michael was born, I hired a mother's helper who was twelve, looked like fourteen, and acted like sixteen. She seemed to know more about babies than I did even after I had had one and was decidedly more than twice her age. She also got along well with Brian, sharing his passion for the Hulk, and for Tinker Toys, and for mint chip ice cream. So the four of us spent some lovely summer days together at parks and beaches and in friends' backyards. We alternated our charges, taking turns cavorting with Brian and carrying Michael. In that way, I was able to form a bond with the baby, while Brian did not feel forgotten.

It would not be surprising if some first children do develop a forgotten feeling. Cambridge researchers Judy Dunn and Carol

Kendrick compared the way mothers treat their older children before and after the birth of a second child. There were very definite changes, and none for the better. The mothers were less likely to give their first children playful attention after the birth, less likely to suggest new activities or initiate verbal games, and more likely to engage in negative confrontation. It would seem that the lowered attention might well be due to the mothers' preoccupation with baby care. But even when the mothers were not involved with their new babies, they gave their older children less attention than before the birth.

Just as you should keep up attention levels, you should keep up routines. Don't omit your child's morning visit to the sprinklers in the playground, or his three o'clock snack, or his bedtime story, if that is what you have always done. Many children find their familiar world disrupted by a move to another home. The arrival of a second child is a common moving time, what with another family member to find room for. In the University of Michigan Medical Center study, it was found that a move to a new home soon after the birth of a sibling was often very stressful. In some children it seemed to contribute to regression, in some, to separation anxiety, in others, to aggression. According to the researchers, ". . . a move, which removes the security of a child's known environment, provides a type of stress that may trigger maladaptive reactions when coinciding with the stress of a sibling's birth." But, they add, the move need not be as stressful as it often is. Parents who are aware and sensitive can help to ease the transition for their children.

Whether you move or not, you should make sure that your child's privacy and possessions are protected. Don't give away any of her toys, even her baby toys, to the baby, without her permission. She may actually find some ingenious use for that rattle or pacifier. Even if she doesn't, she may rather have them stored away in her closet than sucked on by her brother.

Another useful strategy is to extend your child's interests outside the home. Enroll her in a gymnastics class, or swimming class, or painting class. Take her to a concert or a play. Let her sleep over at a friend's house. If her turf is expanded, she won't feel it is being taken over by a bawling, boring baby.

MOVING BACK, MOVING ON

If you do all the right things after the baby is born, if you are loving and supportive and play-going, your older child may not regress as you have been told older children do. You may be able to keep the plastic sheet in the linen closet and the pacifier in the nursery. In fact, some scientists report that an enhancement in development may be associated with the birth of a sibling. Some children become quickly toilet trained after the birth, learn to play independently, separate more easily from the mother, actually relinquish a pacifier. Such progress is more likely, research shows, if the child was prepared early on for the birth, if she had contact with her mother during the hospital stay, and if the father has been actively involved.

But regression can happen even in the best of families. It reflects a temporary longing to be a baby again, and to receive the same total care and attention as a baby does. Some children revert to crawling, some forget their sophisticated sentences and go back to "goos" and "gahs." And, of course, there may be the unsettling of the bowels or the begging for a bottle. "Don't panic. It's normal," says Dr. Berk of Bank Street. "Be reassuring and nonjudgmental. And be patient. Go along with them, within reason. If they say 'dress me,' do. If they want to try a bottle, all right. But if they want only a bottle, and nothing else, say 'You don't just drink milk, you have other foods.' They'll probably lose interest in the bottle after a while." Regression does not occur only after a sibling's birth. Often, as children grow up, they go back to a stage they felt more comfortable in, then they go back to being themselves. If you allow your child to regress temporarily, and return to a former stage, you are providing him with the security he needs to go on.

FANTASIES AND FATHERS

Keep in mind, through all these do's and don'ts, that you are still going to have a competitive child on your hands. You have made it clear that he can't hurt the baby, so what is he to do with his feelings of rivalry and retaliation? You might try providing him with a punching bag or a baby doll. Whenever he expresses hostility to the baby, you can suggest he give the bag a beating or the doll a drubbing. Soon he will be doing it without your suggestions. He will have learned to vent his angry feelings without hurting anyone. As another alternative to violence, you might encourage him to play-act with a doll family, or a teddy bear family, or even a family of socks stuffed with old nylons. In dramatic fantasies his jealousy can rage without bounds and without danger. Competitive games can also help him cope with his rivalrous feelings and safely express his hostility.

It is not only mother who sets the stage for sibling relations; father plays an important part, too. Research has shown that the stress of sibling birth is reduced if the father actively cares for the older child. Apparently, the child uses the increased attention from his father to offset the other changes in his life situation. If the father is wrapped up in the baby to the exclusion of the older child, there is trouble ahead. In one family the father was clearly more attached to his baby daughter than to his older son. She was a "sweet and pleasant" baby while he had been "difficult and colicky." She was Daddy's little girl—but not brother's beloved sister. After her birth, he showed a great deal of regression, as well as a lot of hostility toward Daddy's darling daughter.

In many families, though, the pattern is different. The mother is so consumed by baby's needs that the father "takes over" the older child. The father may choose that role because he is still disgusted with dirty diapers, and anyway, older children are more fun. Such a family alignment may be particularly apparent on family outings. "Usually, the mother is in charge of the baby while the father winds up with the older child," points out psychologist Ilana Reich. "But it's a mistake if it happens all the time. It may even continue when the children are older, and it's not good for anybody. A special effort should be made to have the father sometimes wheel the carriage or carry the baby." In that way, Dr. Reich points out, there won't be any role differentiation between what is right for father to do and what is right for mother to do. And there won't be a family split.

THE PEACE WILL PASS

If you've gotten through the first few weeks, or first few months, and all seems calm and quiet, you might feel a complete success at this sibling rivalry business. But don't start celebrating just yet. Tammy, new mother of two, breezed through the first three weeks. "My husband was home. Company was around. Stacey seemed happy and content with her new sister. We all had a fine old time. I thought I was home free." But then Tammy's husband went back to work and company stopped coming. "After that, the dam broke."

Kim had a few more months of tranquility. "For the first eight months, Robyn slept almost all day. She was good. She never bothered anybody. Andy didn't seem upset at all. But when the baby started walking, and she needed more attention, the problems began. My son would knock her down, hit and bite. I couldn't do anything about it. He took powder and powdered her. He squeezed mustard over her head. He poured shampoo on her and all over the room."

A mobile baby is much more of a threat than a motionless one. A beginning crawler or walker demands more space and attention than ever. Her parents must be ever alert to possible danger to her and possible destruction to the furnishings she is beginning to explore. What's worse, she is beginning to explore her sibling's possessions. She may grab one of his blocks to see how it feels and tastes, only to knock down his intricate construction. Fascinated by the crinkly sounds of paper, she may rip his prized paintings off his wall and into a thousand pieces. By then, he probably feels like doing the same to her. And he probably wishes she was back in the crib, so he can build and paint in peace.

Jealousy may grow worse, yet, as your children pass the age of four. In a study of childhood competition, children aged two to seven were observed while playing with blocks. The children under four usually picked up blocks as they needed them, while the older children more often cornered a supply. Older children were more likely than younger ones to make favorable remarks about their own work. Also, the older the children were, the higher the percentage who showed signs of competition. At three years of age, fewer than half seemed competitive, compared with 86 percent of the six-year-olds.

As your children grow older, you may also notice that their fights last longer. In one study it was found that only 40 percent of the fights between two-year-olds went beyond round one, while 67 percent of the conflicts between four-year-olds lasted two rounds or more.

You may have a long wait before your two children retire from the ring. Generally, siblings don't get on well together until their mid-teens. That doesn't mean there won't be any intermissions between their bouts. As I discuss further in the next chapter, there will likely be a warm and wonderful side to your children's relationship, too. Sibling feelings are often a mixture of the most intense devotion and the deepest disgust. Brian has expressed it so distinctly, I've felt like recording it for use at psychological conventions. He would gaze directly into Michael's eyes, and say, "I love you. I hate you. I love you. I hate you." His feelings were crystal clear.

But how are you to get through all those times when hate seems to be the prevailing emotion? Should you referee the fights or sit them out? Should you root for the less experienced fighter, or remain in the neutral corner? Should you give the fighters trophies of equal size when at last the match is done? There are decisions to be made, and they will come at you fast and furiously. You can make them one at a time, basing them on your mood at the moment, or you can plan ahead, deciding what your general responses will be to certain types of situations. If you are the planning type, this chapter may help you shape some of your responses.

Instead of delivering a dry lecture on the remedies to rivalry, I decided to let parents and psychologists speak for themselves. I asked a number of parents to list their major everyday problems with sibling rivalry, and I asked therapists to suggest solutions. For some problems, there was complete professional agreement; for some, a dissent or two from the majority viewpoint; for others, a wide diversity of opinion. It may be helpful for you to read all the suggestions, and choose the ones that make the most sense to you should the problems arise in your family.

The first problem was presented by the mother of four-year-old Ivan and ten-month-old Brenda.

"Whenever I hold Brenda on my lap, Ivan wants on, too, and even tries to push her off. They fight over me. I feel like I'm being torn in two. What should I do?"

The idea here is to give Ivan something, but not everything, according to the experts I questioned. "Include both children in your affection," advises one psychologist. "Neither one should be excluded." At the same time, make it clear to Ivan that he can't have your whole lap. Point out that you have two legs, one for each child. You might tell him, "You can't have my lap to yourself all the time. Either share it now, or wait until later when it's your special time."

The next three questions were raised by the mother of Cathy, five, and Bradley, two.

"Whenever Bradley plays with one of his toys, Cathy grabs it away from him. Should I intervene?"

Considering Bradley's tender years, one psychologist advised helping him protect his possessions. "A two-year-old can't measure up to a five-year-old. Three years is a lot of difference, so the parents have to intervene. Label the children's possessions. If you see the older taking a toy from the younger, tell her to stop. Tell her, 'If he wants to give it to you, okay.' If she continues grabbing toys without consent, take her out of the room and tell her she can't play there because of what she's doing."

Another psychologist suggested basing your reaction on the younger child's reaction. "If the younger one minds, try to get the older one to cut it out. But if the younger one doesn't mind, who are you protecting?"

Several other therapists leaned toward nonintervention, no matter how loudly the little one cries. "Let her grab," said one. "A two-year-old has to learn how to get along in the world. You can't always step in and protect him. Give him separate time to play with toys and develop normally. Provide a place for her to

play alone, too." Another therapist pointed out that always interfering on Bradley's behalf may only intensify Cathy's obvious
jealousy.

Perhaps more important than her parents' response to *what*
she does is their understanding of *why* she does it. Her constant
grabbing is a common symptom of jealousy, of the feeling that
what she has is not as good as what he has. So a basic solution is
to make her feel more valued, to try to enhance her self-esteem,
to do special things with her that a two-year-old can't be included
in. Before too long, her toy-grabbing may cease, whether you
intervene in it directly or not.

*"Often, when Cathy builds up something with her blocks,
Bradley knocks it right down. Should I let them work it out themselves? Should I punish him? How should I handle it?"*

Again, there is a disagreement between the interventionist
school and the keep-out-of-it camp. According to a representa-
tive of the former, "Children should respect each other's rights.
Be firm. Tell Bradley he can't knock down Cathy's project. It
belongs to her. If he knocks it down, smack him and take him out
of the room."

On the other side, "The older child will have to learn to deal
with that behavior. You might point out that it's not the end of
the world, that you had fun in building it, and that it doesn't take
away from you that he knocked it down."

The idea in this instance is again to look behind the action to
the motive. It seems that a cycle is being set up in this family,
and that younger brother may be getting revenge at big sister for
taking away his toys. One way of handling it, as well as other
family disputes, is to set up a family council to meet once or
twice a week. In this democratic organization, parents and children can talk things over, can determine who is responsible for
what and who is angry at whom, and can find solutions together.
Parents can teach the children how to negotiate to get what they
want, but also how important it is to be concerned with the needs
of others. The key thing about the council is that everyone has a
role, and feels a vital part of the family.

Another issue that this block-knocking dispute touches on is
space. Some space is private space. If a child shuts the door to

his room and works on a project inside, his sibling should be kept out. But if he works in the living room, or other common family area, his younger sibling has the right to be there, too. "You should help your child differentiate special uses of special areas," Dr. Berk suggests. "Common living space is common living space. It's up to the older child to decide where he wants to be and what he wants to do."

"When Cathy has friends over, Bradley often wants to play with them, too. But they tell me to ask him to leave. Should I?"

There is general agreement to this question: The answer is yes. "Get him away, even if he cries," is the consensus. Her right to play with her own friends, in privacy, should be respected. Of course, older children sometimes are willing to include a younger sibling in their play. And a younger sibling would do just about anything to be included. "My son would let his older sister's friends hit him over the head with a Tonka truck if it meant they'd let him play with them," a mother told me.

The problem can be more difficult if it is the older child trying to horn in on his sibling's friends. His sibling may not like it, but the friends may. "Older children can be very seductive," Dr. Berk points out. "When they get involved in games they can take them over, and the second child finds himself without the friends he invited over."

Mrs. Ruth Newman, a New York psychotherapist, found that to be the case with her own preteen sons. "My older son, Richard, charms the pants off Andrew's friends. They all want to see Andrew just so they can see Richard. So I encourage Richard to go out. It's worked out better."

Another solution is to invite friends over for each child. Otherwise, it's up to you to see that the child who is alone has something to do, so he is not just standing around watching everyone else having a good time.

The next two problems were posed by the mother of Alexander, ten, and Craig, eight.

"When I buy something for one child, the other one wants the exact same thing, whether he really needs it or not. Should I

keep the peace and buy it? Or should I buy what I feel is appropriate for each child?"

This problem introduces a much broader subject: Should you treat your children equally or individually? Here, all the votes are for the individual. Although children say they want total equality, it is impossible to achieve, it is a hardship on parents (did you ever try counting the number of sprinkles on two ice cream cones, or the number of Cheerios in two bowls of cereal?), and it is not what the children really want anyway. "Trying to be equal leads to neurotic parents and unhappy children," Dr. Robert Sherman of Queens College asserts. "Children are different, even from the beginning. They come out differently, they're different in their cribs. They have different styles and different preferences."

Dr. Ilana Reich comes right up against the problem with her adolescent daughters. If she buys one daughter a pair of Jordache jeans, the other wants the exact same style. The family recently faced a major decision: Should each girl get a Barbi Doll camper? Or should one get the camper and one the tent, so they can switch off and share? "I presented them with the choice. They went crazy deciding. They asked each other, 'Will you *always* give me the camper if I want it?' 'Will you *always* give me the tent?' 'No, it's mine.' "

A mother of younger children, Lewis, six, and Linda, five, faces the same kinds of demands on a less expensive scale. "If I give each child a cookie, my son will eat it even if he's not hungry. He'll choke it down before he gives it to her. He measures the milk. He has to have the same amount or more. I always try to give them the same to avoid jealousy, but it doesn't help."

That's the point. It doesn't help. Research has shown that a policy of providing two sisters "two of everything"—two swings, two sandboxes, two tricycles, two pairs of similar galoshes—does not prevent rivalry. The reason is that children are not really fighting over the swings, or the cookies, or the Jordache jeans. What they are fighting over is your love. What they need is the reassurance that they have it. So if one child happens to get a smaller cookie, simply point out that they come in different sizes. "That's how they come out of the box. It doesn't mean I love you less. Maybe the next time *you'll* get the bigger cookie." Speak to their feelings, not to their appetites.

"When it's one child's birthday, the other is jealous. He seethes when the presents are opened up. He doesn't understand why he doesn't get one. Should I give him a gift to soothe his hurt feelings?"

The goal should be to give him some recognition, psychologists suggest, without taking the limelight away from the birthday boy. A token present is a good idea so he doesn't feel he has been stranded in Siberia while everyone else is making whoopee. But the present should not be of the same magnitude as the birthday child's. Be careful about that, or you may be in big trouble. One mother bought a token present for one daughter on the other daughter's birthday. She found out, too late, that the birthday girl considered her sister's "token" better than her own gift. "What, you got her that record?" she complained. "That's what *I* really wanted."

If you decide against a small gift, you might take out the gifts your child received on his last birthday, and remind him when his next birthday will be coming up. Whether you choose a gift or not, try giving him some extra hugs and kisses on that day to remind him how special he is to you.

Some parents try really to equalize things by lighting an extra candle for their other child or adding a "Happy Birthday" verse for him. That undermines the meaning of a birthday, and raises the equality versus individuality issue again. If it is not the child's birthday, no such pretense should be made. Today is not his day. His day will come.

The mother of Grant, nine, and Scott, three, asked for advice with the next two problems.

"When my children fight, and they fight a lot, should I allow them to work it out for themselves? When should I step in? They're of very different sizes and ages, but Scott's got the fiercer temper."

The unanimous decision is to let them go at it as long as they are not hurting each other or bursting your eardrums. In that way, they will be able to express their angry feelings, and they will learn to reach some resolution without outside help. In case they are getting hurt (which is rare, despite the sound and fury), or you are going deaf, stop the action and separate them.

Interference generally doesn't do much good. Research has shown that when interfering parents change their ways, and stay out of it, less sibling squabbling goes on. In one study, the number of fights was cut in half when parents did not intervene, and the fights that did occur were much shorter than before.

If you find yourself irritated by the fights, anyway, remember that some fighting is a good thing. It helps children to work out their rivalrous feelings, to protect their territory, to establish their sense of self. Many children even enjoy it. Dr. Ilana Reich recalls going in to try to stop a fight between her daughters. They quickly set her straight. "What are you doing here? There's nothing wrong. We're just trying to decide something." Dr. Reich realized that her daughters' behavior bothered her because it didn't fit in with her own fantasy of a lovely family. "Bickering is just how they talk to each other."

If parents somehow manage to prevent their children from fighting, they shouldn't pat themselves on the back. They are stifling a natural part of the sibling relationship, and producing an unhealthy situation. "Fighting should be allowed," says Dr. Emily Rubinstein of Brooklyn Jewish Hospital. "Unless there's danger, it should be allowed, because it's there."

In the particular problem presented, it is the younger son who generally initiates the fights. Many parents assume that it is always the older or bigger child who is at fault. And even if it obviously isn't, the older child should "know better" than to hit back. That approach will undermine the older child's strength, turning it into a weakness. And it will make him resent his younger sibling, who "gets away" with everything. The younger child will suffer, also, if he thinks he can attack a powerful target without retaliation. He may earn some bruised ribs and blackened eyes at school before he learns his lesson. Of course, if either child is victimized by a bullying brother or sister, he must be offered parental protection.

"Whenever I come in during a fight, each child accuses the other of wrongdoing. 'He hit me!' 'He kicked me!' I don't know who's wrong. Should I try to get to the bottom and find out exactly who did what to whom?"

One expert opinion came in on the positive side of this question. "Children need help in finding out how the fight got started. If one child started it, someone else probably kept it going. So help them figure out how each one contributed to the situation. Give them examples of how to deal with it in other ways and how to avoid it in the future."

On the other side, some psychologists pointed out the futility of getting involved. You can't be a fair referee, they say, and if you place yourself in the middle, you are the one who will end up in the most trouble. Dr. Virginia Pomeranz, the pediatrician, has stated this view most vividly. "Playing judge and jury is dreadful. You come in and hear, 'She started it!' 'She did it!' It's exhausting to get into it. And you come off wrong with both of them anyway. You can't win. You're going to be accused of playing favorites by each one."

So what should you do? Say you don't care, and walk out? Dr. Robert Sherman suggests a bit more compassion. They are your children, and they are hurting. So you might say something like, "Apparently you both have good reasons. I assume you do because you're bright and good. But this is what happens in the end. No one likes it. Can we figure out a different way?" Dr. Sherman emphasizes the importance of stressing the positive. Although your children are fighting, they are good children. By letting them know you know that, they won't feel they have to defend themselves, and will be open to a new approach.

The last problem was presented by the mother of Philip, four, and Bill, two.

"My children don't fight too much physically, but there's a lot of verbal teasing going on at Bill's expense. Should I let it continue?"

Some teasing is part of normal development, psychologists agree. Most children do it to each other to help them feel better about themselves. The barbs are usually general and meaningless. In those instances, the children should be left to work it out for themselves. But some types of teasing can be very hurtful, especially teasing that really tells it like it is. If a boy always calls his overweight sister "fatty," the girl may suffer great emotional distress. It's up to the parents to stop him from doing it. It is also helpful to find out his motives, or else he will find other ways to hurt his sibling. You might ask him, "What's going on with you? Why do you want to hurt your sister? In our family we respect and love each other, and don't want to hurt each other. We hope you feel the same way about your sister." If the recipient of the teasing is old enough to protest, but doesn't, it is important to talk to her, too, perhaps to ask, "Why are you taking this? Do you have any part in egging your brother on? How can we make things better?"

Parents who prohibit physical fighting may find their children going wild with verbal abuse. "If children aren't so physically over-controlled, they don't develop sharpened tongues so early," says Dr. Bernice Berk. She prefers belts to barbs. "I don't want children to throw all their anger into the verbal. I'm less uptight about smacking. I prefer an occasional poke or hit. Saying things can be hurtful. A sock is over in ten minutes."

PARENT'S PET

You may find yourself liking one of your children a whole lot more than you do your other. He is more obedient, or smarter, or livelier, or you-can't-figure-out-what but you just like having him around. You call him the regal Prince, and your other child plain old Stanley. You brag about your favorite's accomplishments, no matter how modest, but you never seem to say anything special about that other child in the house (Stanley, isn't it?). Is there anything wrong in continuing to follow your natural feelings? Should you accept them and forget about it, or reject them and try to change?

If you realized the effects of parental partiality, you would try to do something about it. Certainly, there is nothing wrong with loving each child differently; your relationship with each will be unique. But treating one child like a prince and the other like a pauper will harm them both. The unfavored child will feel inadequate, jealous, and resentful, and may rebel against all your values. Ethan, not yet two, is already beginning to feel the jealousy part. His mother freely admits her differing feelings toward her two children. "Ward, my oldest, is my favorite. He is *my* boy. I know what's going on inside that brain of his. We think the same way. But as for Ethan, I could have picked him off Mars. I have no idea what he's thinking. I try not to let it show, but maybe it does. Maybe that's why Ethan acts so jealous, and comes up and tries to shove Ward and pinch him whenever he's on my lap."

The favored child often suffers as well, feeling guilty toward his sibling. He may unwittingly avoid success to give his sister or brother a share of the limelight. Some favored children react differently, and are terrified of failure for fear they'll fall from favor. "They feel a dread of not being preferred," Dr. Berk points out. "They feel they have to be favored in any social situation to be secure. There's the burden of always having to be 'easy.' " More to the point of this chapter, your children won't like each other very much, what with all the jealousy and all the guilt. Even as adults, they may try to keep their distance. A study of sixty-five adults, aged twenty-five to ninety-three, clearly demonstrated the divisive effects of favoritism. Of the 71 percent who admitted experiencing sibling rivalry at some time in their lives, 40 percent attributed it to parental preference for one child over the other, according to psychologists Helgola G. Ross and Joel I. Milgram of the University of Cincinnati.

The key to changing your actions, as a parent with a preference, is to understand your feelings. Do you prefer a particular child because he is the athlete you always wanted to be? Do you prefer your daughter to your son because you disliked your brother as you were growing up, and boys will be boys? Do you favor your youngest because *you* were the youngest? Do you prefer the child who listens to you, not the one who winks at your warnings and laughs during your lectures? If you find one child unbearable, maybe there is something you can do to straighten him out. Possibly he feels neglected and left out, or maybe the two of you are engaged in a power struggle. It's up to you to discover the basis of your feelings and his actions, and to somehow break the cycle. Whatever your reasons for favoritism, you should try to work them out, with professional help if necessary. Otherwise, everyone in the family is the loser, and sibling rivalry of the vicious variety will be on the loose.

Another spur to fraternal friction is the common practice of comparison. "Your brother cleaned off his plate. Why do *you* still have three peas lurking behind your mashed potatoes?" or "Let's see if you can throw the ball as far as your sister can." Your child may feel like breaking his brother's plate, or ramming the ball down his sister's throat if he hasn't matched her distance. If you can't help comparing, keep it to yourself. And don't try to change one child's behavior by using the other as an example. Your children are individuals, not reflections of each other.

LOOKING AHEAD

As you have noticed, there are no simple solutions to sibling rivalry. When you decide to have a second child, rivalry is part of the deal. You have to make a commitment to handle it. To do it right requires effort, and energy, and time for planning. You may wonder whether all the work is worth it. Once your children are out of the house, what is it to you if they meet for Wednesday luncheons and vacation together at the shore? What is it to you if they put 3,000 miles between them because they still haven't resolved the cupcake caper? Obviously, there are lasting benefits for siblings who remain friends. But if you want to be purely selfish for a moment, Mrs. Newman points out that your interests are very much at stake. "You're creating a situation for your old age. Will your children try to work together in being responsible for you if you're sick and need their help?" Or will a parent's nightmare come true? "Will you have to spend every other Mother's Day with a different child?"

7. Playing and Learning Together

THE CRY CAME LOUD AND CLEAR from her children's bedroom, "She's killing me! She's killing me!" Supermom ran in quickly to rescue her nine-year-old son from the dangerous clutches of her four-year-old daughter. But she was immediately told by embattled Barry to go away and leave his sister alone. "As I walked out of their room I heard him giving it to her. If he can kill her, that's okay with him, but he won't let anyone else touch her."

Another scene of love and violence was played out at a neighborhood park when two-year-old Cary tried to climb up the ladder to the slide. A tough three-year-old, muscles flexed and teeth clenched, blocked his way, and outmatched Cary started to head elsewhere. But then along came an even tougher four-year-old to defend his brother Cary's rights. "You let him up or I'll beat your brains out!" he threatened the toothy tormentor. His choice of words may not have been admirable, but his brotherly feelings of protectiveness were.

The above are examples of sibling loyalty, the best evidence that brothers and sisters really care about each other. Sibling loyalty is not a concept you hear much about. On the contrary, ever since Cain did it to Abel, siblings have been renowned for doing it to each other. Just say the word *sibling,* and *rivalry* (not *loyalty*) trips easily off the tongue. Images come to mind of nasty little boys springing slithering snakes on their unsuspecting sisters, of sly little girls taunting and torturing their still younger sisters. Should a kiss pass between siblings, it is only a "cover-up" for jealousy, parents assume, and they search for telltale toothmarks. Should a brother and sister give each other a hug, parents listen closely for sounds of breaking bones.

Parents aren't the only ones who have ignored the great positive potential of their children's relationship. Until recently, psychologists haven't paid much heed to the sibling experience as a positive force, either. The mother has long been viewed as the exclusive person of importance in a growing child's life. In recent years the father has also been paid his due, and studies of "father power" have proliferated. Now the circle of influence has broadened again, and researchers are taking a long overdue look at what has been termed the "sibling underworld." They are finally beginning to untangle the webs of that often wondrous relationship.

A dramatic episode that helped ignite the scientific interest in siblings involved a nineteen-month-old girl. She had been a perfectly normal, active, and outgoing child, the younger sister of a five-year-old boy and a three-year-old girl. When she was temporarily separated from her siblings she became severely depressed, she suffered retardation, forgetting how to walk and falling continuously, and she came close to starving. Her life was thought to be in danger, so she was reunited with her siblings. After just two weeks with them, all traces of her depression, retardation, and physical weakness were gone.

There is little wonder siblings have a powerful impact on each other. For about the first quarter of their lives they live in intimate daily contact with one another. They usually spend at least as much time together as each spends with the parents, and they are certainly on a more equal footing. As I interviewed Dr. Ruth Lesser, a New York City psychoanalyst, the conversation turned personal for a moment as she looked at me and said, "When you were born, there were *three* other people in your house. Each one had a powerful impact on you, your sister as much as your two parents. That aspect is often neglected."

But it is becoming harder to neglect a relationship that is generally the longest of a person's lifetime. Sibling relationships often last anywhere from fifty to eighty years, compared with the usual parent-child relationship of thirty to fifty years. After their parents die, siblings offer the only tie to the family of origin. After their own children grow up and leave home, siblings may turn to each other for guidance and support.

With today's family structure—or lack of it—siblings are becoming more important than ever. "As the nuclear family is being threatened by fragmenting forces, the sibling relationship helps to keep it together," points out Dr. Albert Solnit, Director of the Child Study Center at Yale University. Children may go from parent to parent to stepparent in this high-divorce era, but they still have each other. The trend to smaller families also portends a closer sibling alliance. Older adults will have fewer and fewer adult children to help care for them, and will come to rely more than ever on their siblings.

Earlier I provided a short summary of the benefits of the sibling relationship for the benefit of parents who feared the worst. But there is much more to it than that, and with every new study researchers are learning just how much siblings mean to each other. Certainly, it may be hard for you to believe, now, that your quarrelsome kids mean anything but trouble for each other. But they are influencing and enhancing each other in countless ways even as you are wondering why they don't get along.

In a paper with the phrase "Sisterhood-Brotherhood Is Powerful" in its title, psychologists Stephen Bank and Michael Kahn of Connecticut describe some of the functions siblings play in each other's lives. For one thing, siblings identify with each other, seeing themselves in the other. Identification is the "glue" of the sibling relationship, say Drs. Bank and Kahn. It allows a child to "expand on possibilities for himself by learning through a brother's or sister's experience." But there is another side to the coin. Siblings also differentiate from each other, intentionally taking on different or even opposite qualities (as in Dr. Frances Schachter's deidentification theory). They can each serve as a model for the other of what he would *not* like to be.

Siblings also serve as sounding boards for each other, providing a safe laboratory for experimenting with new behavior. Before they try out those swell swear words in front of their parents, they might give them a go in front of their siblings. If their new language earns them a swift kick from sister, they may decide not to risk their parents' wrath. Before an insecure adolescent ventures out wearing her latest lipstick, or latest blouse, or latest hairstyle, she may model it for an audience of one—her objective, if uninterested, sibling. After all, who wants to make a fool of yourself in front of your friends, but in front of your sister or brother, who cares?

To get down to more serious business, siblings perform direct and valuable services for each other. They teach each other skills, they lend each other money (after just some minor arm twisting), they introduce each other to friends. Drs. Bank and Kahn described the exchange of services between a pair of brothers aged eleven and eight. The older provided protection for the younger on the way to school, standing up to anyone who picked on him. In return, the younger boy pledged he would never "rat" on his brother to their parents. When the parents found a knife in the eleven-year-old's drawer, the younger boy said that he, not his big brother, had taken it. In that way he fulfilled his part of the bargain.

Having a sibling, say the psychologists, is a great asset when dealing with parents. Siblings can protect each other from their parents' abuse of power, or just plain bad moods. Jacqueline sees it in her own almost-adult children. "I know they're close because they gang up on me. When I get on my high horse and start yelling, they say to each other, 'Let's cool it. Let's not ruffle Mom's feathers.' So I find myself yelling at the walls after they've gone off together." Even younger children can protect each other from hurt. One mother remembers the first time she blew up at two-year-old Merle. Five-year-old Candi ran over to her tearful sister and assured her, "Mommy still loves you, Merle." I couldn't believe my ears when a similar incident occurred in my own strife-torn home. It was one of my bad days. I was cranky and so was Michael. I was tired of his hanging on me and I shooed him away. When Brian saw how upset his brother was, he told him that "Sometimes Mommy is tired, or Mommy is cooking, so she can't be with you all the time." Funny, as soon as I heard that, my mood brightened.

Siblings protect each other not only from wounds by parents, but wounds by friends as well. One day Beth came home from school looking depressed and feeling rejected. "Ali says she's not my friend anymore," she blurted out tearfully. Her older brother tried cheering her up. "What do you care? You have lots of other friends. You don't need her anyway." Few friends can match the loyalty of siblings.

Nor can they match the silence of siblings when secrets need to be kept. Gayle, just fourteen, admits to fighting a lot with her nine-year-old brother. But she also admits to confiding in him. "Being with my brother is different than being with my friends. He's so young. I can tell him anything. I don't have to worry that it'll get back to someone else." Drs. Bank and Kahn refer to a "conspiracy of silence . . . an unbreakable understanding of the children from which the parents feel isolated and excluded. Siblings are the guardians of each other's private worlds."

Siblings also introduce each other to new worlds, turning the outlawed into the acceptable, the prohibited into the possible. When child number one forgets to study and fails his first history test, his parents may forget to spare the rod. But once they are used to seeing red on test papers, they may be happily surprised by any speck of blue appearing on their second child's exams. Smoking dope, driving too fast, staying out too late—calamities all, when they happen to a first child, may be rated as only mild misdemeanors when a second child follows down the same "treacherous" trail. Moving away from home, when I was growing up, was seen as most treacherous of all. When my friend's older sister wanted to move just a borough away, her parents used all their persuasive powers in an unsuccessful attempt to persuade her not to. But when my friend wanted to move 3,000 miles away, she found her bags packed for her, airline tickets and all. Her sister's subway ride across the river had made possible her flight across the country.

Although Drs. Bank and Kahn covered a lot of sibling territory in their "Sisterhood-Brotherhood" paper, there is still some ground for further comment. Dr. Stefanie Wilner, psychologist at the Children's Psychiatric Clinic of the Long Island Jewish–Hillside Medical Center in Queens, sees two additional positive effects of the sibling experience. For one, having a sibling breaks into a child's feeling of omnipotence. "Without a sibling, a child feels the sun rises and sets in him. Some people never give up that feeling of omnipotence—we call them 'infant kings' and 'infant queens.' Siblings help children to learn to share and cooperate, and to develop a realistic view of their place in the family and in the world."

Secondly, Dr. Wilner points to the sibling contribution to sexual identity. "With an opposite-sex sibling, there's a better de-

marcation of your own sexuality. If siblings are of the same sex
—two boys or two girls—that can heighten sexual identity as
well. So siblings benefit in terms of psychosexual development.''

A sister with a brother, or a brother with a sister, may find it
easier to relate to the opposite sex. Nine-year-old Sean is not like
many boys his age, who shun females for football. He puts up
patiently with girls. He even likes some of them. His mother
credits his tolerance to the presence of older sister Andrea. ''He
feels no stigma about having girls as good friends, even as a best
friend. It doesn't embarrass him. He's not afraid of being called
a sissy. That's because there's a girl in the house.''

As you read about the wonders of sisterhood and brotherhood,
you may wonder about all the rivalry I described a chapter back.
It's still there, but it is not the whole story of the sibling experience. It is only part of it, and usually not the most important
part. Parents who can block out the sounds of battle can hear
what is really going on. Lainie, the mother of a school-age boy
and girl, is able to put it all into perspective. ''There's positive
and negative, but it goes in cycles. The bad part, the fighting,
passes. It comes back in a few months in a different form, but
then that passes, too. The good that develops, though, remains,
and is built on.''

The sibling relationship, as Lainie understands, is not a static
one. It changes even as children live together. It changes again
when they live apart, and when their own children grow up, and
when their parents grow old, and when *they* grow old. Scientists
are now looking at each of those stages to understand better the
significance of the sibling experience.

SIBLINGS UNDER STUDY

The most detailed research involves siblings as children—how
they respond to each other, how they play together, how they
learn together. In one study, the interaction between twenty-four
infants and their preschool siblings was observed at two points in
time—first when each infant was twelve months old, then when

each infant was eighteen months old. The sessions took place in a laboratory playroom with one or both parents present at all times. The six-month passage of time didn't make much difference to the sibling interaction. During both play periods the infants watched their older siblings closely, tried to imitate their actions, and took over toys they abandoned or gave them. The investigator, Dr. Michael Lamb, concluded that "older siblings may play an important role in facilitating the infant's mastery of the object environment."

The preschoolers were more likely than the infants to offer toys, to take toys, and to hit. But they also seemed to benefit from having a baby around. Dr. Lamb found that the more the infant smiled at his sibling during the first session, the more the sibling smiled at the infant six months later. That effect of the infants on their siblings' social behavior was totally unexpected, and indicated that both children may influence one another's development.

Dr. Lamb, assistant professor of psychology at the University of Michigan, also found a sex difference that was not unexpected. Girls were much more sociable toward their younger siblings than were boys. (Boys were ahead on only one measure of sociability—touching.) So in a sibling pair headed by a girl, the influence of the older may be especially strong.

Dr. Lamb concluded his work at the eighteen-month mark, but researchers at the University of Toronto took it two months further. They observed how thirty-four babies, each twenty months of age, interacted with an older sibling in their own homes. Each sibling pair was watched twice, for an hour at a time, while the mother went about her ordinary activities. The children did not seem to tire of each other's company; they stayed in the same room 90 percent of the time and interacted a great deal. The older children were more often the initiators of actions—both aggressive actions (physical and verbal) and social actions. Older brothers were the more physically aggressive, older sisters the more nurturant, acting like "little mothers."

Young children were, again, the great imitators: They followed older siblings as they said the ABCs, as they climbed onto a chair to reach the sink, as they put Lego pieces together. If they saw an older sibling pretend to be a monster, they pretended, too. Dancing around the room swinging one's arms, or blowing cake crumbs out of one's mouth, or pointing a cane like a gun, all became attractive pastimes if big brother or sister started the game.

Canadian researchers Rona Abramovitch, Carl Corter, and Bella Lando were amazed at just how much the older and younger children did together. They concluded that "there is a high level of interaction among siblings in the home and that the quality of this interaction is rich and varied." Apparently, what siblings do for each other is at least as important as what they do to each other. Despite the instances of aggression, "sibling interaction clearly is not based predominantly on rivalry."

To take another three-month jump in time, Helen R. Samuels of the University of North Carolina at Chapel Hill observed fourteen infants, each twenty-three months old, playing in the back yard of a private home. She observed each child twice, a week apart, for twenty minutes at a time. Both times, the mother was present, but only once was the older sibling there. The infants acted a lot different when a big brother or sister was around. They left their mothers sooner, they stayed away longer, and they traveled farther. They were more likely to play in an area of the yard where they couldn't see their mothers, and even to leave the yard altogether. They were also more likely to handle and inspect various objects in the yard, such as the shrubbery, a birdbath, a pile of powdered chalk. In summary, said the investigator, "The older siblings stimulated infants to explore a new environment more thoroughly." The infants not only explored more, they also enjoyed themselves more with big brother or sister present; they did less crying and less fretting.

To take an even bigger time jump, school-age siblings have been studied extensively by Dr. Victor Cicirelli, a professor of developmental and aging psychology at Purdue University. In many of his studies, the younger sibling was given a task to do. Either he had to do it alone, or there was a sister or a brother or a nonsibling to help. Dr. Cicirelli found that a sibling helper was better than no helper at all, and that sisters were more effective teachers than brothers. Sisters were also better at teaching their younger siblings than were unrelated children. If there was a four-year age gap between siblings, the younger child was more likely to accept help than if the age gap was just two years.

DIARY OF LOVE

As I looked over the studies I just described, it was hard for me to reconcile what the scientists were finding with what was happening in my own home. All that pleasant interaction . . . all that brotherly and sisterly concern . . . all those lessons being learned. One of my children seemed to fit quite well into that. Though Michael hits and hounds Brian, his hero worship is obvious. Every morning he wakes with the words, "Where's Byan?" If "Byan" takes medicine, he is willing also. "Byan" can make him laugh even more easily than "Byan" can make him cry. But what about "Byan"? I had been certain, all along, that big brother didn't return little brother's feelings, and that he would just as soon be an only child again. How can you love someone you tease, and taunt, and terrify? The most positive Brian seemed to get was the "I love you, I hate you" comment I mentioned earlier. Fortunately, I had been keeping a diary of my children's interactions ever since I decided to write this book. As I read it over I realized that yes, the "bad" incidents outnumbered the "good," but how could I have forgotten how marvelous those "good" incidents were, and how often Brian initiated them? Here is a small sampling of Brian's "goodies," proof that miracles can happen.

April 8: "This is *my* baby," Brian told his friends. "*My* baby has four teeth. *My* baby can walk." (Later, Brian told me that other babies are "yukky." The only baby he claimed to like was Michael. His pride in Michael was obvious, though he seemed to consider him a possession, not a person, at that time.)

May 29: As the three of us sat in a pizza parlor, a little girl toddled over and tried to grab Michael's bottle away. When Brian saw what she was up to, he shooed her away with a show of force and fist.

June 3: Michael was sitting in his high chair making the sounds "Da Da Da." Brian was delighted, and said proudly to his father,

"Look! Michael is saying Daddy!" (When Michael started learning more words, Brian told me that "Michael is starting to talk." I asked him if he *wants* Michael to talk. Brian replied, "I want him to talk to *me*.")

June 30: Brian announced that "I'll be as tall as the tree, but Michael will be as tall as the sky." He hesitated a moment, and then added, "But then I'll grow, and break through the clouds and be the tallest." (Brian wanted big things for his brother—but even bigger things for himself.)

July 16: Michael, as usual, was throwing his food off his tray. His father, annoyed with the mess-making, asked him why he was doing it. Brian piped in, "Because he *feels* like it." (That was the first recorded episode of sibling loyalty within our family, but there have been many more since.)

July 29: Brian made an announcement my husband and I were *not* waiting to hear. "I'm going to marry Michael when I grow up." "Why?" I asked, in horror. "Because we're best friends." (After about a month, his object of marital ardor changed to a little girl across the street. We couldn't have been happier.)

November 7: Brian says he doesn't like Michael to nap anymore because "I get lonely." And he pulls Michael's high chair next to his own chair because "Michael is lonely."

March 20: Brian told me about a nightmare he had. "It was about bad guys and good guys. Me and Michael were the good guys." (Sibling loyalty had even seeped into his subconscious.)

April 16: Michael, as always, preferred being carried to walking. I told him, "You're too heavy to carry." Just then Brian came to his brother's defense. "He is *not* too heavy to carry." (Is there no end to sibling loyalty?)

Some instances of sibling loyalty, however, exist only in the eye of the beholder. One day, at a country fair, Michael pulled his "I won't walk" routine. But we wouldn't carry him and he started to cry. Brian started to cry along with him. My husband and I were unhappy with the whole noisy scene, but touched by Brian's evident concern. "Why are you crying?" I asked Brian, feeling certain of the answer. "Because I'm thirsty!" he wailed. At that moment he cared a whole lot more about soda than he did about his sobbing sibling.

CHILD'S PLAY

If your children are exhibiting a lot more rivalry than loyalty, you may wonder if you can do anything to shift the balance. In addition to the suggestions in the last chapter on dealing with their rivalry, you might try actively encouraging their mutual play. That will be good for them as siblings—it will help to cement their relationship and foster their love—and good for them as individuals. "Emotionally, children of different ages derive so much from each other," says Doris Kramer, director of the Wantagh Jewish Center Nursery School on Long Island. Your younger child will imitate your older in many activities, learning countless skills, proud he can almost keep up. True, he may not learn as much from his siblings as from you, but he will have more fun learning it. One little boy would not give up "yeah" for "yes" until his older sister devised a "yessing" game.

Your older child, contrary to popular opinion, may profit even more than your younger one from their interaction. Through teaching, a child learns, and gains a sense of responsibility. By being with a younger child, an older develops kindness and gentleness. And because an older child is generally more skilled than a younger—balancing better, speaking better, running faster—his sense of accomplishment sharpens and his ego expands.

Before getting down to specific ideas for mutual play, educators stress the importance of organizing the environment.* Every play material should have its place, and every child should have enough of the play material to satisfy him. "If children have enough of something, they're not as tempted to grab from each other," maintains Ruth Selman, codirector of the Village Infant Center in Manhattan. "Give them each their own cup with as much as they want in it. And if they use that up, they can have more from a big pile in the middle. That method of organization leads to less friction and more joy."

*In this discussion I am indebted to Doris Kramer, Ruth Selman, Patricia Henderson Shimm, Eileen Eisenstark, Jimmy Esposito, and Judy McGerald.

The joy can begin early on, when the baby of the family is still only a baby. Don't keep him isolated. At certain times of the day deposit him close to big sister and encourage their interaction. You might say to your older child, "Look, your brother is trying to turn over," or "Pretty soon he'll be able to crawl around and to play with you." You can put the record player on so your children can enjoy music together. Perhaps your older child will sing or dance for your younger, or play a musical instrument, or put on a show with hand puppets. Whatever the specific activity, the important thing is that they are sharing an experience and sharing their time.

As your baby approaches the half-year mark, more activities become possible. Older siblings can make the perennial "peek-a-boo" especially exciting, leaping from behind chairs with a roar and a shout. "Come-and-get-me" is another baby-pleaser, as a hustling toddler pursues his scrambling sibling. "House" is yet another natural, even at this tender age. Baby usually gets to play baby, as he is diapered, fed, and bedded down by his "mommy for a day." Should big sister happen to roll a ball to her seated sibling, she might not get it rolled back, but she might enjoy watching the baby grasping it and pushing it out and dropping it in practice for the real thing.

A few months further along, and baby will be an even more engaging playmate. He can push toy cars or trains across a room and be part of a "race" he doesn't even know he is in. He can play the guest at a make-believe tea party so big brother doesn't have to sip alone. Together, a big sister and little brother can look at picture books and magazines. Even if she can't read yet, she can moo for the cows and oink for the pigs and ho-ho for Santa. Even if she gets it wrong, and oinks for the cows and moos for Santa, your children will enjoy their togetherness.

As your younger child gets older still, the opportunities for mutual play are almost endless. In general, "open-ended" activities are best, so each child can participate on his own level and not feel inadequate. One specific area, unlimited by age restrictions, is art. Siblings can draw together, paint together, punch and pound play dough together (if messes aren't minded). And they can each enjoy the activity in their own way. "An older child may build a house out of play dough, while a younger one just feels it and touches it and sees what happens when he squeezes it," says Jimmy Esposito, a teacher at First Impressions Preschool in New York City. "With paint, the older may make something specific. But the younger may be fascinated with the color or with just holding and moving the brush. Different mediums are enjoyed in different ways at different levels." If you provide crayons for coloring, you might give your younger child thicker ones so he can grasp and work with them easily. To encourage your young artists, you might also provide materials for collage—macaroni, fur, patches of wallpaper, or anything else you can think of. Each child will take pride in his imaginative creations.

Your aspiring artists may decide to switch career mid-collage, and become music lovers instead. Children love the standard singing games, especially when finger play is involved. Good music may soothe your savage beasts, setting loose their rhythm in a duet of dance. They may even pool their musical talents to produce an after-dinner entertainment for your watching and listening pleasure. Veronica, four, and William, one, did just that for their proud parents. Their mother gave their premiere performance a rave review. "Veronica sang and played toy piano. William danced and imitated everything she did. At the end of each song they gave each other a hug and a kiss. It was a riot. We wished we had a movie camera."

Perhaps your talented twosome would like to try their hand at drama? Their first endeavors may be as simple as making faces at each other—you be happy, I'll be sad. Then they might advance to horse and rider, with your little one sometimes squashed underneath a hard-riding cowboy (and getting a lot of practice at making that sad face). Surely you haven't forgotten "doctor," but just as surely you won't explain the rules to your innocent little children. Felicia, three, and Rodney, two, are still playing it in their own innocent way. She gives him her doll and says, "My doll is sick. Can you help her?" or "Will you be my dentist? My teeth hurt." But Jennifer, seven, and Justin, four, have discovered the seamier side of the game. "They play doctor the way *we* know doctor," their father told me. "We've noticed the sexual exploration."

You may find your children's dramatic play reflecting the latest world news, or even stale headlines. Megan, five, and Gail, four, play an interesting game with their matchbox garage and cars. It's called "gas line." Sound familiar? They line up their toy cars one behind another, then one car tries to sneak in the line, only to meet crashes and curses by the others. But then along comes a truck, and is allowed to drive straight to the front to fill up first with the precious commodity.

If you do nothing at all to encourage dramatic play, your children will be dramatic, anyway. But you can help make their play richer and more varied by providing the proper equipment—a big box full of costumes (mostly worn-out clothing and accessories), a place for your children to hide out (if only a sheet thrown over a table), and perhaps some miniature replicas of adult equipment, such as a stove, a refrigerator, an ironing board, telephones.

Your efforts will be well worth it, for you and for them. "My son and daughter really work out a lot with each other through dramatic play," Dr. Joel Sambursky of Brooklyn Jewish Hospital told me. "And I find out what's going on. I can hear my daughter parrot what's happened in school because she'll pretend she's the teacher and my son will be the student. So I know exactly what the day was like for her. I also get an opportunity to see what I've been doing with her because when they play mommy and daddy I can hear myself. 'I am sick and tired of your doing this same thing . . . blah, blah, blah.' It's like looking in a mirror. It's like watching a videotape of yourself."

Once your children tire of the more artistic endeavors of drawing, drama, and dance, they may get down to intricate manipulations with their hands. Here, they will depend a lot on the supplies you provide. If you have on hand puzzles for both their ages, they will both be kept busy. But you may be surprised to see them switching, your older child boosting his confidence on the easy four-piecer, your younger one stretching her skills on the hundred-piece jigsaw. Just one set of blocks—if there are enough in the set—can occupy both children. Your younger child may drop the blocks and inspect them and touch them and taste them. Your older child may build them into something recognizable—until your younger one knocks them down into an unrecognizable mess. Jacks, sorting boxes, bristle blocks that stick together, all appeal to children of varying ages. A cash register means different things at different ages. A young toddler will gain a sense of power from turning the crank and hearing the bell ring. She will enjoy manipulating the coins, pushing the buttons. An older child can incorporate the cash register into dramatic play, as she pretends she is a grocer or baker or shoemaker. And she may learn that a nickel and dime do not a quarter make. Counting beads also can span age groups; younger children learn about colors, older children about numbers.

Now that your children's finger muscles are in shape (and color concepts mastered), how about the rest of their bodies? Their large muscles need some activities, too. "Follow-the-leader" and "Simon says" can get your children moving, and liking it. "Tag," "Hide-and-seek," and "Red light, green light," are just a few games that younger and older children, and even adults enjoy playing together. You can initiate some real exercise sessions on a carpet or exercise mat. For some cash outlay, you can furnish your home with a toddler gym or junior gym, climbing mat or climbing house, rocking boat, or even karate training bag.

Your children can enjoy cooking together as you supervise, giving them each tasks appropriate to their skills. They may enjoy planting together and observing the miraculous transformation of lima bean to plant. And as they grow older, board games and card games can occupy them for hours precious to them, and precious to you. The opportunities for sibling play are indeed endless.

ROCKS AND LEAVES AND REMBRANDT

But one day you may wake to find there are only fifty-one cards in the deck; the play dough has hardened from overexposure; there are no more places to hide and not be found; the cash register comes up with a zero; the make-believe garage is out of make-believe gas, and even the truck can't get any. All of you have just *got* to get out of the house. Where can you go with children who are years apart?

If there are any traces of nature where you live, go out and find them. Nature walks appeal to older children and younger

children and children in between. Encourage them to notice
things, to pick up things (that aren't poisonous or gooey), to talk
about what they have found. If they pick up rocks, they can use
them for counting games at home. If they collect leaves, teach
them about the different kinds. Later, they can paste them or
make leaf prints.

You might just take your children on a trip to the store and talk
about what is healthy to eat and what is not. If you are a bit more
ambitious, you might take them to a zoo, or aquarium, or botan-
ical garden. If your younger child is old enough, a roller skating
or ice skating outing is a lot of family fun. And nothing beats the
seventy-six trombones of a good parade for a good time.

If you get really ambitious, you might decide that a good concert is just what your children need. But you might be wrong.
Doris Kramer, mother of four as well as nursery school director,
tried it when her children were young. "I took them to young
people's concerts at Lincoln Center. One son put his hands over
his ears and yelled, 'Get me out of here!' I thought to myself,
'What am I doing here, schlepping them from Queens for this?' "
She ran into similar resistance at museums. "My kids were
bored. They just rolled on the floor." Some children, though, are
mesmerized by music and mad about museums. Try it—but don't
be too disappointed if your children don't like it.

THE TENDER TEENS

As your children grow older your influence over their play activities, and their work activities, and everything else, will probably
diminish, but their influence over each other will grow. They may
act tough to you, but they will be getting soft on each other.
Researchers from Washington State University and Stirling University questioned more than 7,000 junior high and high school
students on their feelings toward family members. A sizable 65
percent reported feeling close to an older or younger sibling.
(That compared with 71 percent feeling close to their mother, 68
percent to a best friend, and 61 percent to their father.) Only 3
percent said they were "not at all" close to their siblings. "The
picture, then," wrote investigators Charles E. Bowerman and

Rebecca M. Dobash, "is one of fairly high levels of affect among the majority of brothers and sisters, with relatively few living in a state of conflict and rivalry producing negative feelings." Sisters were more likely than brothers to feel close to a sibling, and each sex felt closer to a sibling of the same sex. Younger siblings generally felt closer to older siblings than olders did to youngers. And despite the popular image of big happy families, adolescents in two-child families felt closer to siblings than did the teens from larger families.

As the researchers found, it is often the younger who feels most fortunate to have a sibling, come the scary age of thirteen. Shari didn't much like her big brother before then, but she started to notice that his presence, if not his personality, was doing her a lot of good. First of all, it gave her an advantage with her girlfriends. "They all liked my brother. When they found out I was his sister they started treating me a lot better, trying to make a good impression." Even more important to Shari, it gave her an advantage with her boyfriends. "They treated me with respect because they knew who my brother was. They acted differently to me than to my friends. With me, they had second thoughts about getting out of line."

Having an older sister isn't bad, either. I can personally attest to that. What my parents neglected to tell me about sex, which was just about everything, my sister filled me in on. I couldn't understand why the boys on American Bandstand didn't leave their hands on their partners' waists, but inched them upward as they danced. Diane told me why, and assured me that up was better than down. I spent hours sitting on the bathroom radiator watching Diane apply her make-up and tease her hair. (I also spent hours plotting to hide behind the living room drapes to watch her tease her boyfriends, but I never dared do it.)

Younger siblings do have a little bit to offer their elders. They can provide a brief respite from having to act sixteen and look eighteen, even if you are just fourteen. "I like being with my little brother sometimes. I become a kid again," says fourteen-year-old Simone, sounding as if her days of being a kid were eons ago. "Sometimes Nicholas and I go outside and play ball or something. Sometimes we go to the store. We kid around and play stupid word games. It's fun."

Even as teen-agers reach college age, the fun goes on. According to a study by Kathleen Marra of 350 college freshmen and sophomores, 60 percent said siblings made home life more pleasant, and 41 percent said they had more friends because of siblings. More recent research, conducted by Purdue University's Victor Cicirelli, looked at the strength of feelings of 100 college women toward family members. The most striking finding was that the women felt as strongly toward their siblings as their mothers on items of emotional support; siblings were viewed even more positively than were fathers in the role of confidante or helper. "This indicates the importance of siblings and their influence in this stage of life," wrote Dr. Cicirelli. In another finding, the college students expressed stronger feelings toward siblings spaced close in age than toward siblings spaced far apart.

GETTING OLDER, GETTING BETTER

When siblings move out of their parents' home, they still don't move entirely out of each other's lives. True, if they live far from each other, they generally don't get together often, but if they live within a hundred miles, there's a fifty–fifty chance they interact with each other at least once a month, research indicates. In another study by Dr. Cicirelli, 19 percent of older adults saw their closest sibling at least once a week, and 56 percent saw that sibling more often than yearly. They telephoned about as often as they visited, and those who didn't telephone or visit, wrote letters instead. Only a few had lost complete contact. Dr. Cicirelli concluded that "the majority of siblings continue to interact after they leave home and through their adult years into old age."

But just because they see each other, does that mean they like each other? Scientists seem to think so. In one study, 220 people aged fifty to eighty were asked which relatives (apart from those living with them) they felt closest to. About three of every four siblings made the grade. In another study of adults, almost half of those asked said they felt close to their siblings. Again, sisters came out very sisterly. An impressive 61 percent of the sisters questioned reported feeling close to their sisters, and most said they felt closer as adults than as children. But brothers were still haunted by their Cain and Abel origins. Only 39 percent of brothers felt close to brothers. Cross-sex pairs came out in between. The investigator Bert Adams, who authored a book on kinship, attributed the sisterly bonds to their common adult interest in marriage and children. But brothers often carried along the competitiveness and jealousy of childhood into adulthood, especially if one brother was socially and economically much better off than the other. One scientist noted this paradox: ". . . the families of siblings with least contact with each other are those of two brothers, the only ones with the same last name. . . ."

Not unexpected is the finding, also by Bert Adams, that the amount of interaction adult siblings have is related to the feelings of closeness they experienced as children. Their early relationship has lifelong significance. But things can happen to change that relationship, for better or for worse. Shana had been very close to her brother Richard, four years her senior. "When we were growing up there was no sibling rivalry between us. But things changed when he got married. I think his wife influenced him in his feelings. She came between us." In addition to mate trouble, there was mother trouble. "Our mother moved to Florida after our father died. She put a lot of responsibility on me for her personal life. She feels I have more time than Richard does because I'm single, and I'm more responsible. My brother feels Mom doesn't trust him. He resents me for it." But things have changed for the better again. "Our relationship got special again after he was ill. He mellowed after that. Now, the closeness is back."

The themes of adolescence and adulthood continue into old age—brotherly and sisterly love, especially the latter. Remember that figure of 65 percent—the proportion of teen-agers who reported feeling close to a sibling? That exact figure came up again in a study of the elderly. Of 300 people asked, 65 percent said they felt "close" or "extremely close" to the sibling with whom they had the most contact. Both males and females tended to name sisters as the closest sibling.

Siblings, in old age, can be important parts of each other's worlds, caring for each other, emotionally supporting each other, challenging each other, stimulating each other, loving each other. Of course, the ambivalence of childhood may still be carried along as they compare their own life's accomplishments with the other's. But despite any remnants of rivalry, the sibling relationship is rarely severed. In this time of marital instability and geographic mobility, with mates and friends falling by the wayside, sisters and brothers endure.

8. Making One Room Big Enough for Two

THIS CHAPTER WOULD NEVER HAVE BEEN INCLUDED in a book written a generation or two ago. Then, everybody did it. Well, almost everybody, except for the chosen few with the maids and the mansions. No one thought twice about two or more children sharing a bedroom, or even a bed. Sometimes whole families slept in one room, with children snuggled together on one of those sofas that even a four-year-old could transform into a bed. Most children took it for granted. They knew no other way.

Today, as more people have more space, those who *don't* have it think twice about it, or can't stop thinking about it. The thoughts often begin during a second pregnancy. Roseanne and Joel live in a desirable apartment complex, complete with playgrounds and patrol cars, on Manhattan's East Side. The only drawback is that three-bedroom apartments are impossible to come by. Roseanne and Joel spent hour upon hour of her second pregnancy sitting in their son Blake's room wondering how it could possibly absorb the sounds and fury of yet another active child. They rearranged the furniture countless times in their minds and still weren't satisfied that it could all fit in. The effort apparently drove them to mad imaginings. When I asked what they finally decided, Roseanne told me, "We've come up with the perfect solution. Joel and I will simply jump out of the window, and our children will have plenty of space." When I asked another couple who had gone through the same torment how they managed, they said, simply, "We moved."

Will your children really be deprived without a room to call their own? Some parents feel that the opposite is true. They see their children kissing and cuddling and loving each other, sharing secrets at bedtime, having friendly pillow fights and songfests, being comforted that the other is there. Jeanette feels that her daughters, Molly, twelve, and Miriam, seven, have benefited from sharing a room. "They're very close. They have to cooperate and respect each other in terms of space, both physical and psychological. They're sensitive to that." That's the *good* part. Children will learn to share because they have to learn to share. And they will learn, early on, that they can't always have things their own way. Many children say they wouldn't want it any other way—they like sharing a room. But that's not always so good.

"It may be a rationalization, because they're stuck together," points out Dr. Bernice Berk, school psychologist at the Bank Street College of Education. "Or they may be fearful about being alone, and suffer separation anxiety."

THE TROUBLE WITH SHARING

A single room can be shared successfully—and happily—by siblings. The problems that such an arrangement presents are solvable, as I will show in a moment. But first those problems must be confronted.

According to Dr. Berk, and many other psychologists, sharing a room is *not* the best way to grow up. If a newborn baby is unceremoniously dumped into its older sibling's room, the problems can begin immediately. Big brother (or sister) has literally been invaded. All his fears have come true, and are confronting him day and night: the lost time and space; the endless crying; the continual diapering and feeding and rocking. His child's room has been turned into a nursery, his parents into nursemaids. According to a University of Michigan Medical Center study, some children respond with regression and hostility, wetting their sheets and battling their brothers.

In Renée and Jay's apartment, a bedtime problem was created that hadn't existed before. Four-year-old Craig had always liked to talk a lot before he went to sleep. So Renée or Jay would stand by his bed and listen until his talking trailed off into slumber. But then little sister Toni came along, crib and all, and his talking sessions couldn't continue in the room they shared lest she wake up. So his parents put him to sleep in their bed. "I lie down with him until he falls asleep," Renée told me. "Later, Jay carries him back into his own room. Apparently it's confusing to Craig. He's said to Jay, 'How come you carry me back? I want to sleep in your room. I want you to sleep in my bed.' It's awkward, but we don't know how to deal with it differently. We don't want to make him be quiet, but Toni wakes up from every little noise. If only we had another room!"

As the children get older, the problems get worse. They may want to be alone, but can't. "Having their own room gives them an opportunity to get away from each other," says Dr. Joel Sambursky, clinical psychologist at Brooklyn Jewish Hospital. His own children, aged seven and four, do have separate bedrooms. "Our daughter can go in her room and say 'Nobody comes in here,' even when she's angry with us. Fine. It's her room. She can lock out the world if she wants. Sometimes a child needs that. When you have two people in the same room, you can't do that." Dr. Sambursky mentioned still other drawbacks of shared bedrooms. "Your toys are out and privy to everybody. And when you come in with a friend, where do you go if you don't have your own room?"

Where children share a room, parents report trouble at night —the children keep each other up—and trouble in the morning —one wakes the other up. They report trouble if one child is messy and the other neat, trouble if one child likes a night light and the other doesn't, trouble if one likes listening to the New Wave, and the other to the New York Yankees, trouble if one likes to do her homework aloud and the other needs quiet, trouble finding room for all the toys and clothes and junk that keep piling up and just won't go away. It's not the situation most parents would choose if they had a choice. Ronna, mother of a ten-year-old boy and seven-year-old girl, put it most succinctly. "Do I love it? It's what I have now. Do I want another bedroom? Sure."

BOYS AND GIRLS APART

What it comes down to, basically, is space—children need a lot of it to explore, to express themselves, to develop as individuals —and to the privacy that growing children crave. Privacy can be especially crucial to siblings of the opposite sex. Some parents are apparently aware of that. In fact, a few of my friends used that insight to "console" me after I had a second son. "Well, at least you can put them in the same bedroom. If you had a girl, you'd need a separate room for each." But some parents are not so psychologically attuned. They keep a teen-aged boy and girl together in the same bedroom or, less commonly, in the same bed. That's only asking for trouble, psychologists say—big trouble.

"For a girl to be standing in her room in her bra and panties, and to have her adolescent brother come in and gape or poke fun, can be very traumatic," says Dr. Sambursky. "And vice versa. For a boy who's going to sit there in his jockey shorts and have an erection, and for a sister to be walking in, can be very embarrassing." When lights are out, the embarrassment may escalate. "It's a problem to have to hide masturbation or wet dreams from the person in the next bed. To have a sibling of the opposite sex become aware of those activities can be traumatic for both children. It becomes very arousing sexually and creates problems."

Sexual activity between siblings is probably more common than you think. Of 796 New England college students recently surveyed, 13 percent reported having had sexual experiences with a sibling. And they didn't all wait until adolescence to have them. Forty percent were under the age of eight at the time of their experience. Many psychologists suggest that opposite-sex siblings have separate bedrooms by the time they reach school age, when they become more conscious of their sexual differences.

HERE, THERE, OR ANYWHERE?

If this discussion has increased your pregnancy pangs, or driven you to the want ads in search of a second job to finance a third bedroom, relax. If you plan carefully, and anticipate the problems, your current apartment may suit your family's needs just fine. Take first things first: infancy. When you bring your second child home from the maternity center, just where should you put her? You have three basic choices: Your older child's room, your room, or someplace else. Let's look at those alternatives, one at a time.

Put her immediately in your first child's room, and you may arouse some of the hostile feelings I described earlier. If they become hostile enough, your baby may be in real danger. Better wait until your older child has become somewhat adjusted to the new situation, and until the baby's sleep patterns are a little more stable. After a while, older children often announce that they *want* the baby in their room. If your child makes that request, and lives happily through the first few days of togetherness, you are home free, at least for a while.

Many parents choose to keep the new infant in their own bedroom during the early months. That arrangement can work out well, but in some families it makes at least one member unhappy. The most obvious malcontent is the member left out of it—big sister (or brother). Every time that *she* has tried to crawl in with Mother and Dad she has been swiftly removed, no questions asked. So where does this scrawny, screaming little baby come off sleeping with her parents, while her sister is banished to her own lonely bedroom? If she hasn't thought about hating the baby until now, this might be a fine time to start. She may well be resentful and confused, unable to understand why the baby is in and she is out. According to researchers at the University of Michigan Medical Center, this sleeping arrangement "epitomizes feelings of exclusion and displacement," and often produces sleeping disturbances and regression. One older sister asked for a bottle at night when she saw her baby brother sleeping with her parents. A sixteen-month-old boy woke frequently to ask if his new brother was in their parents' room.

What about you? To be selfish for a moment, you might consider what life will be like with an infant in your bedroom. Will you whisper, not talk, for fear of waking him? Will you make love under cover, if at all, for fear his eyes will be on you? Hannah and Owen kept little Eliza in their room for a whole year, until they moved to a house. They don't have fond memories of that year. "We were afraid to talk. We were afraid to make love. We were afraid to do anything. We tiptoed around our own bedroom. It was not pleasant going through it. But looking back on it, it seems totally absurd." When you are tired of whispering and making furtive love, and want to sleep, you may not be able to. The baby turns over, and you're up. The baby whimpers, and you're at her crib, checking her diaper, or smoothing her bedclothes, or doing anything else you can manage in the dark. Reva and Hillel went through it for fifteen months, way too long, they now agree. "Ari wasn't a restful sleeper," Reva recalls. "I heard everything. If he'd been in another room, I wouldn't have heard all his noise. It disturbed my sleep. That's why I was always so tired. And I went to him and woke him sooner than I might have. Sometimes children are fretful and then just go back to sleep. But since he was here I'd wake up, and everyone would be up."

If you are willing to sacrifice your intimacy, and privacy, and sleep, for the good of your second child, consider that it may not be so good for your second child. If you pick him up for every peep and squeak, you may be creating sleeping problems, and a baby who just won't stay bedded down for the night. Also, you may not be giving him the best start for life as a unique individual. "A child is a separate person from the two parents who are married and have a relationship," Dr. Emily Rubinstein, psychologist at Brooklyn Jewish Hospital, points out. "A child should start life developing on his own."

If the arrangement is just for a few weeks, there are some compensatory advantages. The parents learn the rhythms of their new baby, learn to be sensitive to his signals and his needs. If the child is premature, or requires a close watch for any medical reason, there may be no choice. To make things easier for your older child, explain just what the reason is. You might also say, "The baby cries at night. He'd wake you up if he were in your room. And you'd smell his diapers. So for a short time he'll be with us. Later he'll share your room, and you'll be buddies in there."

In addition to these two choices, there is always "elsewhere." And just where is that—anywhere else you can find a cozy corner in your home to fit a crib or a bassinette. It can be a section of your dining room, or hall, or foyer. You can wheel the baby there at night (keeping him in your room by day). Or by dividing that area off from the rest of the apartment, you can make it almost a tiny bedroom for baby for day and night. There are a number of ways you can accomplish this. Most simply, you can place some bookcases or room dividers around the area to create a symbolic separation. Another good solution is to put a track on the ceiling and floor and hang vertical or horizontal blinds around the alcove. They can be opened for air circulation or closed for privacy. Still another alternative is to have a carpenter build a plywood wall around the area. To help keep out noise, interior designer Lynn Bressler of New York City suggests padding the wall and upholstering it with fabric—you can do it yourself with a staple gun. And to keep down the expense, you can have louvre doors put in. You may decide to mix things up a bit and have a plywood wall form one side of the alcove and blinds the other. If you are willing to put in some planning time, you can create a private haven for your baby, and safeguard the privacy of the rest of the family as well.

A DEN FOR ME OR A ROOM FOR YOU?

But there will come a time when your second child will need more than an alcove. Should you put him in with your older child at that point and risk all the problems that that move may create, or should you look elsewhere again? If you have a den, you have an obvious place to look. But sometimes the needs of the parents, or of one parent, take on disproportionate significance. "My husband's comfort has always come first," Lois told me. When Lois and Dan chose an apartment, one of the three bedrooms was earmarked as his personal den for reading and television watching. All was fine until second child Estie turned eighteen months and decided that night was not for sleeping. "She slept from seven until nine in the evening, but then she woke up and wanted to get out and play. I wouldn't let her out, so she stayed in her crib singing and playing. My five-year-old son woke up screaming when he heard her." It got so bad, Frankie even became afraid to walk into his room in the evening to attempt sleep—afraid that Estie would still be up. He told his mother, "Oh, she's up. I can't go in. She'll bother me." Lois tried to reassure him. "But then I would go crazy myself. I'd tell him it's her room, too, that he should turn his head the other way. If it was my crazy day, I'd scream. If not, I'd put him on the couch." Frankie ended up on the living room couch many a night for two or three months. Estie is finally sleeping better, but Lois still leaves a pillow and blanket on the couch, just in case.

During all that nocturnal turmoil, Dan spent evenings relaxing in his private den. What does Lois think of that? "He wants his room, but sometimes I feel that it's not right, that I should put one child in that room. When Estie had sleep problems, I was up all night. It was driving me up a wall. But my husband had his room."

In that situation—where sharing did *not* work out—perhaps the living room or parents' bedroom could have doubled as a den. Flexibility is important when the emotional needs of children are at stake. Some families use an extra room as a playroom, rather than as a den or as a third bedroom, and sleep their children together. But it is still preferable for each child to have the privacy of a separate bedroom. If you follow some of the space-saving ideas I outline later in this chapter, each bedroom can serve as a playroom as well.

A few valiant parents do more than give up a den to meet their children's needs—they give up their own bedroom. They reason that their children need a lot of space for playing and creating, and they only need space for sleeping. So they go into the child's room, and the children share their larger room. Or else they move to the living room, and the children each have a separate room.

Those maneuverings present some interesting design challenges. For one, how can two large adults and a king-sized mattress find happiness in one small bedroom? It can be done, even in an eight-by-twelve room, says interior designer Bernice Finkelstein. She suggests putting the mattress on the floor wall-to-wall, and then having built-in cabinets for clothes and books and everything else all around the walls. Even the television can be placed up on the wall, so you don't have to feel at all deprived.

Choosing to sleep in the living room on a high-riser or a pull-out sofa may seem out of the question at first, but on second thought, not so bad. Once your children are tucked in for the night, you have your own area for relaxing, for entertaining, for making merry in any way you like. And you will feel secure that what your children are doing in their separate quarters is sleeping, not scaring each other with ghost stories, or making merry in a way you don't like.

So should you make the big sacrifice to give each child a separate room, or at least one half of a big room? If you find yourself thinking of it as a big sacrifice, you will probably resent it and it won't work out. But if you can do it with grace, do it. Dr. Bernice Berk of Bank Street points out its importance. "Parents do have rights. But if a choice has to be made between a big bedroom for the parents and no space for the children, or between a bedroom and den for the parents and a shared room for the children, there's only one choice to make. It's better if the parents do without the big bedroom, or the bedroom and den. Children in one small room just don't have a chance to develop as individuals as well as they should."

DIVIDE AND CONQUER

But your apartment may not lend itself to any of the solutions I've suggested. Perhaps your bedroom is just as small as the children's. Or perhaps your children have compatible personalities and sleeping habits, and you think they would do well together. You are still not off the decorating hook. You have some work to do in their room to make it a bedroom fit for two.

Even when they are young, it is important that each child have a separate space in the room, a place for working alone, playing alone, even for just daydreaming his own private daydreams. Some parents hesitate breaking up an already small room into still smaller parts, but small is okay for kids, points out James Morgan, professor of interior design at Pratt Institute in Brooklyn. "Kids are little, so the scale of space is different to them. Spaces in their areas can be smaller than adults would want to be in. To children, small is cozy." Professor Morgan suggests providing the older child with some private space as soon as the new baby is brought into the room. "Privacy is necessary so he feels he hasn't given up everything the room used to represent. He should have a nook or corner of his own, where he can feel the eyes of the infant, and to some extent even his mother's eyes, are not on him." Psychologists agree that each child should have a definable place all his own, even if it looks like a sad little cubbyhole to his large-scale parents.

Private space can be accomplished in ways elaborate or simple. It is possible actually to have two layers in a single room by building a raised platform, or balcony, as a private play space, with a ladder to reach it. The room can really be two in one by placing a bed up there, also. But the child living in the upper must be old enough to manage getting up and down, and not falling off. Also, you should be planning to stay put in that apartment or house long enough to make the building effort worthwhile.

More practically, and easily, you can adapt the suggestions for closing off the infant alcove. If you use a plywood wall, you can attach a blackboard or bulletin board to it to make it even more functional. You might simply use shelves as a room divider, closed on the bottom to provide visual privacy, open on the top to allow a flow of air and light. Designer Bernice Finkelstein provides still another idea: Pile up modular storage units to divide the children's areas. If you pile up more units near the wall, and progressively fewer out into the room, you can create a dramatic decorating effect (and climbing fun for your children). If you are convinced the room is simply too small for any real division, a symbolic division may do. Perhaps even some plants or trees can do the trick, making each child feel king of his own small castle. (If your children are small, make sure you choose greenery that is not harmful when eaten.)

You can divide the room up by time, not just by space. Try setting up time blocks for each child to have the room alone, and keep the other child busy elsewhere in the house or outside. You can set up special hours for homework for each child, when the other is expected to keep quiet or keep out. You and the clock and the carpenter (or just a simple curtain) can make each child feel like his room is his own.

DOING IT THEIR WAY

There is another need that should be met in a shared room or any room: the need for individual expression. Sherry, the second daughter of two, felt deprived of that in the room she shared with her sister. "We couldn't create our own space. We were't allowed to put anything on the walls. We had no control over our furnishings. I should have been encouraged to express my personality. I felt it just wasn't my room, anyway."

One way to individualize a room is to give each child as many of her own things as possible: her own clock, her own cubes to keep toys in, her own dresser to keep clothes in, her own work space, even her own half of the closet by partitioning it with wood or installing two rods. And each child should have her own area of the wall for displaying creative efforts. You might provide them each with a bulletin board with a different color frame, or with an individual tack board. If your children are of very different ages, it is important that their furnishings and belongings are age-appropriate, even if the disparity gives the room an uneven look. Don't force your four-year-old to use a big desk because you want it to match that of your ten-year-old; don't keep your tall and gangly twelve-year-old in a youth bed just because your six-year-old still prefers one.

Another good way to personalize a shared bedroom is to use your children as decorating consultants. Even five-year-olds have definite preferences in color. When shown an array of wall coverings, they can pick out a favorite. By allowing your children to help decorate, you give them some control over their environment and help them develop their taste. But what if one likes orange and the other red, one prefers sleek contemporary lines and the other ornate Mediterranean? How do you please them both and still create a livable room? You can do your part by providing a coordinated, neat background with the floor coverings, curtains, and bedspreads. Then let them create their designing magic on fabrics, throw pillows, wall posters—anything that can be changed easily with their evolving tastes. If they each have their own section of the room, it makes it easy to decide who does what where. The total effect may not qualify the room for *House Beautiful,* but it will make your children proud of their room and themselves.

If a boy and girl share a room, some extra care must be taken to keep the room from being too "masculine" or "feminine." Suellen remembers the room she grew up in with some amusement; her brother's half was papered with a map, her half with a "girlish" weave. But a shared room does not have to be schizophrenic. It should simply have a neutral, clean look. Designer Lynn Bressler uses lots of lemon yellows, whites, and greens in rooms shared by boys and girls. Bernice Finkelstein recently designed such a room in gray, red, and white. Another interior designer, Jody Locker of New York, leans toward plaids and bright, primary colors. The children can, of course, individualize the room with cushions and artwork and assorted paraphernalia. There may come a time, however, when the girl wants more "feminine" furniture and the boy something more "mannish." That's a clue that you should start thinking about separate bedrooms.

STRETCHING SPACE

A major complaint in a shared room is that there just isn't enough room to fit in everything. But there are a number of ways you can make the most of the space you have. When you initially move in your second child with your first, your infant will have two main furnishing needs: a place for sleeping and a place for changing. If space is cramped, sleeping can be done in a portable crib for the first year or so. If you are buying or borrowing a crib, be on the look-out for one with drawers underneath. That can save the space of a separate dresser. If your crib doesn't have drawers, don't waste that valuable area underneath. Use it to store blankets, presents, boxes of diapers, or other bulky items. And don't waste the wall space above the crib, either. You can put cubicles for toys running up the walls along the side and front of the crib.

You can also save the space of a large changing table. Many infant-supply stores sell pads you can attach to the top of a chest of drawers. To make it soft, you can cover it with terry cloth. Also available is a small changer—a plastic tray with a pad and a belt—that fits onto the rails of a crib. If you need a new dresser for the baby, you might choose one with a flip-top changing table on top. (There are also desks that convert to changing tables, but I doubt your older child would enjoy studying on such a dual-purpose surface.) Some parents forego all the above and change the baby in the crib or on a bed or even on the dining room table.

As your baby gets older, you should throw out or give away or store elsewhere things she no longer uses. If she is bored with the swing, get rid of it. If the playpen has become a prison, take it away. Free up the space for more interesting activities.

There will come a time when your baby is too big for a portable crib or even a crib. It's bed time. What should you do? If you had used some foresight, you would have already done it. Your first child would be sleeping in a bunk bed or a high-riser, and there would be a bed all ready for your second child.

Bunk beds are perfect for privacy and for saving space. Each child has his very own wall space to decorate. Each child has privacy from his sibling's roving eyes. And what would have been sleeping space can now be play space. A child of five is generally mature and cautious enough to occupy the upper deck. If you decide to shop for a bunk bed, make sure the mechanism locking the beds together is strong and child-proof, and that the guard rail along the top bunk is high enough and sturdy. Also, see that the ladder for climbing to the top provides good footholds, with a stable method of attachment to the bunk. Slats are more comfortable for barefoot climbing than are rungs. Some bunks convert to single beds. That's a good option to look for in case you move, or if either child decides he has had quite enough of bunking with his brother. (Teen-agers often feel too grown-up for bunk beds.) Some bunk beds also have storage drawers under one or both beds. When space is tight, the more drawers the better. If you plan to put the bed in a corner, you might choose a bunk with one bed at a right angle to the other. In the empty area under the top bunk, you can place a desk or a chest of drawers.

As a variation of the bunk bed, you might decide on loft beds —beds built on raised platforms. The space underneath can be used for a desk and dresser or anything else. Each child would have a private, quiet area, and space would be saved. But there are some disadvantages to loft beds. If your ceilings aren't high enough, your children may suffer a lot of head bangs. If you don't have high windows with fans for good air circulation, your children may stifle in their sleep. (Hot air rises.) And if the room isn't brightly lit, the area under the loft may be depressingly dark.

Another popular space-saving choice is a high-rise bed. One bed fits neatly under the other during the day and can be pulled out and raised up at night. In some models, the two beds can be completely separated. Some parents keep them apart not only at night, but during the day as well, so they serve as compact versions of regular twin-sized beds. Those parents feel it is important that both children can see their beds during the day, and can plop down on them whenever they want to read, to entertain, or just to while away the time.

If the thought of bunk beds and high-risers leaves you up in the air, perhaps you would prefer a captain's bed (also known as a storage bed), an efficient space saver with its drawers underneath. Whatever you decide on, don't waste the area underneath the bed. Whether you use it for another bed, for drawers, for storage, or for hiding away the drum set you want your child to forget he has, use it.

If you have some extra money to spend, and want to be daring, you can decide on one (or two) of those beds that pop right out of the wall at night. Or you can have an architect build one that slides smoothly out. The disappearing bed will free up space for daytime play. But your child may miss the security of knowing his bed will stay put, just where he left it last.

Once you have decided where to put your kids at night, you still have to figure out where to put all the things they play with during the day. If you can get those out of the way, you will be amazed at just how much free space your children's room has.

As your main storage area, you might have shelves or a multi-drawer storage unit built up along the walls. It would be good if at least part of the unit is open so your children can see what they have, take it out, and most importantly, put it back by themselves. For extra games and toys, you can use wood or plastic stack boxes, or metal vegetable stack-ups, or even baskets hanging by chains or ropes from the ceiling. Some children's tables can double as storage boxes, and chairs open up to a surprise storage space. If you design your children's closet right, you may even save the space of chests and dressers. Put in an extra rod for hanging extra clothes, shelves inside the door and along one wall, clear plastic drawers on the bottom (or as much of the above as you can fit in without wrinkling everything), and you have created the equivalent of two dressers and a closet all in one.

If your children sometimes need a lot of work space, but not always, you might look for a desk with a drop leaf that can be lifted to create a bigger work area. If your children have a lot of space-consuming projects going, and you are handy or have a carpenter handy, you might build a desk top that can fold flat against a wall, or even against the inside of a closet door, and be flipped down for use. If your children have a train set but nowhere to lay down the tracks, you can try hinging the train tables to the wall so they will collapse when not being used.

ALL THROUGH THE HOUSE

As creative as you are, there is just so much you can do with one small room. There will be times your children won't want to be cooped up there—spacious or not—and will transform other areas of the apartment into play areas, whether you like it or not. But you can keep the damage down if you do the transformation yourself. If you fold up your dining room table during the day, your dining area can make a fine, safe play space. What about your neglected terrace? Sweep it up, maybe screen it in, and you have a first-rate playroom. If you have a basement, don't let it waste away, gathering molds and mildew. Put in some elbow grease and some toys, and your kids won't stay away. Even your living room can serve as a playroom if you store away your museum pieces and your glass coffee table. Buy casual, sturdy furniture that resists stains and toothmarks. More formal furniture can wait until your children are old enough to write on composition paper, not the couch, and to get a basketball through a hoop, not the top of the lampshade.

If you think you have sacrificed a lot for your children, consider Flo and Irwin. They actually turned their very own bedroom into a child's playroom. Out went the king-sized bed, headboard and all. Out went the triple dresser. Out went the armoire. In came a high-rise bed and one wall unit for themselves. In came a little table, and little chairs, and toy shelves, and a toy chest, and lots of toys for their two children. Why did they do it? "We never used our bedroom during the day," Flo related, "and our children really needed the space. Now they have two playrooms—their own room and ours—so they can play separately if they want." How has it worked out? "So far, so good," Flo told me, after two months of sleeping in a playroom. "I actually use my room more now than I used to, reading or sewing on the high-rise." She has only two minor complaints: She misses her old headboard, and she can't seem to find a comfortable position for watching television from her bed.

Some parents make a lesser concession to their children; they store some toys or games in their own bedroom. One couple found a clever way to do it. They built toy shelves on the walls behind their drapes so no one would ever know that Mr. Potato Head and the Incredible Hulk lurked nearby. You might prefer to build shelves or cabinets for toys in a hallway, in a garage, or even under a stairway. One woman was so fed up with her children's playthings strewn all over the place, she had a wing built onto her house solely for the storage of toys.

FRIENDS, FIGHTS, AND LIGHTS

Once you have solved the design problems and figured out what to do with all the furnishings and footballs, you are still left with the personal problems involved in room-sharing. Those problems can create frustration for your children, and require finesse from

you. One of the major problems I remember in sharing a room
with my sister came around bedtime. She liked to read late into
the night; I preferred sleeping. So I had a choice of being blinded
by the light or suffocated by the covers I pulled over my face to
keep the light out. If that same battle is going on in your home,
you might set aside a special reading area outside the children's
room for your lover of great literature or great comic books. But
if you are very clever about the lighting inside the room, that
might not even be necessary. You should install an overhead
light for daytime play, and small, individual reading lamps for
night use. Look for reading lamps with very focused light and
with dimmers, so that your reader can read without awakening
your sleeper. Such lamps can usually be attached to the wall or
to the headboard of a bed. If your children sleep in a loft or bunk
bed, you can attach a lamp to the safety rail.

Bedtime can bring still other problems to mismatched roommates. One child likes to sleep with a night light in the room or
the light on in the hall; the other needs total blackness. One child
likes to talk and tease and giggle before she settles down for the
night; the other prefers lights out, mouths shut. Your only re-
course is to send one child to sleep before the other. Generally,
the younger child will have the honor of being first to bed. It may
only take ten minutes or so before it is safe to send in your other
eye-rubbing, yawning sleepyhead, and shut the night light off (or
put it on). Chances are your older child won't object strenuously
to being "forced" to watch some more television or to listen to
one more record.

Once you have the nights down pat, you may think your trou-
bles are over. But things may seem worse, not better, in the light
of day. Your little one may start getting into your big one's toys,
dragging them out of boxes and knocking them off shelves. Your
big one may feel his possessions, and privacy, are being invaded.
It is your job to see they are protected. Keep your older child's
toys up high, too high for little fingers to reach. You might even
keep some toys in a chest or cupboard with a padlock, and give
your older child the key.

What about the inevitable fights—those times you would love
to say to each child, "Go to your room!"? You certainly don't
want them to go to the *same* room, where arguing might escalate

into screaming and harmless hitting into a bedroom brawl. You want some quiet. You want a cooling-off period. Try sending one child to your room and the other to their room. Or use the living room or den as a temporary "isolation booth" for one of your children. But if the fights start suddenly to escalate in number, investigate. Your children may be having too good a time in your room, especially if it is decked out with telephone, phonograph, and color television, and they may be "fighting" to get in.

As your children get older, you will have different problems to deal with. The inevitable fighting over friends can be especially acute for children who share a room. "It's my room, too!" is the common refrain of the child told to scram. Your options are limited. If the room is very small, you may not want to invite a friend over for each child for fear of crushed ribs and claustrophobia. Your best bet is to invite a friend over only when your other child is out. Otherwise, it is important that you establish a separate play area in your home so that the brother who has been bounced has somewhere to retreat.

Once your children reach school age, you will be haunted by their homework, especially if they can't manage to do it in the same room at the same time. In this case, you may be called on to make the sacrifice, as one child converts the kitchen table into a makeshift desk. The other alternative, which I already discussed, is to have them do their homework at different times. You may find that the whole problem disappears if you give them separate desks on opposite sides of the room so their eyes don't meet and shoulders rub while they are conjugating verbs or contemplating Plato.

Bringing up two children in one room is not ideal. Your children will have less privacy. You will have more problems. But it is your attitude that can make it a livable, workable situation or a congested, chaotic mess. Roz has an attitude that makes it work for her preteen daughters. "It's crowded here, but they don't ask for much. They're pretty satisfied. I don't tell them 'This is terrible. Look at how we live. If only you each had your own room.' I'm quite content, even if it is crowded. I've lived in worse. In comparison, this is luxury." If you make the most of what you have, it will be more than enough for your children.

9. Meshing Schedules and Making Time

ONCE YOU HAVE FOUND SPACE in a two-bedroom apartment, you face an even tougher challenge: how to find time in a 24-hour day. It takes a lot of time to be a mate to one spouse, perhaps an employee to one employer, a parent to two children, and a home-maker to a score of walls, ceilings, and floors, and everything in between. Can there be anything left over just for you, for your dreams and your daydreams, your hobbies and your goals?

Many second-time parents think not. Time is something other people serve if they have done something bad; it is something other people make if they have met someone good. But person-ally, the only thing second-timers notice about time is its lack.

Some parents are frustrated by their endless duties, by the newspaper that never gets read, by the shower that has gone from a leisurely interlude of song and solitude to a soap-and-splash affair. Others accept it as the price they pay for dual parenthood. But that price is too high, even if it is only for a few years. "Parents need personal time in this madness," says Dr. Jane Nemiroff, assistant professor of home economics at New York University and the mother of two. "Many women feel they must be at their family's service every minute, that no one can do it as well, that they must meet everyone's demands. It's tied in with a guilt trip, with a fear of letting go. They may find they can meet their family's needs, but what do they sacrifice? They sacrifice time to themselves."

You probably don't need convincing that time to yourself will make you feel better. If you know that evening will be yours, alone or with your mate, you can better make it through your daily dose of spit-up milk and muddied floors and battling brothers. But won't it psychically scar your children to find out you are reading Russian literature by yourself rather than *The Three Little Pigs* to them? What if they want you to bathe them, but you are out bathing yourself in a hot whirlpool or a cold lake? Actually, if you don't overdo it (and if you see that when you are not there, someone reliable and loving is), your children will be better off for your sometime absences. They will find you less irritable and resentful when you are around; they may learn to respect you as a person, not just love you as a mommy or a daddy; they may even become better people themselves. "Too many parents suffocate their young children by waiting on them," points out Dr. Nemiroff. "They should begin letting go, even in infancy. In that way children will find out about the world and establish their own independence."

LETTING IT LAY

Okay, it's good for you, it's good for them. But how to turn the fantasy of free time into a reality when there are mouths to be fed and dishes to be washed at least twenty-one times a week, laundry to be done twice a week, or twice a day, diapers to be changed and burps to be burped and hurts to be soothed? What's gonna give? If your baby is screaming for a bottle, you have got to do something about it, even if it's just to check his diaper to see if he is really screaming about something else. But if socks that were worn a day too long are screaming to be put into the washing machine, you have got some choice about it. So your first place to look for leeway—if you can stand it—is the house-work.

With a toddler and a new baby in the house, many parents choose simply to do less of it—a lot less. When Sarah and Marshall had two children a year apart, their standards of cleanliness took a sharp downward dive. "I used to be immaculate," Sarah recalls, dimly. "If you had dinner here, I'd be on the floor picking up from the carpet. I had this thing about lint." Nowadays, the lint is undisturbed, and so is the dust. "It's gotten so you can write your name on the glass table."

Naila, the mother of three-year-old Brad and eighteen-month-old Drew, staves off the invading dust and dirt—well, at least she does once a month. "The name of the game, when you have two children, is to find yourself a cleaning woman." That's how she manages one out of every four weeks. "The other three weeks, wherever things fall, that's where they lay."

If a nonparent is reading this chapter, overcome with disgust at this parental "slovenliness," consider the causes: the consuming tasks of child care, especially when two children need the caring; the consuming clutter of carriages and crayons, bats and balls, diapers and dolls. And consider the clothes that are drooled on and walls that are written on and floors that are spilled on. Try to clean it up? Come back an hour later and it looks like you didn't. "Whenever I clean the bathroom, my children [aged four and three] come in and drip water over the floor, they get black marks on the soap from their dirty hands, they put the towels back crooked," says one disgruntled mother. "It looks like I never laid a sponge to it. Vacuuming is just as futile. Two hours later, there are cookie crumbs all over. You'd never know I vacuumed. For all my cleaning, the house still looks like a cyclone hit it."

If you are the parent of two, it is important to figure out just what means the most to you. Is time for your family and yourself worth a little more clutter and a little less clean? "With two young children, it may be unrealistic to think you can maintain the house in the same order as when you had one child," says Dr. Ruth Allen, assistant professor and coordinator of consumer affairs at Brooklyn College, and also mother of two. "It depends on individual priorities. For some people, order is more important than children, though they wouldn't admit it. If they're not organized, it eats away at them. But for this period, if you truly feel human beings are more important than material resources, you'll have to change your standards of cleanliness, and block out the disarray." What if you just can't? What if you can't read your child a bedtime story if you remember a soiled cup lies unwashed in the sink? What if you can't file your nails until you have filed your bills? "If you're so concerned with order, you should try to figure out why," suggests Dr. Allen. "Is it because other people may judge you, or does it truly bother you? If it's really you, not other people, then why? What does disarray sym-

bolize to you? What does untidiness represent?'' For this time in
your family's life cycle, some disarray and untidiness may be
inevitable, especially if you want to preserve a piece of time for
yourself.

PREVENTIVE HOUSEKEEPING

So let's forget about clean for a while. How about livable? You
may not enjoy your leisurely shower if you slip on a roller skate
on the way in and break a leg, or enjoy your favorite television
show if the screen is smudged with jelly. But you can manage
your little pleasures easily with the help of preventive housekeeping. It is sort of like preventive dentistry, but instead of preventing cavities, you are preventing chaos. A good way to start is to
choose furnishings that can't be hurt too badly by a pair of stomp-
ing, spilling, staining siblings. That means washable wallcover-
ings, curtains, floors, and slip coverings, and rugs and upholstery
that resist soils and stains. It also means getting rid of fragile
items—and anything around the house you don't really need. (If
it's there, you may one day be tempted to clean it.) Of course,
none of the above may appeal to you. Perhaps, you would as
soon give away your second child as you would your crystal
figurines and Oriental pottery. Keep it if you must—but some
day you may have to put in the time to pick up the pieces.

Some parents are lulled into a false sense of security by the
model behavior of their first child. Watch out for number two!
"Some children don't touch things and some do. You can have
one of each," cautions NYU's Dr. Nemiroff. "The first child
may leave your valuables alone. But your second may be the
kind that turns things over and drops them on the floor to see if
they'll bounce."

It may be too late for you to decorate your house, or too
expensive to redecorate. But there are other things you can do to
prevent child-made messes. Some of the potentially messiest
times are mealtimes. If you are a parent, no need to say more
about the disasters that can occur when child and food come into
contact. To reduce the spillage, you might try using well-balanced, heavyweight bowls and cups that can't be easily tipped

over. If one child is in a high chair, there will be less food splattered on the walls if you place the chair toward the center of the room while he is eating. Once your child starts molding his Jell-O into footballs, or mashing his green peas with his elbow, it is time to remove his plate and the sickening mess on it. He is no longer hungry—it's prime time for mess-making. Right after the meal, hands should be washed. If your child can't make it to the bathroom without leaving a trail of soggy, sticky handprints, do the wash-up in the kitchen.

A good mess-prevention rule is to limit all eating and drinking to the kitchen or dining area. Of course, there are exceptions to every rule. Jordan is one very stubborn exception. His older sister eats daintily at the table and always did. Jordan, however, doesn't eat at the table. As his mother puts it, "He eats at the house. He eats all over, and won't take 'no' for an answer. He takes his French toast into my den so he can watch my color TV. It annoys me, but I'm more flexible with his messes than I was with Lindsay's. So I clear the crumbs after him."

Clever children can make messes anywhere, so clever parents should keep bottles, jars, and other containers out of reach of both their children. Cosmetics, pencils, ballpoint pens, and ink should also be kept out of their grasp. When your children do messy work with crayons or paints or play dough—the kind of work so important to their growth and creativity—you might stay around to limit the damage without limiting the fun.

Some homes are kept very clean, but you would never know it because you can't see past the toys. Toys are on the floors. Toys are on the windowsills. Toys are lurking under the radiators. Toys fall from the closets and roll down the stairs and hide under bedcovers to surprise unsuspecting parents. Toys are here, there, and everywhere.

It is not easy to live in a house like that. You can't walk without fear of falling or sit down for fear of a more personal injury. Besides being an eyesore and a footsore, a takeover by toys can be psychologically damaging. "If every space is your children's space, it does something psychologically to the parents," says Dr. Nemiroff. "Just as parents need personal time, they need personal space, a space clear of their children's toys." She recommends setting aside different areas of the home for different activities, including playing, and limiting the toys to those areas. "It shouldn't be a rigid constraint, with three square feet to play in. But there should be areas off-limits to lots of toys."

It also helps in keeping down the chaos to have convenient, plentiful storage, as I discussed in the last chapter. If you are creative about the storage, you may even get some help from the perpetrators of the problem. If you store some of their toys in boxes, your children may actually enjoy filling them up. Keep some games on a rolling cart, and cleanup time will just roll right along. If you can convince your children that cleanup is fun, not work, and they can't wait to do it, you are halfway to your French class or bingo game. You might say, "Let's see if we can count five toys and get them into the box," or "Let's put away all the red toys." Or you can have a race to see who can clean up faster. I used a rhyme with Brian when he was a lot younger and more naïve. "Let's put the blocks into the box." The idea is to start them out young, so you don't get old before your time— hunched over from bending for toys and bleary-eyed from looking for the last red bead buried in the red carpet. Which reminds me, did you ever get a gift-wrapped present for your child, and shake it to see how much it rattled, and pray that it didn't? Those hundred-piece toys can kill any hope you have of getting out to the movies or into a bath, especially if you can't have any peace if a piece is missing. You might suggest to friends and relatives that a toy with more than ten or twenty pieces (or any number you think you can manage to keep track of) will not be warmly received.

BROOMS, BRILLO, AND BACKPACKS

Now that the toys are taken care of, what about the rest of your house? How can you manage to clean it quickly? In fact, with two tornadoes around, how can you manage to clean it at all? Since my main concern here is children, not houses, I would suggest you find a housekeeping handbook for tips on efficient cleaning. There are also books on time management that may be helpful—if you can find the time to read them. What I will try to help you with is what to do with the children while you are being so efficient and saving so much time. How can you cook with them crawling up your legs? How can you make the beds if they are undoing one side while you are struggling with the other?

Many parents don't even attempt to clean unless the children are safely sleeping or safely out of the house. Those are times, however, when you could be reading, or having a friend over for coffee, or sleeping yourself. The trick is to do the cleaning while your children are awake and around. It may sound impossible, but it can be done. If your second child is still a baby, you have a couple of options. You can carry her around in a backpack (or a carrier worn in front) while you are doing some light house-work. She will love being close to you and close to the action, and she won't squawk for your attention and disturb your work. Or you can put her in a playpen for a little while, if you keep it close to what you are doing so she can see you and hear you. For an older child, take out her favorite game and hope she will be kept busy. But she may also want to be near the action. Try talking to her while you are working. Talk about what you are doing now, what she will be doing later. Let her trail along as you are bringing the laundry downstairs. Answer questions she has about her homework while you are ironing. You *can* get your work done without turning your back and a deaf ear to your children.

But there may be a time when you wish you were deaf. You are trying to clean up last week's mess, and your children are performing a realistic re-enactment of World War II in their room. Should you drop your mop and break it up? Unless you suspect bodily injury, keep on mopping. "My children start fighting whenever I start cleaning," says one mother. "I put the stereo on loud and the vacuum on high and I ignore them."

What if you are vacuuming, and your children want to help, but you are having company over, and you can't afford the time their help will take? You might get away with diverting them to another task. "Why not help me with the dusting instead?" Or if they offer to help you with the cooking, but you have no time to peel mashed bananas off the walls or sticky rice off the pans, you might suggest setting the table instead. A knife placed in the wrong position won't set your schedule off, unless you try eating your soup with it.

LITTLE HELPERS

Your children's offers of help should not always be rebuffed or redirected. When you have the time for their assistance, it can do the whole family a lot of good. Your children will learn about cooperation, and responsibility, and will feel like important members of the family group. And, believe it or not, if you put up with their fumbling attempts now, they may develop skills you will depend on later. One day, when you are in a hurry, you may *want* them to do the vacuuming and the cooking, and the carpet and food will be none the worse for it. Even a two-year-old can do more than help put away toys. She can also empty wastebaskets, and a three-year-old can sort laundry. Children start off by thinking of housework as fun. You can encourage that misperception by making a game of it, as you did with the toys. "First put away all your dad's black socks. Now put away all his red [ugh] socks. Aren't we having a good time?" If you keep your tone light and cheery, they may not even realize they are being had.

Try to make it easy, as well as enticing, for them to help. If you want them to hang up their clothes, make sure the rods or hangers are low enough for them to reach. If you want them to make their beds, make sure they can roll them out easily from the walls. If you want them to set the table, make sure the dishes are low enough for them to grasp.

As they get older, you will have more of a choice of jobs to give them. Try to choose chores that are appropriate to their age, interests, and size. A young child may be perfectly suited for low, under-the-table dusting jobs, while a long-limbed teen-ager is a natural for cleaning ceiling light fixtures. But don't keep the young child down or the older child hanging. Give them new jobs every once in a while to keep them enthusiastic.

Their enthusiasm will wane quickly if you can't control yourself and you correct what they do. "When young children set the table, it's generally a mess, with everything in the wrong place,'' says Dr. Nemiroff. ''But you must discipline yourself not to change a thing. Otherwise, you're conveying the message that Mommy always does it right, and you always do it wrong.'' They may just give up on helping, not willing to risk doing it wrong again.

BEDMATES CAN BE HELPMATES, TOO

There is someone else lurking in the woodwork who can sometimes give the wood and the walls and your home's other vital parts a good cleaning. Yes, I'm talking about your mate. And unless there has been a remarkable revolution between the time this book was written and the time you are reading it, the house-shy mate is the male. Most women are still given, whether they like it or not, the chief responsibility for the home and the family (even if both partners work outside the home). And some women perpetuate this inequity as much as the men do. When their husbands lift a dustcloth, they are not simply doing their fair share, they are ''giving me a hand.'' When their husbands stay with the children for an evening, they are not simply being a parent, they are being a ''babysitter.''

You are in this thing together, and when you both understand that, you can sit down to discuss your needs and negotiate your duties. Dr. Ruth Allen of Brooklyn College suggests an open and honest exploration that goes something like this: ''This is the work that has to be done. This is what I like to do. This is what you like to do. And there's a couple of things left over that no one likes. Let's each take one of those leftovers for a week, or trade one for one.''

Whatever the words you use, the important thing is to end up with definite, and fair, work assignments. If you don't, you may not like the results. ''If it's left nebulous, like that whoever's home should do the vacuuming, you know who would end up doing it,'' Dr. Nemiroff cautions. ''There's no question in the world about that.''

Juggling the needs of the household is a formidable task, but it is just the beginning. You also have to juggle the needs of your children. Getting them synchronized, to some extent, is not easy, because of their different ages, temperaments, and biological clocks. Whether they are close in age or far, you will have some scheduling problems. What if your one-year-old child is ravenous whenever your infant is nursing? What if you have to rush your five-year-old to gym class just when your baby settles in for a nap? The challenges vary, depending on age and spacing, so I can't set down rules to cover every conflict you will encounter. I will, however, discuss some scheduling difficulties you may face, now or later, and some ideas for solutions.

GETTING MOVING IN THE MORNING

As soon as you hear the first signs of life—your second child crying, or the first flushing the toilet—the day, and the problems, begin. When your second child is still a baby, you may hope to hear the crying well before you hear the flushing. Many parents prefer time alone with their baby before having to deal with their toddler. That arrangement evolved naturally in Evelyn and Harry's home, and they are glad of it. "The baby wakes up before Brandon does. We feed and change him, and then he goes back for a nap. Brandon wakes up about an hour later, when the baby is out of the way. It's very convenient, because Brandon is horrible when he gets up. He's screaming, and he needs a lot of comforting and loving. With Sean napping, Brandon can get our full attention." Evelyn and Harry just have one minor complaint: The time this idyllic schedule begins is five o'clock in the morning. "If it all happened just two hours later, it would be perfect."

The difference in wake times often does happen naturally, since babies are notorious early risers. But what if it doesn't? You might be able to manipulate the baby's waking hour a bit by giving him his evening feeding earlier or later. As for your older child, you might be able to keep him sleeping by keeping the crying baby out of earshot. Take the baby out of the room, if they sleep together, and shut the door. If they are in separate rooms, be careful the baby doesn't crawl next door and coo or cry into big sister's ears.

If they awaken simultaneously, and you can't deal with both

of them so early in the morning, you might encourage your older child to climb into the baby's crib to entertain him for a while. Both children often love this, and can go at it for an hour or more while you luxuriate for another hour in bed.

What if they both wake up hungry, and they won't play until they are fed? A possible solution is to leave out, the night before, a bowl of cereal on the kitchen counter and a small pitcher of milk on the bottom shelf of the refrigerator so while you are feeding the baby, your older child can help herself to breakfast.

As children pass the baby stage, many parents prefer them up and about at the same time. They find it easier to handle because the children can occupy each other, and a set morning routine often develops. Isabelle, the mother of a four-year-old and a seventeen-month-old, does it like this: "My older child dresses himself and I dress Noah. Then I send Daniel into the bathroom to wash and brush his teeth. Meanwhile, I go down to the kitchen, put Noah in the high chair with juice to keep him quiet, and I make breakfast. Then Daniel comes down and we eat together. If *Captain Kangaroo* is on, they watch it while they eat, so it's quiet for half an hour. It took a while to get it like this, but now it's fine."

The dressing part is a stumbling block in some families. Even when you have convinced your older child to dress herself, she may want your rapt attention while she is doing it. You could try dressing your second child in the same room so at least your older child has your presence, if not your attention. Or you might announce that "This is the family dressing time," so your time isn't monopolized watching your daughter trying to wriggle her fanny into her tight designer jeans.

DINNER—OR DISASTER—FOR TWO?

Mealtime can be an unnerving time of the day, especially if your older child is not yet an independent diner. Even if he has already mastered the intricacies of eating, he may forget all about them once a new baby is on the scene, and demand to be spoonfed again.

Your first feeding problems will occur when you are still

breast- or bottle-feeding your second child, and your first child announces he is faint with hunger. Your best bet is to prepare ahead of time. If your older child is still on the bottle, get one ready before your feeding period, and give it to him when he asks. Use a straw in the bottle if your child does better with it. Or you might leave out snacks, like crackers or carrot sticks, where he can reach them. If you are breast-feeding, you are at a slight advantage—you have a free hand to fetch something from the refrigerator, or even make a sandwich, if you are dexterous and desperate enough.

Breast-feeding can work against you, however, if Little League and feeding time coincide. If you don't want eight-year-olds gaping, what do you do? Try throwing a blanket over your shoulder while you are putting the baby to your breast; while you are nursing, have your blouse or sweater lifted from the bottom to frame the baby's head. Those curious miniature Mantles won't know what you're doing. Even if they do, they have probably seen it all before.

You may encounter a different sort of problem. Your baby may scream for breast or bottle whenever he sees his older sibling eating. Jane and Stuart can tell you all about it. "Whenever Jaimie eats, the baby yells. But Jaimie wants our undivided attention or he won't eat. So we've taken to feeding him mainly when Craig naps. That way, we can give him individual attention and don't have to hear the background screams." Jaimie is no longer fed lunch exactly at noon or dinner exactly at six. The family has learned to be flexible. Yours may learn that lesson, too.

Your next challenge occurs when both children are on solid foods—especially if they are both still in high chairs. To save feeding time, beg, borrow, or buy a second high chair so you can feed your children together, not in shifts. Or see if your older child will be comfortable and safe in a less costly booster chair. Pamela has gone the two-high-chair route. "I put the high chairs close together, I have two forks and two spoons ready, and I feed them at the same time. And they eat!" You won't be quite as busy as Pamela if your children are eating finger foods. It is a big time-saver if you can hold off with solids until they can pick up their food themselves—but only try that if your pediatrician agrees. In my case, I had no choice. Michael acted as if he was allergic to the spoon, and subsisted on my milk, crusts of bread, and squirts of vitamins until the ripe old age of eight months.

As your children get older still, they may demand different menus. Try not to let it get that far, or you can cancel your long-awaited bridge lessons. You are not a restaurant. You don't have time to be a restaurant. So try to serve them what they both like, and occasionally make a special treat for one that the other would refuse to eat.

PLAYING TIME OR GRAYING TIME?

What should be the best time of day for fun and frolic can turn into the worst. Fran and Bill's younger child is only four months old, but the haggard parents are already pulling out each other's gray hairs. "Play is the biggest problem," sighs Fran. "The children's interests are totally different. When I go goo-goo to Larry, Kevin is not excited. I'm with one for two minutes, and the other cries and pulls at me. When I lie down on the floor to play with Larry, Kevin climbs on my back for a horsey ride. I don't want him there—he's a heavy two-year-old. I find it very hard to pay attention to both children."

The problems don't ease up with the passing months or years. If anything, they get worse. Meredith and Alan have a five-year-old and a two-year-old and not a few headaches. "Morgan will want me to do something with her at the table, like play dough, but I can't, because Tim will get into it. Once I let him, and it was disgusting what he did with it. It was in his ears. He even pressed it into the cracks between the bathroom tiles." Meredith and Alan have made things easier by restricting Morgan's activities when Tim is around. There are certain things she is not allowed to do, like finger painting, or playing with her Erector Set because of its tiny pieces. Morgan seems to accept the limits, but some children will not. What's a parent to do?

Playtime is easiest when there is an equal ratio between adults and children. If one of your children is sleeping or away, take that time to play with the other. Make it your special time together, and whip out those toys and games that would be endangered by (or dangerous to) your other child. If both parents are around, or one parent and one popular babysitter, you can go one on one—or divide and conquer. Try to switch off your charges so neither one feels short-changed.

But there will probably be many times you will find yourself alone with your two children, and they will both be after you for a good time. During some of those all too frequent occasions, you can try the activities suggested earlier (chapter seven) for them to do together. However, your children will often want to do their own thing. You could try setting up one child in an activity—getting all the play pieces out and arranged—and hope she will stay busy with it while you play with the other. Or you could try talking to one child about what he is doing—the colors he is painting with, the model rocket ship he is building—at the same time as you are working on a project with the other. Your children may accept this split attention if they know they frequently get your full attention. And you will learn the art of splitting yourself in two, if you haven't learned it already.

SYNCHRONIZED SLUMBER

That first yawn after lunch, those scrunched-up fists rubbing those half-closed eyes, are sights of joy to time-starved parents. Finally, nap time has arrived, time to escape from parenthood for a few brief but shining hours (or minutes, if you're not so lucky). At least, that's how it is for parents of just one tired toddler. But what if your second child is not so accommodating as to yawn and rub on cue with her older sibling? What if your children's nap times come at different times, robbing you of your time? Should you let nature take its course, or tinker with its biological beat?

Every child, every person, has his own biological clock. During infancy, that clock is all-important, regulating wake times and sleep times and mealtimes. It is best to let the clock do the scheduling, not you, for that time. After a while, however, you may find that your baby is somewhat flexible, and isn't too cranky if you keep her up a little longer, or too resistant if you put her down a little sooner. You may even be able to tinker with your older child's schedule, though that takes a little more doing.

If it is a question of napping him earlier than usual, consider what makes him sleepy—a bottle, perhaps, or a bath, or maybe the whole bedtime ritual of story and song? To keep him up past his normal nap time, try tempting him with his favorite activity. If you are willing to participate, you may find him very awake and very alert. One mother told me a good tickle works wonders in reviving her daughter's flagging spirits. For some children, baths stimulate rather than soothe.

If you have children who are lulled to sleep by motion, you have a perfect solution to out-of-synch schedules. Take them outside for a stroll, and when they are asleep, get them upstairs and into bed. (You could try the same thing in your car. But if you can't transport them easily from car to bed, you may find yourself spending your wonderful free time taking an inventory of the glove compartment.)

Even if only one of your children is still napping, nap time can be a problem time. If you have just *got* to get your older child to school, or a sports club, or a dance class, what do you do with your sleeping baby? Some parents find they can just tote the baby along without ill effects—the baby does not seem to mind sudden wakenings, quick dressings, and a heavy schedule of travel. But some are less cooperative. If they are awakened they are miserable, and you will be miserable, too. If you try to time their naps around their sibling's schedule, they will be a mess of tears and temper tantrums all day. If your baby needs to be on his own individual schedule, try to make it possible, for the good of your whole family. That might mean hiring a sitter for the baby while you chauffeur your schoolchild. Or you might decide that a bus service or a carpool to school is the only way to keep everyone happy and to keep yourself sane.

WALKING ALONG

Some parents of two young children become stay-at-homes because they don't know how to get about. The carriage or stroller they wheeled their first child in can't accommodate two, but their first child is still unable, or unwilling, to walk distances. So how to get from here to there without another adult to help with the pushing? If you do some smart shopping, you will find vehicles built for two. If you do some smart thinking, you may choose one appropriate to your children's ages, weights, and napping needs.

One inexpensive possibility is to purchase a toddler seat that can be placed on your current carriage. There are seats especially designed for that purpose, with seat belts and all. Some toddlers enjoy their high perch, but safety is a concern with these seats. Tipping over is a common cause of carriage accidents, and the added weight of a toddler near the handlebar makes tipping over more likely. Some salespeople at carriage stores recommend the toddler be under twenty-five or thirty pounds, and that the carriage be especially sturdy, with a metal body or a frame with metal. Even if those recommendations are followed, it is vital that you keep your hands on the handlebar at all times.

Another caution about carriages: Never let your older child wheel the baby. A short child will likely pull down on the handle, perhaps tipping the carriage backward. Also, don't let your first child play with the carriage or it might fold accidentally, injuring infant and toddler.

If you decide that a carriage seat is not safe enough for you, or not suited to your needs, you might consider strollers made for two. Again, safety is a factor. A recent study by the U.S. Consumer Product Safety Commission (CPSC) found that two-seat strollers, particularly those with seats mounted one in front and one in back, appear to be less stable than other types. Tip-over is most common when the children are being put in or taken out in the wrong order. (One seat may be further from the stroller's balance point, and if that is the only seat occupied, the stroller may tip.) So be careful, first of all, that the stroller is a stable one. Says George Rutherford, co-author of the CPSC report, "A vehicle built for two must be stronger and sturdier and made with better materials than a vehicle for one, because of the added weight and stress." And when you use the stroller, be careful not to leave one child in the "wrong seat" with the other seat empty.

There are a number of varieties of two-child strollers. In some, the seats are side by side. The stability problem may be less with these, but the getting-through-the-doors problem is more. (I did see one model in which the children were seated next to each other in one broad seat, and the stroller could fit through doors without being folded. But the seat did not recline for napping.) Also in the side-by-side mode, you can buy special clamps to attach an umbrella stroller you already have to an equally light-weight stroller. That is another thrifty solution, and once your older child is walking distances, you won't be saddled with a two-seated stroller for one. Again, however, there is the door problem and the napping problem. And with all the side-by-sides, it is easy for the children to jab and kick one another. So there are a lot of trade-offs to consider.

More common are strollers with seats facing each other, or one behind the other. (Some have seats that can be turned either way.) When you bought your original stroller for your first child, it may have contained a "hitchhiker" seat for packages, a seat you now plan to use for your second child. But don't do it, unless you can attach a restraint system to it. Remember that strollers can be dangerous. During 1979, there were approximately 7,900 stroller- and carriage-related injuries treated in U.S. emergency rooms. If you do use the "hitchhiker" for two, it is less likely to tip over if the heavier child is in the seat farther from you.

With strollers as with carriages, don't let your older child wheel it, or he may pull down on the handle and tip the whole thing over. When it is not being used, fold it and keep it out of both your children's reach. Otherwise, it may accidentally col-lapse on a child playing with it and fracture or lacerate hands and fingers—or cause even more serious injuries.

If none of the above alternatives appeal to you, a baby carrier may be just the thing. Carry the baby in front or back, and wheel your toddler in her trusty old stroller. A soft carrier is appropri-ate for a baby up to four or five months (until she can sit up unaided), while a frame carrier can be used for older babies and toddlers. Some parents buy the soft variety, but never use it because they can't figure out how to get it on. It is a good idea to try out models your friends may have before you choose one of your own. If a child is in it, so much the better; you will get some idea of whether your neck and back can take the strain. (My back, not the strongest, started to protest when Brian passed the twelve-pound mark.) I recently saw a large man loaded down with one child in a front carrier and one child in a back carrier—

a good idea for balance, but not ideal for making it through re-volving doors.

You may be taking some trips by car, not foot. If you are planning to pass on your first child's car seat to your second, your economizing may be dangerous. Unless your older child is more than four years of age and over forty pounds, borrow or buy another car seat so both your children will be safe.

SPLISH, SPLASH, IT'S TIME FOR THEIR BATH

Bath time used to be that pleasant interlude between dinnertime and bedtime, when your child would play contentedly with rub-ber ducks and toy boats while you perched nearby reading the newspaper, occasionally glancing over to make sure his head remained safely above water. Now, it is a harried time, with two soapy, slippery, splashing siblings fighting over space and toys, and then two wet bodies to be dried and dressed. How to restore some order without ruining the fun of the fights and the lure of the water? When baby number two is still an infant, there is little problem. You simply bathe her separately in a small plastic tub. If the thought of two baths tires you, you can just sponge her down on some days. You may not be as crazy-clean with your second child as with your first. Dana finds she alternates days bathing toddler Kevin and baby Bruce. "When Kevin was Bruce's age, I thought the world would end if I didn't bathe him every day. Now, every other day is fine for both of them." Dana had first tried a different approach—bathing them in different tubs at the same time. "Just as I was washing Bruce down, Kevin would try to kill himself. He climbed, or stood up and walked around in the tub, and sometimes went under. So there I was, holding a dripping baby in one hand, and slipping and sliding trying to rescue Kevin." That approach was short-lived.

Even with two older children, some parents prefer separate baths. "That way, there's no fighting," said Lucille, the mother of a preschooler and a toddler. "They each have a chance to relax and play by themselves." But drawing two baths a day and cleaning two rings can be a real burden, so she also chooses to alternate days.

Most commonly, parents put the children in together because it saves time. While they soap the older, they can seat the younger in a special bathtub anchor with suction cups on the bottom. Despite the fights, children often have a great time bathing together. Kelly, six, and Amanda, one, wouldn't have it any other way. "She splashes him. He washes her. He showed her how to put her face in the water, how to wash herself, how to make bubbles, how to splash the bathroom walls."

Some parents give in to a dangerous temptation when two children are in the tub. If the telephone rings, they ask the older to watch the younger, and they leave for a long conversation. But babies should never be left in a bathtub without an adult present; they can drown in just a few inches of water. And it's not fair to put such a serious responsibility on an older child.

The end of the bath presents another problem: How can you towel and dress your younger child and still keep an eye on the older? The safest and quickest way is to line up the towels and clothing in the bathroom ahead of time. Take the younger out first, dry and dress and seat her, and then do the older child.

ASLEEP AT LAST

Evening is finally approaching, that time of the day when you and your mate can be alone together, free of whines and whimpers and whiffle balls. Many parents look forward to a long evening without the children, and get them off to bed before the seven o'clock news drones to a close. That's fine, if you can do it and want to do it. But in some families, one or both parents come home late from work, and the children have saved up all their energy for a play session with Mommy or Daddy. To kiss them hello and whisk them off to bed may not foster the closeness you want with your children. So in that case, you might do with a little less time for yourself at night, and try to find time at other points of the day.

Getting them off to bed, at any time, may be a problem if you are alone with them. What do you do with one while you are reading to and tucking in the other? A solution some parents have found is to have a joint reading session in neutral territory

—have each child bring a favorite book or two to the living room, and take turns reading them. Then tuck in the younger, or sleepier, child, and finally put the other to bed.

What if one, or both, children just won't go? What if they kick and scream and carry on to stay up just a little longer even after you have played with them plenty? You can't make your child sleep, but you can explain that Mom and Dad need time alone at night. So have them stay in their rooms, door closed, reading or playing quietly, until they are bored enough or tired enough to turn in. If you let them run around the house as long as they want, they will tucker you out, and finally, they may tuck you in at night.

BUILDING BOUNDARIES, SEEKING SAFETY

Even some parents who have their homes organized and children coordinated have problems because they haven't learned to defend their rights. They can't sit down to read a newspaper without their children plopping down beside them, talking and giggling and trying to grab the paper away. They can't lie down in bed without one child sitting on their head and the other on their feet. Dr. Jane Nemiroff of NYU realized a problem existed when she found herself sitting on the toilet with a child on her lap. "I felt idiotic. 'What nonsense!' I thought. 'I can't get to the toilet without a child on top of me.' But what's the alternative? If you lock yourself in the bathroom you'll hear the inevitable banging on the door, and you'll feel guilty." She suggests that children be told that Mommy has the right to her own time. "Communicate that message to them, and reassure them it doesn't mean you don't love them." If you don't set up some protective boundaries between yourself and your children, you will find that time to yourself is gone, and your sense of self diminished.

Many parents spend a lot of time following their toddlers around, making sure they don't get hurt. If they see them toddling to the medicine cabinet, they turn them around so they can toddle away. If they see them applying a key to the socket, they rush to the rescue. Making your home as child-proof as possible can save you time and your child injury. There are many guides to child-proofing, which you may have followed when your first child started making mischief. Now that you have your second child, you will have to do a better job of it. With two children to watch, you won't be able to watch each as carefully, and may be too emotionally or physically exhausted to watch even one well. Also, your children will be at different developmental levels. They can each find danger in different ways, and you will have to guard against them all. You may have already let down your guard some as your older child has matured; for example, you may have removed the safety caps from the outlets because he "knows better" now. But there is a little one around again, so put them back in.

There's a new danger confronting second children that first children don't face, at least not at an early age: the clutter created by first children. There may be balls on the stairs to trip over, scissors on the table to be cut by, marbles on the floor to swallow. Many of the toys that are just right for your older child— intricate contraptions with small, easily swallowed parts—can be dangerous to your younger. That is another good reason to control the clutter, and to put toys hazardous to your second child too high for him to reach.

Another reason to think again of safety is that children develop at different rates. Your second may be climbing before your first was walking. And while your first may have been more of a listener, your second may be more of a doer. That is the experience in Shelly's and Dennis's home. "Eric's the problem. He's more physical than Robert. If I said no, Robert would listen. But the baby is deaf and dumb and blind. And he's a climber. I had to put hooks and eyes on the closets because he stands on a chair —Robert never did that. I had some coffee tables in front of the couch. They had sharp corners, so I put weather stripping around them. That was enough to prevent Robert from hurting himself. But the baby would peel it off and eat it, so the tables are now in a friend's basement."

Your second child may not only be naturally more agile and ingenious, he may also learn from his older sibling. If he sees big sister working the safety latch on the cabinet door, or opening the child safety cap on the aspirin bottle, he may follow suit. So you may have to keep your medicines and other potential poisons under lock and key this time, even if you didn't the last. It may take a lot of time to give your home a good child-proofing, but you will be able to relax your minute-by-minute vigilance a bit, and earn the time back quickly.

YOU CAN'T DO IT ALONE

Parents who find life with two children easiest are parents who aren't always with the children. They are willing to trust other people to take over the job from time to time. Carla loves being with her daughter and son, and also loves being without them. "I use babysitters in my home and out. I'm not afraid to put my children in new environments so that I can enjoy something, as long as it's a good safe place with a conscientious person watching." When her younger child was just nine months, she put him in a nursery at the tennis courts so she could enjoy an hour of her favorite sport. "He's none the worse for it, and I'm a whole lot better. A friend of mine just couldn't bring herself to leave her kids anywhere. So after her second child was born, she was like a madwoman."

Some parents won't trust anyone else to watch their children, not even friends and neighbors, so they suffer alone. But more parents are getting wise. They use babysitters, or switch off babysitting duties with another parent. Some go further and form babysitting cooperatives or play groups. Dr. Ruth Allen of Brooklyn College is a vocal advocate of the latter. "There may be five women on the block going out of their minds in their own little places. They should get together. That was my saving grace with one of my daughters. When she was one and a half years old, we formed a group that met three mornings a week. It's as easy to watch three children as one, and we each had six or nine hours to ourselves on our 'free' weeks. Play groups are critical if you want time for yourself."

If time to yourself is difficult to come by for all parents, it can seem totally elusive to parents who have outside jobs. When I was a staff writer on a magazine, two of my favorite times of the day were my rides to and from work. I was free of the demands of child-rearing and writing. I could relax behind the wheel, listen to the radio, and think. Whether you go to work by car, train, or bus, try to make it a time to enjoy. Don't travel with someone you don't like; don't think about the work that awaits you. Just treasure this small part of the day that is yours alone.

If you ever get extra time off from work, don't rush home to relieve the babysitter. During the summers, when my workday ended at four on Fridays, I'd head straight for the park to lie in the sun. If it was raining, I'd even sit in the lobby of my building reading my mail instead of going right up and resuming motherhood. No, I didn't hate my child. I simply guarded my bit of freedom.

AS TIME GOES BY

As your children grow older, you will have more and more time to yourself. There may even come a day when you feel you have too much of it, and you wish your children would share it with you. Why don't they visit, or even just write? You may look back with longing to the days when they were little, when you had the great joy of bringing up your first child, matched only by the enchantment of bringing up your second. These are the days you will be remembering, so relish them, and relish your children, in all of their likenesses and in all of their differences.

Bibliography

1. PLANNING FOR YOUR SECOND CHILD

Allan, G. Sibling solidarity. *Journal of Marriage and the Family*, 1977, *39*, 177–184.

Arnold, F., and Fawcett, J. T. *The value of children: a cross-national study, vol. 3: Hawaii.* Honolulu: East-West Population Institute, East-West Center, 1976.

Belmont, L., Stein, Z., and Zybert, P. Child spacing and birth order: effect on intellectual ability in two-child families. *Science*, 1978, *202*, 995–996.

Blood, R. O., Jr., and Wolfe, D. M. *Husbands and wives: the dynamics of family living.* Glencoe, Ill.: Free Press, 1960.

Bowerman, C. E., and Dobash, R. M. Structural variations in inter-sibling affect. *Journal of Marriage and the Family*, 1974, *36*, 48–54.

Brazelton, T. B. *Toddlers and parents.* New York: Delta, 1976.

Bulatao, R. A., and Arnold, F. *Relationships between the value and cost of children and fertility: cross-cultural evidence.* Paper prepared for the General Conference of the International Union for the Scientific Study of Population, Mexico City, August 8–13, 1977.

Cherry, S. H. *Understanding pregnancy and childbirth.* New York: Bantam Books, 1975. Page 166.

Christensen, H. T., and Philbrick, R. E. Family size as a factor in the marital adjustments of college students. *American Sociological Review*, 1952, *17*, 306–312.

Cicirelli, V. G. The effect of sibling relationship on concept learning of young children taught by child-teachers. *Child Development*, 1972, *43*, 282–287.

Cornoldi, C., and Fattori, L. C. Age spacing in firstborns and symbiotic dependence. *Journal of Personality and Social Psychology*, 1976, *33*, 431–434.

Current Population Reports. Population characteristics. Trends in child spacing: June 1975. U.S. Department of Commerce, Bureau of the Census. Series P-20, No. 315, issued February 1978.

Current Population Reports. Population characteristics. Population profile of the United States: 1979. U. S. Department of Commerce, Bureau of the Census. Series P-20, No. 350, issued May 1980.

Current Population Reports. Population characteristics. Fertility of American women: June 1979. U.S. Department of Commerce, Bureau of the Census. Series P-20, No. 358, issued December 1980.

Espenshade, T. J. *The cost of children in urban United States.* Population Monograph Series, No. 14. Berkeley: Institute of International Studies, University of California, 1973.

————. Raising a child can now cost $85,000. *Intercom,* a publication of the Population Reference Bureau, Inc., 1980, *8.*

————. The value and cost of children. *Population Bulletin,* a publication of the Population Reference Bureau, Inc., 1977, *32.*

Fenton, N. The only child. *Journal of Genetic Psychology,* 1928, *35,* 546–556.

Goodenough, F. L., and Leahy, A. M. The effect of certain family relationships upon the development of personality. *Journal of Genetic Psychology,* 1927, *34,* 45–71.

Hawke, S., and Knox, D. *One child by choice.* Englewood Cliffs, N. J.: Prentice-Hall, 1977.

Johnson, R. C., and Medinnus, G. R. *Child psychology,* New York: John Wiley and Sons, 1974.

Knox, D., and Wilson, K. The differences between having one and two children. *The Family Coordinator,* 1978, *27,* 23–25.

Koch, H. L. Children's work attitudes and sibling characteristics. *Child Development,* 1956, *27,* 289–310.

————. The relation of certain formal attributes of siblings to attitudes held toward each other and toward their parents. *Monographs of the Society for Research in Child Development,* 1960, *25* (4, Serial No. 78), 1–124.

————. Some emotional attitudes of the young child in relation to characteristics of his sibling. *Child Development,* 1956, *27,* 393–426.

————. Some personality correlates of sex, sibling position, and sex of sibling among five and six year old children. *Genetic Psychology Monographs,* 1955, *52,* 3–50.

————. The relation of certain formal attributes of siblings to attitudes held toward each other and toward their parents. *Monographs of the Society for Research in Child Development,* 1960, *25* (4, Serial No. 78), 1–124.

Lasko, J. K. Parent behavior toward first and second children. *Genetic Psychology Monographs,* 1954, *49,* 97–137.

Lewis, M., and Kreitzberg, V. S. Effects of birth order and spacing on mother-infant interactions. *Developmental Psychology,* 1979, *15,* 617–625.

Monthly Vital Statistics Report. Advance Report, Final Natality Statistics, 1978. From the National Center for Health Statistics. DHHS Publication No. (PHS) 80-1120, *29,* Supplement, April 28, 1980.

Nuttall, E. V., Nuttall, R. L., Polit, D., and Hunter, J. B. The effects of family size, birth order, sibling separation and crowding on the academic achievement of boys and girls. *American Educational Research Journal,* 1976, *13,* 217–223.

Nuttall, R. L., and Nuttall, E. V. *Family size and spacing in the United States and Puerto Rico.* Washington, D. C., Center for Population Research, National Institute of Child Health and Human Development, U.S. Department of Health, Education, and Welfare, 1975.

Peck, E. *The joy of the only child.* New York: Delacorte Press, 1977.

Pomeranz, V. E. with Schultz, D. *The first five years.* Garden City, New York: Doubleday and Co., 1973.

Rosenberg, B. G., and Sutton-Smith, B. Sibling age spacing effects upon cognition. *Developmental Psychology,* 1969, *1,* 661–668.

Salk, L. *What every child would like his parents to know.* New York: Warner Paperback Library, 1973.

Stott, L. H. General home setting as a factor in the study of the only versus non-only child. *Journal of Personality,* 1939, *8,* 156–162.

Sutton-Smith, B., and Rosenberg, B. G. *The sibling.* New York: Holt, Rinehart and Winston, 1970.

Terhune, K. W. *A review of the actual and expected consequences of family size.* U.S. Department of Health, Education and Welfare; Public Health Service; National Institutes of Health. Pub. No. (NIH) 75-779, July 31, 1974.

The 1980 Virginia Slims American Women's Opinion Poll. A study conducted by the Roper Organization. Page 64.

The one-child family. Brochure published by the National Organization for Non-Parents, Baltimore, Md.

Turchi, B. A. *The demand for children: the economics of fertility in the United States.* Cambridge, Mass.: Ballinger, 1975.

Turner, R. H. Some family determinants of ambition. *Sociology and Social Research,* 1962, *46,* 397–411.

Wagner, M. E., Schubert, H. J. P., and Schubert, D. S. P. Sibship-constellation effects on psychosocial development, creativity, and health. *Advances in Child Development and Behavior,* 1979, *14,* 57–148.

Whelan, E. M. A second baby? . . . If yes, when? *American Baby,* 1978, *40,* 41–42.

———. Personal communication, 1979.

White, B. L. *The first three years of life.* Englewood Cliffs, N.J.: Prentice-Hall, 1975.

Williamson, N. E. Boys or girls? Parents' preferences and sex control. *Population Bulletin,* a publication of the Population Reference Bureau, Inc., 1978, *33.*

Wray, J. D. Population pressure on families: family size and child spacing. *Reports on population/family planning,* 1971, Number 9.

Yarrow, L. Right and wrong reasons for having another baby. *Parents' Magazine,* 1979, *54,* 45–47.

Zajonc, R. B. Family configuration and intelligence. *Science,* 1976, *192,* 227–236.

Zajonc, R. B., and Markus, G. B. Birth order and intellectual development. *Psychological Review,* 1975, *82,* 74–88.

2. PREGNANCY AND CHILDBIRTH THE SECOND TIME AROUND

Alk, M., editor. *The expectant mother.* New York: Pocket Books, 1969.

Baldwin, A. L. Changes in parent behavior during pregnancy: an experiment in longitudinal analysis. *Child Development,* 1947, *18,* 29.

Chase, H. C. The relationship of certain biologic and socio-economic factors to fetal, infant, and early childhood mortality: 1. Father's occupation, parental age and infant's birth rank. Albany, N. Y., State Department of Health, 1962.

Cherry, S. H. Understanding pregnancy and childbirth. New York: Bantam Books, 1975.

Clark, M., and Lord, M. Too many caesareans? *Newsweek,* October 6, 1980, *96,* 105.

Clifford, E. Expressed attitudes in pregnancy of unwed mothers and married primigravida and multigravida. *Child Development,* 1962, *33,* 945–951.

Cohen, M. B. Personal identity and sexual identity. In J. B. Miller (ed.), *Psychoanalysis and women,* New York: Brunner/Mazel, 1973. Page 141.

Colman, A. D., and Colman, L. L. *Pregnancy: the psychological experience.* New York: Bantam Books, 1977.

Consumer Reports. Do women need iron supplements? September 1978, *43,* 502–504.

Dommel, D. Nutrition report: The need for iron during pregnancy. *American Baby,* November 1978, *40,* 33.

Doty, B. A. Relationships among attitudes in pregnancy and other maternal characteristics. *The Journal of Genetic Psychology,* 1967, *111,* 203–217.

Gause, R. Dear Doctor: Dr. Gause discusses the causes and prevention of premature labor. *American Baby,* April 1979, *41,* 18 + .

Guttmacher, A. F. Pregnancy, birth and family planning. New York: The Viking Press, 1973.

Hall, R. E. *Nine months' reading.* New York: Bantam Books, 1973.

Hausknecht, R. H., and Heilman, J. R. *Having a cesarean baby.* New York: E. P. Dutton, 1978.

Heilman, J. R. Breaking the caesarean cycle. *The New York Times Magazine,* September 7, 1980, pages 84 + .

Jarrahi-Zadeh, A., Kane, F. J., Jr., Van De Castle, R. L., Lachenbruch, P. A., and Ewing, J. A. Emotional and cognitive changes in pregnancy and early puerperium. *British Journal of Psychiatry,* 1969, *115,* 797–805.

Kay, L., Jacobson, L., and Nilsson, A. Postpartum mental disorder in an unselected sample: the influence of parity. *Journal of Psychosomatic Research,* 1967, *10,* 317–325.

Kliot, D. A. OB update. *Parents Expecting,* Winter 1979–80, *12,* 8 + .

Kolb, L. C. *Modern clinical psychiatry.* Philadelphia: W. B. Saunders Co., 1977.

Larsen, V. L. Stresses of the childbearing years. *American Journal of Public Health,* 1966, *56,* 32–36.

Leifer, M. Psychological changes accompanying pregnancy and motherhood. *Genetic Psychology Monographs,* 1977, *95,* 55–96.

Lesinski, J. Family size: its influence on family's health, economic status and social welfare. *Obstetrical and Gynecological Survey,* May 1976 (supplement), *31,* 419–452.

Measey, L. G. Psychiatric problems in obstetrics. *The Practitioner,* 1978, *220,* 120–122.

Newton, N. Emotions of pregnancy. *Clinical Obstetrics and Gynecology,* 1963, *6,* 639–668.

Panter, G. G. Once a cesarean, always a cesarean? *Parents' Magazine,* June 1979, *54,* 28.

Percent distribution of live births by period of gestation, race and live birth order: total of 42 reporting states and the District of Columbia, 1977, Department of Health, Education and Welfare, Public Health Service, Work Table W-22.

Schaefer, E. S., and Manheimer, H. *Dimensions of perinatal adjustment.* Paper read at Eastern Psychological Association, New York, April 1960.

Sears, R. R., Maccoby, E. E., and Levin, H. *Patterns of child rearing.* Evanston, Ill.: Row, Peterson, 1957.

Shereshefsky, P. M., and Yarrow, L. J. *Psychological aspects of a first pregnancy and early postnatal adaptation.* New York: Raven Press, 1974.

Tabulations of 1978 case reports. *Bulletin of the National Clearinghouse for Poison Control Centers,* U.S. Department of Health and Human Services, Food and Drug Administration, Bureau of Drugs, Division of Poison Control. Volume *24,* October 1980.

The women and their pregnancies. The collaborative perinatal study of the National Institute of Neurological Diseases and Stroke. The U.S. Department of Health, Education and Welfare, Public Health Service, National Institutes of Health. Philadelphia: W. B. Saunders Co., 1973.

Westbrook, M. T. The effect of the order of birth on women's experience of childbearing. *Journal of Marriage and the Family,* 1978, *40,* 165–172.

Whelan, E. M. Preparing for fatherhood. *American Baby,* June 1979, *41,* 18+.

3. PREPARING YOUR FIRST CHILD FOR YOUR SECOND CHILD

Alovus, J. Dolls which give birth for educating young children. *Birth and the Family Journal,* 1977, *4,* 79.

Ames, L. B., and Ilg, F. L. *Your four year old.* New York: Delacorte Press, 1976.

Anderson, S. V. Siblings at birth: a survey and study. *Birth and the Family Journal,* 1979, *6,* 80–87.

Chase, E. *Home births in Salt Lake City in 1975.* Master's thesis, University of Utah College of Nursing, 1976.

Church, J. *Understanding your child from birth to three: a guide to your child's psychological development.* New York: Random House, 1973.

Ginott, H. G. *Between parent and child.* New York: Avon Books, 1965.

Goodell, R. Bringing up the children by taking them to a birth. *The New York Times,* February 24, 1980, page E9.

Jimenez, S. M., Jones, L. C., and Jungman, R. G. Prenatal classes for repeat parents: a distinct need. *The American Journal of Maternal Child Nursing,* 1979, *4,* 305–308.

Legg, C., Sherick, I., and Wadland, W. Reaction of preschool children to the birth of a sibling. *Child Psychiatry and Human Development,* 1974, *5,* 3–39.

Leonard, C. H., Irvin, N., Ballard, R. A., Ferris, C., and Clyman, R. Preliminary observations on the behavior of children present at the birth of a sibling. *Pediatrics,* 1979, *64,* 949–951.

Mullaly, L. M., and Kervin, M. C. Professionally speaking: changing the status quo. *The American Journal of Maternal Child Nursing,* 1978, *3,* 75+.

Nelson, W. E., Vaughan, V. C. III, McKay, R. J., and Behrman, R. E., editors. *Nelson textbook of pediatrics.* Philadelphia: W. B. Saunders Co., 1979.

Parma, S. A family centered event? Preparing the child for sharing in the experience of childbirth. *Journal of Nurse-Midwifery,* 1979, *24,* 5+.

Perez, P. Nurturing children who attend the birth of a sibling. *The American Journal of Maternal Child Nursing,* 1979, *4,* 215–217.

Riley, H. D., Jr., and Berney, J. Meeting the new arrival. *American Baby,* October 1980, *42,* 86+.

Salk, L. *Preparing for parenthood.* New York: Bantam Books, 1975.

———. *What every child would like his parents to know.* New York: Warner Paperback Library, 1973.

Spock, B. *Baby and child care.* New York: Pocket Books, 1976.

Stein, S. B. *That new baby.* New York: Walker Publishing Co., 1974.

Sweet, P. T. Prenatal classes especially for children. *The American Journal of Maternal Child Nursing,* 1979, *4,* 82–83.

Trause, M. A. Birth in the hospital: the effect on the sibling. *Birth and the Family Journal,* 1978, *5,* 207–210.

Wesley, C. Becoming a big sister. *La Leche League News,* 1979, *21,* 61–63.

SPECIAL NOTE: To find out the prices of the rag dolls described on page 00, plus more details about the available models, write to Monkey Business, Rt. 3, Box 153a, Celina, TN 38551.

4. THE HIGHLIGHTS AND HAZARDS OF SECOND-TIME PARENTHOOD

Bossard, J. H. S. Family modes of expression. *American Sociological Review,* 1945, *10,* 226–237.

Chittenden, E. A., Foan, M. W., Zweil, D. M., and Smith, J. R. School achievement of first- and second-born siblings. *Child Development,* 1968, *39,* 1223–1228.

Cohen, S. E., and Beckwith, L. Caregiving behaviors and early cognitive development as related to ordinal position in preterm infants. *Child Development,* 1977, *48,* 152–157.

Hilton, I. Differences in the behavior of mothers toward first- and later-born children. *Journal of Personality and Social Psychology*, 1967, *7*, 282–290.

Jacobs, B. S., and Moss, H. A. Birth order and sex of sibling as determinants of mother-infant interaction. *Child Development*, 1976, *47*, 315–322.

Kilbride, H. W., Johnson, D. L., and Streissguth, A. P. Social class, birth order, and newborn experience. *Child Development*, 1977, *48*, 1686–1688.

Lasko, J. K. Parent behavior toward first and second children. *Genetic Psychology Monographs*, 1954, *49*, 97–137.

Lewis, M., and Kreitzberg, V. S. Effects of birth order and spacing on mother-infant interactions. *Developmental Psychology*, 1979, *15*, 617–625.

McArthur, C. Personalities of first and second children. *Psychiatry*, 1956, *19*, 47–54.

Phillips, E. L. Cultural vs. intropsychic factors in childhood behavior problem referrals. *Journal of Clinical Psychology*, 1956, *12*, 400–401.

Rosen, B. C. Family structure and achievement motivation. *American Sociological Review*, 1961, *26*, 574–585.

Rothbart, M. K. Birth order and mother-child interaction in an achievement situation. *Journal of Personality and Social Psychology*, 1971, *17*, 113–120.

Schaller, J. A critical note on the conventional use of the birth order variable. *The Journal of Genetic Psychology*, 1978, *133*, 91–95.

Sears, R. R. Ordinal position in the family as a psychological variable. *American Sociological Review*, 1950, *15*, 397–401.

Sears, R. R., Maccoby, E., and Levin, H. *Patterns of child rearing*. Evanston, Ill.: Row, Peterson, 1957.

Sutton-Smith, B., and Rosenberg, B. G. *The sibling*. New York: Holt, Rinehart and Winston, 1970.

Tessler, R. Birth order, family size, and children's use of physician services. *Health Services Research*, 1980, *15*, 55–62.

Thoman, E. B., Barnett, C. R., and Leiderman, P. H. Feeding behaviors of newborn infants as a function of parity of the mother. *Child Development*, 1971, *42*, 1471–1483.

Thoman, E. B., Leiderman, P. H., and Olson, J. P. Neonate-mother interaction during breast-feeding. *Developmental Psychology*, 1972, *6*, 110–118.

Thoman, E. B., Turner, A. M. Leiderman, P. H., and Barnett, C. R. Neonate-mother interaction: effects of parity on feeding behavior. *Child Development*, 1970, *41*, 1103–1111.

5. THE SECOND-CHILD SYNDROME: SLOW BUT STEADY?

Adams, B. N. Birth order: a critical review. *Sociometry*, 1972, *35*, 411–439.

Adler, A. *Understanding human nature*. New York: Greenberg Publishers, 1927. Page 154.

———. *What life should mean to you*. New York: Capricorn Books, 1958.

Ahe, K., Tsiyi, K., and Suzuki, H. The significance of birth order and age difference between sibs as observed in drawings of kindergarten children. *Folio Psychitrica et Neurological Japonica*, 1963, *17*, 315–325.

Altus, W. D. Birth order and its sequelae. *Science*, 1966, *151*, 44–49.

Arrowood, A., and Amoroso, D. Social comparison and ordinal position. *Journal of Personality and Social Psychology*, 1965, *2*, 101–104.

Bakan, P. Lefthandedness and birth order revisited. *Neuropsychologia*, 1977, *15*, 837–839.

Bayley, N. Comparisons of mental and motor test scores for ages 1–15 months by sex, birth order, race, geographical location, and education of parents. *Child Development*, 1965, *36*, 379–411.

Beller, E. K. *Dependence and independence in young children*. Ph.D. Dissertation, State University of Iowa, 1948.

Belmont, L. Birth order and family size associations with mental and physical development. In Morton Bortner (ed.), *Cognitive Growth and Development*, New York: Brunner/Mazel, 1979. Pages 221–243.

Belmont, L., Stein, Z., and Zybert, P. Child spacing and birth order: effect on intellectual ability in two-child families. *Science*, 1978, *202*, 995–996.

Bharathi, V. V., and Venkatramaiah, S. R. Birth order, family size and anxiety. *Child Psychiatry Quarterly*, 1976, *9*, 11–17.

Boone, S. L. Effects of fathers' absence and birth order on aggressive behavior of young male children. *Psychological Reports*, 1979, *44*, 1223–1229.

Bossard, J. H. S., and Boll, E. Adjustment of siblings in large families. *American Journal of Psychiatry*, 1956, *112*, 889–892.

Bradley, R. W. Birth order and school-related behavior: a heuristic review. *Psychological Bulletin*, 1968, *70*, 45–51.

Brazelton, T. B. *Infants and mothers*. New York: Dell Publishing Company, 1969.

Breland, H. M. Birth order, family configuration and verbal achievement. *Child Development,* 1974, *45,* 1011–1019.

――――. Family configuration and intellectual development. *Journal of Individual Psychology,* 1977, *33,* 86–96.

Brock, T. C., and Becker, G. Birth order and subject recruitment. *Journal of Social Psychology,* 1965, *65,* 63–66.

Burton, D. Birth order and intelligence. *The Journal of Social Psychology,* 1968, *76,* 199–206.

Caplan, F., editor, *The first twelve months of life.* New York: Grosset & Dunlap, 1973.

Carmichael, L. *Manual of child psychology.* New York: John Wiley and Sons, 1946, Chapter 10.

Carrigan, W., and Julian, J. Sex and birth-order differences in conformity as a function of need affiliation arousal. *Journal of Personality and Social Psychology,* 1966, *3,* 479–483.

Chittenden, E. A., Foan, M. W., Zweil, D. M., and Smith, J. R. School achievement of first- and second-born siblings. *Child Development,* 1968, *39,* 1223–1228.

Cicirelli, W. Children's school grades and sibling structure. *Psychological Reports,* 1977, *41,* 1055–1058.

Clarke-Stewart, K. A. Interactions between mothers and their young children: characteristics and consequences. *Monographs of the Society for Research in Child Development,* 1973, *38* (6–7, serial no. 153).

Collard, R. R. Social and play responses of first-born and later-born infants in an unfamiliar situation. *Child Development,* 1968, *39,* 325–334.

Conley. J. J. Family configuration as an etiological factor in alcoholism. *Journal of Abnormal Psychology,* 1980, *89,* 670–673.

Croake, J. W., and Olson, T. D. Family constellation and personality. *Journal of Individual Psychology,* 1977, *33,* 9–17.

Cushna, B. *Agency and birth order differences in very early childhood.* Paper presented at the meeting of the American Psychological Association, New York, September 1966.

Dean, D. A. *The relation of ordinal position to personality in young children.* Unpublished master's thesis, State University of Iowa, Iowa City, 1947.

Dimond, R., and Munz, C. Ordinal position of birth and self disclosure in high school students. *Psychological Reports,* 1968, *21,* 829–833.

Douvan, E., and Adelson, J. *The adolescent experience.* New York: John Wiley and Sons, 1966.

Eisenman, R. Birth order and artistic creativity. *Journal of Individual Psychology,* 1964, *20,* 183–185.

Faris, R. E. L. Sociological causes of genius. *American Sociological Review*, 1940, *5*, 689–699.

Farley, F. H. Notes on creativity and scholastic achievement of women as a function of birth order and family size. *Perceptual and Motor Skills*, 1978, *47*, 13–14.

Forer, L. *The birth order factor*. New York: Pocket Books, 1976.

Franklin, B. J. Birth order and tendency to "adopt the sick role." *Psychological Reports*, 1973, *33*, 437–438.

Freud, S. *A general introduction to psycho-analysis*. New York: Garden City Publishing Co., 1938.

Friedman, J. H., Jackson, B. J., and Nogas, C. Birth order and age at marriage in females. *Psychological Reports*, 1978, *42*, 1193–1194.

Garner, A. M., and Wenar, C. *The mother-child interaction in psychosomatic disorders*. Urbana: University of Illinois Press, 1959.

Gewirtz, J. L. *Succorance in young children*. Ph.D. thesis, Sate University of Iowa, Iowa City, 1948.

Grant, M. W. Rate of growth in relation to birth rank and family size. *British Journal of Preventive Social Medicine*, 1964, *18*, 35–42.

Grotevant, H. D. Sibling constellations and sex typing of interests in adolescence. *Child Development*, 1978, *49*, 540–542.

Grotevant, H. D., Scarr, S., and Weinberg, R. A. Intellectual development in family constellations with adopted and natural children: a test of the Zajonc and Markus model. *Child Development*, 1977, *48*, 1699–1703.

Hansson, R. O., Chernovetz, M. E., Jones, W. H., and Stortz, S. Birth order and responsibility in natural settings. *The Journal of Social Psychology*, 1978, *105*, 307–308.

Harris, I. D. *The promised seed: a comparative study of eminent first and later sons*. Glencoe, Ill.: Free Press, 1964.

Helmreich, R. L. Birth order effects. *Naval Research Reviews*. Office of Naval Research, Washington, D. C., 1968, 1–6.

Helmreich, R. L., and Collins, B. E. Situational determinants of affiliative preference under stress. *Journal of Personality and Social Psychology*, 1967, *6*, 79–85.

Henry, A. F. Sibling structure and perception of disciplinary roles of parents. *Sociometry*, 1957, *20*, 67–74.

Hilton, I. Differences in the behavior of mothers toward first- and later-born children. *Journal of Personality and Social Psychology*, 1967, *7*, 282–290.

Johnson, R. C., and Medinnus, G. R. *Child psychology*. New York: John Wiley and Sons, 1974.

Kaltsounis, B. Creative performance among siblings of various ordinal birth positions. *Psychological Reports*, 1978, *42*, 915–918.

Kawin, E. *Children of the preschool age.* Chicago: University of Chicago Press, 1934.

Koch, H. L. Sibling influence on children's speech. *Journal of Speech and Hearing Disorders,* 1956, *21,* 322–328.

———. Some emotional attitudes of the young child in relation to characteristics of his sibling. *Child Development,* 1956, *27,* 393–426.

Lewis, M., and Kreitzberg, V. S. Effects of birth order and spacing on mother-infant interactions. *Developmental Psychology,* 1979, *15,* 617–625.

Maccoby, E. E., Doering, C. H., Jacklin, C. N., and Kraemer, H. Concentrations of sex hormones in umbilical-cord blood: their relation to sex and birth order of infants. *Child Development,* 1979, *50,* 632–642.

MacDonald, A. P., Jr. Birth order effects in marriage and parenthood: affiliation and socialization. *Journal of Marriage and the Family,* 1967, *29,* 656, 661.

MacFarlane, J. W., Allen, L., and Honzik, M. P. A developmental study of the behavior problems of normal children between twenty-one months and fourteen years. *University of California Publications in Child Development,* 1954, *2.*

Mayer, R. First thoughts, first words. *Parents' Magazine,* 1979, *54,* 70–74.

McArthur, C. Personalities of first and second children. *Psychiatry,* 1956, *19,* 47–54.

Miller, N. and Maruyama, G. Ordinal position and peer popularity. *Journal of Personality and Social Psychology,* 1976, *33,* 123–131.

Murdoch, P., and Smith, G. Birth order and affiliation. *British Journal of Social and Clinical Psychology,* 1969, *8,* 235–245.

———. Birth order and age at marriage. *British Journal of Social and Clinical Psychology,* 1966, *5,* 24–29.

Mussen, P., Conger, J., and Kagan, J. *Child Development and Personality.* New York: Harper & Row, 1969.

Nisbet, J. Family environment and intelligence. *The Eugenics Review,* 1953, *45,* 31–40.

Nisbett, R. E. Birth order and participation in dangerous sports. *Journal of Personality and Social Psychology,* 1968, *8,* 351–353.

Patterson, R., and Ziegler, T. W. Ordinal position and schizophrenia. *American Journal of Psychiatry,* 1941, *98,* 455–456.

Pfouts, J. H. Birth order, age-spacing, IQ differences, and family relations. *Journal of Marriage and the Family,* 1980, *42,* 517–531.

Phillips, E. L. Cultural vs. intropsychic factors in childhood behavior problem referrals. *Journal of Clinical Psychology,* 1956, *12,* 400–401.

Princeton Center for Infancy. *The parenting advisor*, Frank Caplan, editor. Garden City, N. Y.: Doubleday and Co., 1977.

Rosen, B. C. Family structure and achievement motivation. *American Sociological Review*, 1961, *26*, 574–585.

———. Family structure and value transmission. *Merrill-Palmer Quarterly*, 1964, *10*, 59–76.

Rosenow, C., and Whyte, A. H. The ordinal position of problem children. *American Journal of Orthopsychiatry*, 1931, *1*, 430–434.

Rubinstein, J. Maternal attentiveness and subsequent exploratory behavior in the infant. *Child Development*, 1967, *38*, 1089–1100.

Sampson, E. E., and Hancock, F. T. An examination of the relationship between ordinal position, personality and conformity. *Journal of Personality and Social Psychology*, 1967, *5*, 398–407.

Schachter, F. F. Studies in sibling deidentification and split-parent identification. In B. Sutton-Smith (Chair), *Life Span Perspectives on Sibling Socialization*. Symposium presented at the meeting of the American Psychological Association, New York, 1979.

Schachter, F. F., Gilutz, G., Shore, E., and Adler, M. Sibling deidentification judged by mothers: cross-validation and development studies. *Child Development*, 1978, *49*, 543–546.

Schachter, F. F., Shore, E., Feldman-Rotman, S., Marquis, R. E., and Campbell, S. Sibling deidentification. *Developmental Psychology*, 1976, *12*, 418–427.

Schachter, S. Birth order and sociometric choice. *Journal of Abnormal and Social Psychology*, 1964, *68*, 453–456.

———. *The psychology of affiliation*. Stanford: Stanford University Press, 1959.

Schooler, C. Birth order effects: not here, not now! *Psychological Bulletin*, 1972, *78*, 161–175.

Sears, P. S. Doll play aggression in normal young children: influence of sex and sibling status, father's absence. *Psychological Monographs*, 1951, *65* (Whole No. 323).

Sears, R. R. Ordinal position in the family as a psychological variable. *American Sociological Review*, 1950, *15*, 397–401.

Sears, R. R., Maccoby, E., and Levin, H. *Patterns of child rearing*. Evanston, Ill.: Row, Peterson, 1957.

Sells, S. B., and Roff, N. Peer acceptance-rejection and birth order. *American Psychologist*, 1963, *18*, 355.

Skipper, J. K., Jr., and McCaghy, C. H. Strip-teasers: the anatomy and career contingencies of a deviant occupation. *Social Problems*, 1970, *17*, 391–405.

Smart, R. G. Alcoholism, birth order, and family size. *Journal of Abnormal and Social Psychology*, 1963, *66*, 17–23.

Smith, E. E., and Goodchilds, J. D. Some personality and behavioral factors related to birth order. *Journal of Applied Psychology,* 1963, *47,* 300–303.

Stevens, J. H., Jr., and Mathews, M., editors, *Mother/child, father/child relationships.* National Association for Education of Young Children, Washington, D. C., 1978.

Storer, N. W. Ordinal position and the Oedipus complex. *Laboratory of Social Relations of Harvard University Bulletin,* 1961, *10,* 18–21.

Sutton, J. M., Jr., and McIntire, W. G. Relationship of ordinal position and sex to neuroticism in adults. *Psychological Reports,* 1977, *41,* 843–846.

Sutton-Smith, B. *Child psychology.* New York: Appleton-Century-Crofts, 1973.

Sutton-Smith, B., and Rosenberg, B. G. Modeling and reactive components of sibling interaction. In J. Hill (ed.), *Child Psychology,* Vol 3. *Minnesota Symposia on Child Psychology,* Minneapolis: University of Minnesota Press, 1969.

———. *The sibling.* New York: Holt, Rinehart and Winston, 1970.

Terhune, K. W. *A review of the actual and expected consequences of family size.* U.S. Department of Health, Education and Welfare; Public Health Service; National Institutes of Health. Pub. No. (NIH) 75-779, July 31, 1974.

Thurstone, L. L., and Jenkins, R. L. *Order of birth, parentage, and intelligence.* Chicago: University of Chicago Press, 1931.

Tolstrup, K. On psychogenic obesity in childhood. 1V. *Acta Pediatrica,* 1953, *42,* 289–304.

Toman, W. *Family constellation.* New York: Springer, 1969.

———. Family constellation as a basic personality determinant. *Journal of Individual Psychology,* 1959, *15,* 199–211.

Wagner, M. E., and Schubert, H. J. P. *The all-male sibships and the male without brothers.* Paper presented at the 24th Annual Convention of the American Society of Adlerian Psychology, Vancouver, B. C., 1976.

———. Sibship variables and United States Presidents. *Journal of Individual Psychology,* 1977, *33,* 78–85.

Warren, J. R. Birth order and social behavior. *Psychological Bulletin,* 1966, *65,* 38–49.

Weller, G. W., and Bell, R. Q. Basal skin conductance and neonatal state. *Child Development,* 1965, *36,* 647–657.

White, B. L. *The first three years of life.* Englewood Cliffs, N. J.: Prentice-Hall, 1975.

Whiting, J. W. M., and Child, I. L. *Child training and personality.* New Haven, Conn.: Yale University Press, 1953.

Zajonc, R. B. Family configuration and intelligence. *Science,* 1976, *192,* 227–236.

Zajonc, R. B., and Markus, G. B. Birth order and intellectual development. *Psychological Review,* 1975, *82,* 74–88.

Zajonc, R. B., Markus, H., and Markus, G. B. The birth order puzzle. *Journal of Personality and Social Psychology,* 1979, *37,* 1325–1341.

6. THE COMBAT ZONE: CHILDREN AT WAR

Appel, M. H. Aggressive behavior of nursery school children and adult procedures in dealing with such behavior. *Journal of Experimental Education,* 1942, *11,* 185–199.

Calladine, C., and Calladine, A. *Raising siblings.* New York: Delacorte Press, 1979.

Dunn, J., and Kendrick, C. The arrival of a sibling: changes in patterns of interaction between mother and first-born child. *Journal of Child Psychology and Psychiatry,* 1980, *21,* 119–132.

Foster, S. A study of personality make-up and social setting of fifty jealous children. *Mental Hygiene,* 1927, *11,* 13–77.

Freud, S. A general introduction to psycho-analysis. New York: Garden City Publishing Co., 1938.

Ginott, H. G. *Between parent and child.* New York: Avon Books, 1965.

Greenberg, P. J. Competition in children: an experimental study. *American Journal of Psychology,* 1932, *44,* 221–248.

Hendershot, G. E. Trends in breast feeding. *Advance Data from Vital and Health Statistics,* National Center for Health Statistics, DHEW, No. 59, March 28, 1980.

————. *Trends and differentials in breast feeding in the United States, 1970–75: Evidence from the National Survey of Family Growth, Cycle II.* Paper presented at the annual meeting of the Population Association of America, Washington, D.C., March 26–28, 1981.

Hurlock, E. B. *Child development.* New York: McGraw-Hill, 1978.

Jersild, A. T. *Child psychology.* Englewood Cliffs, N. J.: Prentice-Hall, 1968.

Kendrick, C., and Dunn, J. Caring for a second baby: effects on interaction between mother and firstborn. *Developmental Psychology,* 1980, *16,* 303–311.

Koch, H. L. The relation of certain formal attributes of siblings to attitudes held toward each other and toward their parents. *Monographs of the Society for Research in Child Development,* 1960, *25,* 1–124.

Landreth, C. *Early childhood: behavior and learning.* New York: Alfred A. Knopf, 1967.

Legg, C., Sherick, I., and Wadland, W. Reaction of preschool children to the birth of a sibling. *Child Psychiatry and Human Development,* 1974, *5,* 3–39.

Levi, A. M., Buskila, M., and Gerzl, S. Benign neglect: reducing fights among siblings. *Journal of Individual Psychology,* 1977, *33,* 240–245.

McFarland, M. B. *Relationships between young sisters as revealed in their overt responses.* Child Development Monographs, No. 23. New York: Teachers College, Columbia University, 1938.

Nelson, W. E., Vaughan, V. C. III, McKay, R. J., and Behrman, R. E., editors. *Nelson textbook of pediatrics.* Philadelphia: W. B. Saunders Co., 1979. Pages 71–72.

Pomeranz, V. E. with Schultz, D. *The first five years.* Garden City, N. Y.: Doubleday and Co., 1973.

Popper, A. Playing favorites. *Parents' Magazine,* August 1979, *54,* 35–38.

Ross, B. M. Some traits associated with sibling jealousy in problem children. *Smith College Studies in Social Work,* 1931, *1,* 364–373.

Sewall, M. Two studies of sibling rivalry, I. Some causes of jealousy in young children. *Smith College Studies in Social Work,* 1930, *1,* 6–22.

Sobel, D. Siblings: studies find rivalry, dependency revive in adulthood. *The New York Times,* October 28, 1980, page C1 +.

Spock, B. *Baby and child care.* New York: Pocket Books, 1976.

Sutton-Smith, B., and Rosenberg, B. G. *The sibling.* New York: Holt, Rinehart and Winston, 1970.

Tooley, K. M. The young child as victim of sibling attack. *Social Casework,* 1977, *58,* 25–28.

7. PLAYING AND LEARNING TOGETHER

Abramovitch, R., Corter, C., and Lando, B. Sibling interaction in the home. *Child Development,* 1979, *50,* 997–1003.

Adams, B. N. *Kinship in an urban setting.* Chicago: Markham Publishing Co., 1968.

Allan, G. Sibling solidarity. *Journal of Marriage and the Family,* 1977, *39,* 177–184.

Bank, S., and Kahn, M. D. Sisterhood-brotherhood is powerful: sibling sub-systems and family therapy. *Family Process,* 1975, *14,* 311–337.

Bowerman, C. E., and Dobash, R. M. Structural variations in inter-sibling affect. *Journal of Marriage and the Family,* 1974, *36,* 48–54.

Caplan, F., general editor, *The First Twelve Months of Life.* New York: Grosset & Dunlap, 1975.

Cicirelli, V. G. A comparison of college women's feelings toward their siblings and parents. *Journal of Marriage and the Family,* 1980, *42,* 111–118.

——. The effect of sibling relationship on concept learning of young children taught by child-teachers. *Child Development,* 1972, *43,* 282–287.

——. Effects of sibling structure and interaction on children's categorization style. *Developmental Psychology,* 1973, *9,* 132–139.

——. Relationship of siblings to the elderly person's feelings and concerns. *Journal of Gerontology,* 1977, *131,* 309–317.

——. *Sibling influence throughout the life span.* Paper presented at the 87th Annual Convention of the American Psychological Association, New York, Sept. 1, 1979.

——. *Social services for elderly in relation to the kin network.* Report to the NRTA-AARP Andrus Foundation, May 31, 1979.

Cumming, E., and Schneider, D. Sibling solidarity: a property of American kinship. *American Anthropologist,* 1961, *63,* 498–507.

Irish, D. P. Sibling interaction: a neglected aspect in family life research. *Social Forces,* 1964, *42,* 279–288.

Lamb, M. E. The development of sibling relationships in infancy: a short-term longitudinal study. *Child Development,* 1978, *49,* 1189–1196.

——. Interactions between eighteen-month-olds and their preschool-aged siblings. *Child Development,* 1978, *49,* 51–59.

Lesser, R. M. Sibling transference and countertransference. *Journal of the American Academy of Psychoanalysis,* 1978, *6,* 37–49.

Meyendorf, R. Infant depression due to separation from siblings: syndrome of depression, retardation, starvation, and neurological symptoms. *Psychiatria Clinica,* 1971, *4,* 321–335.

Reiss, P. J. The extended kinship system: correlates of and attitudes on frequency of interaction. *Marriage and Family Living,* 1962, *24,* 333–339.

Samuels, H. R. The effect of an older sibling on infant locomotor exploration of a new environment. *Child Development,* 1980,*51,* 607–609.

8. MAKING ONE ROOM BIG ENOUGH FOR TWO

Brothers, J. *New York Post,* July 25, 1980, page 22.

Caplan, F., editor, *The parenting advisor.* Garden City, N. Y.: Doubleday and Co., 1977.

Conran, T. *The bed and bath book.* New York: Crown Publishers, 1978.

Davidson, M. A place to grow in. *Parents' Magazine,* September 1978, *53,* 104–107.

Finkelhor, D. Sex among siblings: a survey on prevalence, variety, and effects. *Archives of Sexual Behavior,* 1980, *9,* 171–194.

Foa, L., and Brin, G. *Kids' stuff.* New York: Pantheon Books, 1979.

Freeman, K. Kids' rooms that really work! *Parents' Magazine,* January 1979, *54,* 70–73.

Glamour. Make room for baby. February 1979, pages 198 + .

House & Garden Decorating Guide. Planned for children. Fall 1979, pages 112 + .

Legg, C., Sherick, I., and Wadland, W. Reaction of preschool children to the birth of a sibling. *Child Psychiatry and Human Development,* 1974, *5,* 3–339.

Schram, J. F. *Successful children's rooms.* Farmington, Mich.: Structures Publishing Co., 1979.

Seebohm, C. The appeal of small. *House & Garden,* August 1979, *151,* 84 + .

Seventeen. Double occupancy. August 1979, *38,* 306–309.

Sunset. Raise the bed? January 1979, pages 58–59.

9. MESHING SCHEDULES AND MAKING TIME

Consumer Reports. Baby carriers. November 1975, *40,* 667–671.

―――. Folding baby carriages. February 1975, *40,* 110–115.

―――. Lightweight strollers, August 1976, *41,* 456–460.

Davidson, M. Shortcut housekeeping tips and time savers for busy families. *Parents' Magazine,* April 1978, *53,* 20 + .

Fitzsimmons, C., and White, N. *Management for you.* Philadelphia/New York: J. B. Lippincott Co., 1964.

Flynn, J. *About the house.* Cambridge/New York: Dorison House Publishers, 1977.

Gould, L. How to liberate your entire family. *Reader's Digest,* July 1978, *113,* 47 + .

Gruenberg, S. M., editor. *The new encyclopedia of child care and guidance.* Garden City, N. Y.: Doubleday and Co., 1968.

Guide to buying for babies. By the editors of *Consumer Reports.* Mt. Vernon, N. Y.: Consumers Union, 1975. Pages 115–130.

Harper's Bazaar. Parents' security guide: The lazy mother's approach to child-rearing. An interview with Virginia E. Pomeranz, M. D. July 1979, pages 70 + .

Redbook's Young Mother. Cutting down on household chores. 1978, page 52.

Riley, H. D., Jr., and Woodworth, K. L. Play it safe: How to babyproof your home. *American Baby*, July 1980, *42*, 64+.

Rutherford, G. W., Jr., and Miles, R. *Hazard analysis: Injuries associated with strollers and carriages.* Washington, D. C.: U.S. Consumer Product Safety Commission, 1980.

Skelsey, A. *The working mother's guide to her home, her family and herself.* New York: Random House, 1970.

Wilder, R. Home safe home: A room-by-room guide to child-proofing. *Parents' Magazine*, September 1979, *54*, 40–45.

Yarrow, L. The time squeeze. *Parents' Magazine*, December 1979, *54*, 35–37.

Index

A

Abramovitch, Rona, 204
Achievement, 120, 149–51
  effects of birth order on, 20
Adler, Alfred, 133–34, 148
Adolescence, 28, 126–27
  sibling loyalty, 212–14
Afterbirth pains and pleasures,
  80–81
Age spacing, *see* Interval between
  births
Aggression, 142–43, 149, 171
Album pictures, 117–18
Alcoholism, 145
Allen, Dr. Ruth, 237, 243, 256
Alternative gratification, 37
American College Entrance
  Examination, 39
American Council on Science and
  Health, 33
Anemia, 71

Anger, 18, 89, 92
Angiotensin (hormone), 72
Anxiety, 51, 61, 88, 89, 96, 106,
  108, 112, 121, 144
Apgar score, 75
Astrology, 133

B

Baby equipment, recycling of, 30
Babysitting cooperatives, 256
Backache, during pregnancy, 69
Ballard, Dr. Roberta, 103–4
Bank, Stephen, 199, 200, 201
Bank Street College of Education,
  84, 171–72
Bath time, 252–53
Belmont, Lillian, 153–54
Berk, Dr. Bernice, 84, 86, 89, 96,
  102, 107, 111, 171–72, 179,
  183, 194, 218, 225

Birth, sibling participation in, 101–6
Birth control, 23, 38
Birth order differences, 133–68
 achievement, 149–51
 Adlerian theory, 133–34
 adult-like attributes, 141–42
 aggressive tendencies, 142–43
 deidentification, 145–47
 dependency, 137, 138
 disease and danger, 136–37
 emotional, 137
 friendliness and playfulness, 139–41
 hormone level, 134–35
 intelligence gap, 151–58
 middle child, 148–49
 need for people, 137–39
 obesity, 135–36
 parents' role and, 159–68
 physical size, 135
 self-esteem, 143–45
 sexual identity, 147–48
"Blighted ovum," 70–71
Bond between siblings, 23, 36
Bossard, James, 120
Bottle-feeding, 114, 177, 246
Bowerman, Charles E., 212–13
Breast-feeding, 40, 80–81, 94, 114, 177, 178, 179, 246
Breech birth, 75
Breland, Hunter, 153, 155
Bressler, Lynn, 223
Bunk beds, 229–30
Bureau of the Census, 32, 38

C
Caesarean birth, 40, 77–80, 81
 "low-flap," 79
 reasons for, 78–79
Cain-and-Abel syndrome, 18

Center for Population Research, 35
Child-rearing tactics, disagreements on, 31
Cicirelli, Dr. Victor, 204–5, 214
Clothing, recycling of, 30
"Cluster" births, 41–44
 advantages of, 41–42
 drawbacks to, 42–43
Collard, Roberta, 140
College attendance, 150
Committee on Maternal Nutrition (National Research Council), 71
Competition, 36, 47
Confluence model theory, 157–58
Conformity, effects of birth order on, 20
Conley, James, 145
Consumer Product Safety Commission (CPSC), 250
Contraception, 23
Corter, Carl, 204
Cranch, Gene, 54
Creativity, effects of birth order on, 20
Croake, James W., 149

D
Deidentification theory, 145–47, 199
Diabetes, 78
Discipline differences, 128–29
Dobash, Rebecca M., 212–13
Down's Syndrome, 72
Dunn, Judy, 177, 181–82

E
East Carolina University, 31
Educational Testing Service, 47, 119, 153, 155

Eisenstark, Eileen, 207
Emotional health, effects of birth
 order on, 20
Episiotomy, 76
Espenshade, Thomas J., 29
Esposito, Jimmy, 207, 209

F
Failure, fear of, 144
Fantasies, family life, 28
Fathers, bond between first child
 and, 19
Father-to-be, second time, 62–64
Favoritism, 194–96
Fear, 18, 19, 33, 48, 54, 59, 88,
 137, 144
Fetal heartbeat, 57, 66
Financial costs, 28–30, 46
Finkelstein, Bernice, 228
First child, preparing for second
 child, 83–111
 announcement, 85–87
 coming home from hospital,
  110–11
 family planners, 94–95
 fathers and, 95–96
 goal of involvement, 99–101
 hospital visit, 83, 107–10
 ideas to consider, 90–96
 jealousy and reassurance, 87–
  89
 lifting and hugging, 95
 meeting mother's doctor, 92
 meeting other babies, 93–94
 minimizing mother-child
  separation, 106–7
 pets, 91
 during pregnancy, 83–84
 reading and making books, 90–
  91
 sibling participation in birth,
  101–6

starting early, 84–85
 what not to do, 96–99
Florida State University, 149
Forrest, Dr. Tess, 34
Freud, Sigmund, 133, 169
Friendliness and playfulness,
 139–41

G
Galton, Sir Francis, 134
Genetic disease, 72
Gittelson, Dr. Roger, 65, 74
Grimm's fairy tales, 170
Gross, Dr. Dorothy, 160, 161,
 164, 165, 167
Grotevant, Harold D., 147, 155
Guilt feelings, 11, 18, 54, 96

H
Hand-me-down clothes, 20
Head Start, 85, 171
Health Insurance Plan (HIP), 94
Heartburn, during pregnancy, 68–
 69
Hemorrhoids, 68–69
High blood pressure, 71
Hilton, Irma, 126, 138
Hostility, 85, 91, 143, 221
Housework, 235–44
 children's offers of help, 242–
  243
 juggling needs, 243–44
 preventive cleanliness, 238–40
 "slovenliness," 236–38
Housework hours, per child, 30–
 31

I
Intelligence, effects of birth order
 on, 20

Intelligence gap, 151–58
  confluence model theory, 157–158
  reasons for, 154–57
  results of, 151–54
Interval between births, 37–49, 56
  "cluster" births, 41–44
  decision on spacing, 49–50
  more than four years apart, 46–49
  two to four years apart, 44–46
Iowa Basic Skills test, 153

J
Jacobs, Blanche, 119
Jealousy, 18, 20, 24, 35, 42, 44, 87–88, 120, 171, 172–73, 174, 177, 178, 185, 188, 197; *see also* Sibling rivalry

K
Kahn, Michael, 199, 200, 201
Kekst, Carol Schapiro, 161, 162, 165
Kendrick, Carol, 177, 181–82
Kramer, Doris, 207, 212
Kreitzberg, Valerie S., 47, 119

L
Labor, division of, 32
Labor process, 73–77
  difference between first and second, 74–76
Lamb, Dr. Michael, 203
Lando, Bella, 204
Lasko, Dr. Joan, 46, 131
Lesser, Dr. Ruth, 129, 132, 198
Lewis, Michael, 47, 119
Lissak, Dr. Louis, 95
Locker, Jody, 228
Long Island Research Institute, 135

Love, 88, 91, 95, 113, 118
"Low-flap" scar, 79
Lubic, Ruth Watson, 102

M
McGerald, Judy, 207
Marital adjustment, planning for, 31–32
Markus, Gregory B., 157–58
Marra, Kathleen, 214
Maruyama, Geoffrey, 140–41
Maternity Center Association (MCA), 54, 80–81, 99, 102, 104, 105
Maternity clothes, 56–57
Meltzer, Dr. Steven, 64
Metzger, Dorothy, 108
Middle child, 148–49
Milgram, Joel I., 195
Miller, Norman, 140–41
Miscarriage, 70–71
MMPI (psychological test), 149
Morgan, James, 226
Morning sickness, 67–68
Moss, Howard, 119
Mother's little helper, 179–80

N
Napping and nap time, 248–49
National Center for Health Statistics, 38
National Institute of Child Health and Human Development, 35
National Institute of Mental Health, 122, 130
National Institutes of Health, 79
National Merit Scholarship Qualification Test, 153
National Research Council, 71
Nausea and vomiting (during pregnancy), 67–68

Nemiroff, Dr. Jane, 235, 236, 238, 239, 243, 254
Neuroticism, 145
Newman, Ruth, 102, 111, 189, 196
New York University, 164–65

O
Obesity rate, 135–36
Old Testament, 170
Olson, Terrance D., 149
One-child families, 34–35
Only child, personality attributes, 34–35
Overprotection, 11–12

P
Parents' role, birth order differences and, 159–68
  change, 166–67
  cry of the child, 161–62
  fathering, 167–68
  living and learning, 166
  loving and touching, 162
  patterns of parenting, 161
  playpens, 163–64
  tag-along kid, 167
  talking, 162–63
  toys, 164–65
  See also Second-time parenthood
Personality, 34–35, 49
  attributes (only child), 34–35
Personality development, 20, 46, 142
  birth order differences, 133–68
Photography, 117–18
Planned Parenthood, 69, 70
Planning, for second child, 25–50
  child-rearing and division of labor, 31–32

family pressure and choice in, 25–26
financial costs, 28–30
interval between births, 37–49
marital adjustments, 31–32
more housework considerations, 30–31
parenting approach, 26–28
reasons and advantages, 32–37
Playground warfare, 18
Playpens, 163–64
Pomeranz, Dr. Virginia, 45, 48, 117, 121, 160, 174–75, 180–181
Population Reference Bureau (PRB), 29
Port-A-Cribs, 63, 93
Postpartum blues, 82
Pregnancy, 22, 39–40
  average length of, 67
  awe (first pregnancy), 57
  See also Second pregnancy
Preparation books, 90–91
Pressures, family, 25–26, 33
Preventive housekeeping, 238–40
Privacy, importance of, 220, 223
Program in Infant and Parent Development (Bank Street College of Education), 160
Program in Infant and Toddler Development (New York University), 163
Project Talent intelligence test, 153

Q
Quickening, 66

R
Reich, Dr. Ilana, 85, 89, 97, 98, 99, 171, 184, 190

Reich, Dr. Leonard, 94, 96, 174, 179
Reinbrecht, Janet, 102
Rejection, feelings of, 19
Relaxin (hormone), 69
Rh disease, 73
Rhogam (vaccine), 73
Room-sharing, 217–34
  alternatives to, 221–25
  bedtime problems, 218–19, 233
  fights, 233–34
  need for individual expression, 227–28
  opposite-sex, 220
  personal problems involved in, 232–34
  play areas (outside the room), 231–32
  separate space, 225–27
  storage areas, 231
  stretching the space, 228–31
Ross, Helgola G., 195
Rubinstein, Dr. Emily, 89, 176, 192, 222
Rutherford, George, 250

S
Sambursky, Dr. Joel, 54–55, 169, 175, 210, 219, 220
Samuels, Helen R., 204
Schachter, Frances Fuchs, 146, 147, 199
Schachter, Stanley, 137, 141, 145
Schaller, Joseph, 127
Schedules, meshing (and making time), 235–57
  bathtime, 252–53
  bedtime, 253–54
  help from others, 256–57
  housework, 235–44
  mealtime, 245–47

  in the morning, 244–45
  nap time, 248–49
  playtime, 247–48
  safety factor, 254–56
  walking along, 249–52
Schwartz, Louise, 76
Second child:
  birth order differences, 133–68
  challenge of two children, 17–19
  introduction to, 17–24
  parenthood, 112–32
  planning for, 25–50
  pregnancy and childbirth, 51–82, 83
  preparing first child for, 83–111
  room-sharing, 217–34
  schedules and making time, 235–57
  second born, second best, 19–20
  seeking help, 20–24
  sibling loyalty, 197–216
  sibling rivalry, 21, 23, 28, 36, 47, 95, 103, 143, 146, 169–96
Second pregnancy, 51–82, 83
  afterbirth pains and pleasures, 80–82
  attitudes, 60–62
  backache, 69
  birth experience, 73–77
  Caesarean births, 40, 77–80, 81
  caring for first child during, 52–53
  compared with the first, 55–57, 58
  complications, 70–73
  dealing with emotions, 59–60
  disappointment with baby's sex, 76
  existing child and, 53–55
  experience and maturity, 61–62
  father-to-be, 62–64

heartburn, 68
labor process, 73–77
nausea and vomiting, 67–68
physical facts, 64–67
planning considerations, 51–52
postpartum blues, 82
quickening, 66
reaction of others, 58–60
stretch marks, 69–70
swelling, 69
varicosities, 68–69
Second-time parenthood, 112–32
album pictures, 117–18
differences, 112–14, 128–29
effects of déjà-vu, 116–17
fall-off in attention, 118–21
feeding the infant, 114–15
hands-off policy, 125–27
lower expectations, 127–28
parents' birth order and, 132
practical factors, 129–30
relaxed attitude, 121–25
schedules and making time,
235–37
unchanged "style of
mothering," 130–32
Security, child's sense of, 45–
46
Self-esteem, 143–45
Selman, Ruth, 207
Sex control, 33
Sex education, 87
Sexual activity (between siblings),
220
Sexual identity, 34, 201–2
Sharing a room, *see* Room-
sharing
Sherman, Dr. Robert, 148, 170,
173, 190, 193
Shigaki, Dr. Irene, 161, 163, 166–
167
Shimm, Patricia Henderson, 207

Sibling loyalty, 197–216
in adolescence, 212–14
adulthood, 214–16
diary of, 205–6
encouraging mutual play, 207–
211
nature walks, 211–12
studies of, 202–5
Sibling rivalry, 21, 23, 28, 36, 47,
95, 103, 143, 146, 169–96
children spaced two to four
years apart, 45
effects of, 169–72
fathers and, 183–84
feeding decision, 177–79
fights, problems, and
suggestions, 185–94
handling on day-to-day basis,
174–76
holding without hurting, 180–82
and mother's little helper, 179–
180
Old Testament, 170
onset of, 18
parental partiality and, 194–96
regression, 183
See also Jealousy
Sleep, lack of, 31
Solnit, Dr. Albert, 199
Spock, Dr. Benjamin, 170
Stanford University, 126, 135
Stirling University, 212
Stretch marks, 69–70
Strollers, 249–52
Sutton-Smith, Dr. Brian, 36, 42,
141, 143, 151
Swelling, during pregnancy, 69

T
Tag-along kid, 167
Tay-Sachs disease, 72

Teacher's pet, 151
Teasing, 193–94
Television, 28, 162
Temper tantrums, 20, 27
Terhune, Dr. Kenneth, 35
Tessler, Dr. Richard, 122
Thoman, Dr. Evelyn, 115
Toilet training, 98, 123–24, 183
Toxemia, 72
Toys, 176, 232, 239
    recycling of, 30
Tyrer, Dr. Louise, 69, 70

U
Uniqueness, feeling of, 51, 56
U.S. presidents, number of first-
    borns, 149–50
University of California, 120
University of Maine, 145
University of Michigan Medical
    Center, 93–94, 171, 182, 218,
    221
University of Minnesota, 99, 141
University of New Mexico, 149
University of Tulsa, 142

University of Washington, 118–
    119

V
Varicose veins, during pregnancy,
    68–69

W
Washington State University, 212
Weaning, 123–24
Welson, Reed, 93, 101–2, 111
Welson, Stephanie, 93, 109, 111
Western Carolina University, 136
Whelan, Dr. Elizabeth, 33, 45
White, Dr. Burton, 47
Who's Who, 149, 150
Wilner, Dr. Stefanie, 201–2
World War II, 38

Y
Yarrow, Dr. Leon, 159
Young, Dr. Bruce, 75, 78

Z
Zajonc, Dr. R. B., 149, 157–58